hRya

Buffy
THE RECKONING
the vampire slayer™

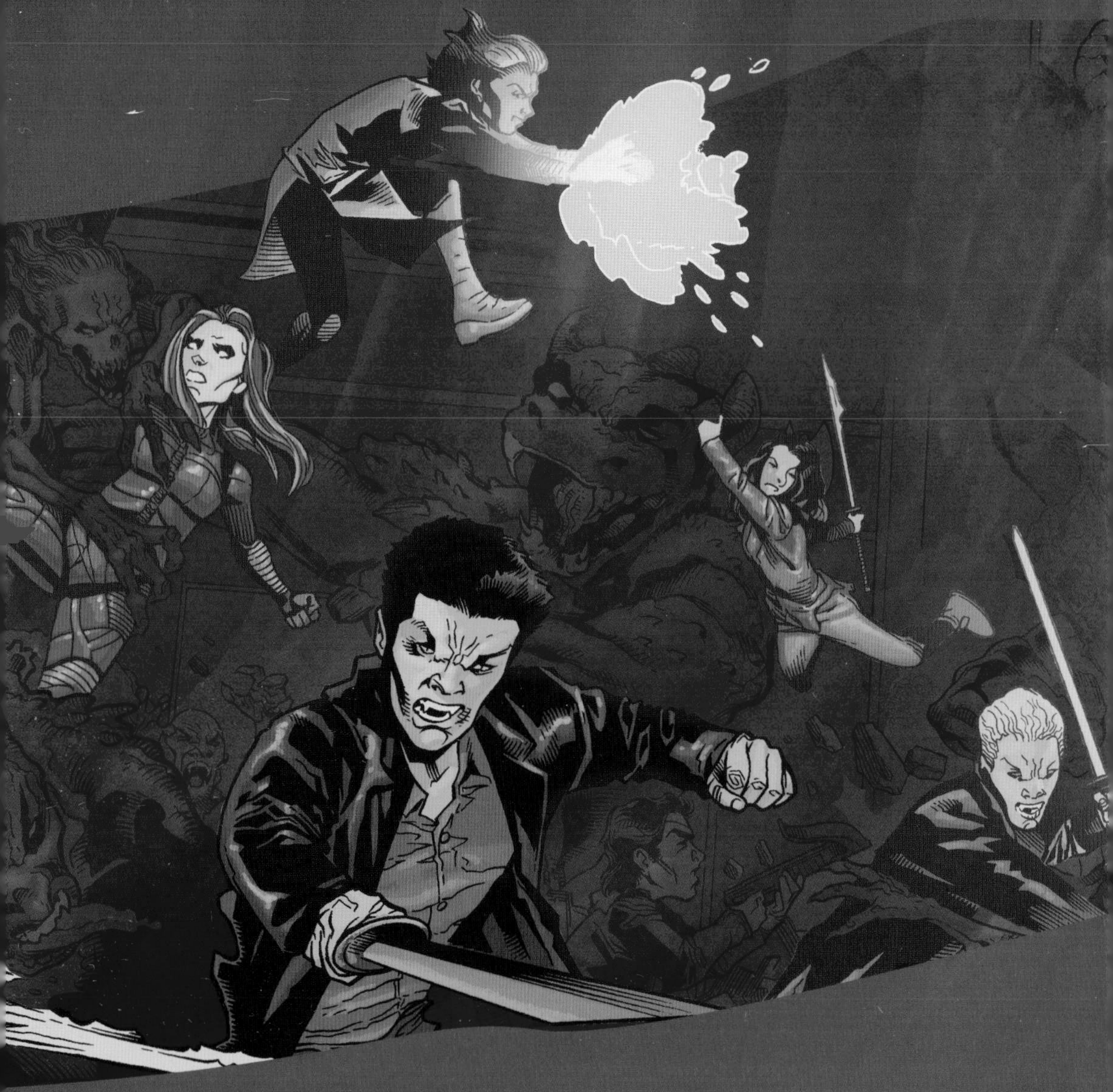

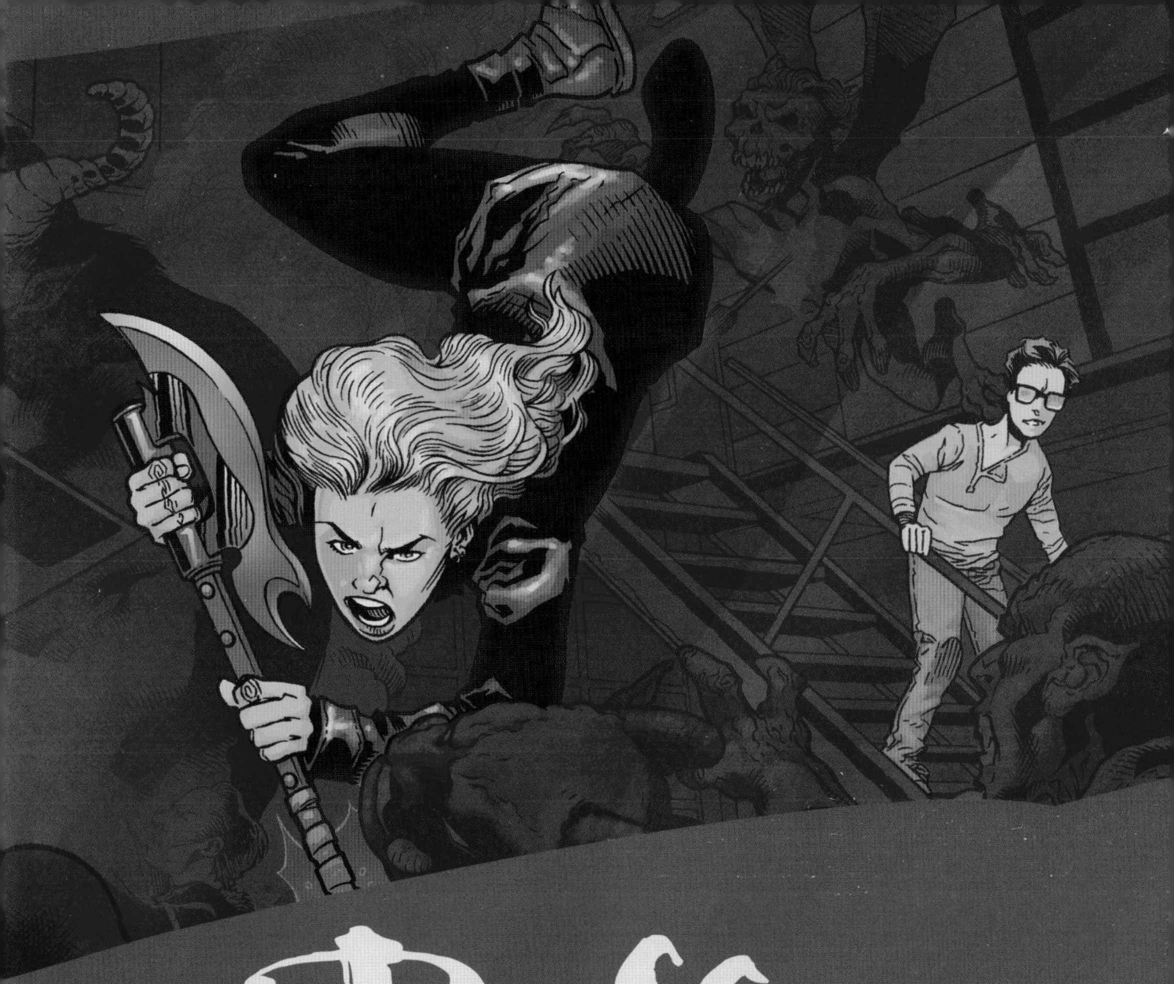

Buffy the Vampire Slayer™

THE RECKONING

Season 12

STORY
JOSS WHEDON & CHRISTOS GAGE

SCRIPT
CHRISTOS GAGE

PENCILS
GEORGES JEANTY

Inks KARL STORY, ANDY OWENS (*pages 62–68, 88, 95*), DEXTER VINES (*pages 69–74, 92, 94*)

Colors DAN JACKSON

Letters RICHARD STARKINGS & COMICRAFT'S JIMMY BETANCOURT

Cover and Chapter Break Art STEPHANIE HANS

DARK HORSE BOOKS

President & Publisher **Mike Richardson**

Editor **Freddye Miller**

Assistant Editors **Judy Khuu, Kevin Burkhalter, Jenny Blenk**

Designer **Anita Magaña**

Digital Art Technician **Christianne Gillenardo-Goudreau**

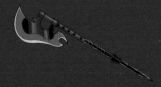

Special thanks to Nicole Spiegel and Carol Roeder at Twentieth Century Fox, and to Melissa Rotonto and Becca J. Sadowsky.

This story takes place after the events in *Buffy the Vampire Slayer* Season 11, created by Joss Whedon.

DarkHorse.com
First edition: December 2018
ISBN 978-1-50670-915-4
1 3 5 7 9 10 8 6 4 2
Printed in China

Published by Dark Horse Books
A division of Dark Horse Comics, Inc.
10956 SE Main Street | Milwaukie, OR 97222

This volume reprints the comic book series *Buffy the Vampire Slayer* Season 12 #1–#4 from Dark Horse Comics, originally published June 2018 through September 2018.

Neil Hankerson *Executive Vice President*, Tom Weddle *Chief Financial Officer*, Randy Stradley *Vice President Of Publishing*, Nick McWhorter *Chief Business Development Officer*, Dale LaFountain *Chief Information Officer*, Matt Parkinson *Vice President Of Marketing*, Cara Niece *Vice President Of Production And Scheduling*, Mark Bernardi *Vice President Of Book Trade And Digital Sales*, Ken Lizzi *General Counsel*, Dave Marshall *Editor In Chief*, Davey Estrada *Editorial Director*, Chris Warner *Senior Books Editor*, Cary Grazzini *Director Of Specialty Projects*, Lia Ribacchi *Art Director*, Vanessa Todd-Holmes *Director Of Print Purchasing*, Matt Dryer *Director Of Digital Art And Prepress*, Michael Gombos *Director Of International Publishing And Licensing*, Kari Yadro *Director Of Custom Programs*, Kari Torson *Director Of International Licensing*

To find a comics shop in your area, visit comicshoplocator.com

Library of Congress Cataloging-in-Publication Data
Names: Gage, Christos, author. | Whedon, Joss, 1964- author, creator. |
  Jeanty, Georges, penciller. | Story, Karl C., inker. | Owens, Andy, inker.
  | Vines, Dexter, inker. | Jackson, Dan, 1971- colourist. | Starkings,
  Richard, letterer. | Betancourt, Jimmy, letterer. | Hans, Stephanie,
  colourist.
Title: The reckoning / story, Joss Whedon & Christos Gage ; script, Christos
  Gage ; pencils, Georges Jeanty ; inks, Karl Story, Andy Owens, Dexter
  Vines ; colors, Dan Jackson ; letters, Richard Starkings & Comicraft's
  Jimmy Betancourt ; cover and chapter break art, Stephanie Hans.
Other titles: Buffy, the vampire slayer (Television program)
Description: First edition. | Milwaukie, OR : Dark Horse Books, December
  2018. | Series: Buffy the Vampire Slayer season 12 | "This story takes
  place after the events in Buffy the Vampire Slayer Season 11, created by
  Joss Whedon."
Identifiers: LCCN 2018032589 | ISBN 9781506709154 (paperback)
Subjects: LCSH: Comic books, strips, etc. | BISAC: COMICS & GRAPHIC NOVELS /
  Media Tie-In. | COMICS & GRAPHIC NOVELS / Fantasy. | COMICS & GRAPHIC
  NOVELS / Horror.
Classification: LCC PN6728.B84 G48 2018 | DDC 741.5/973--dc23
LC record available at https://lccn.loc.gov/2018032589

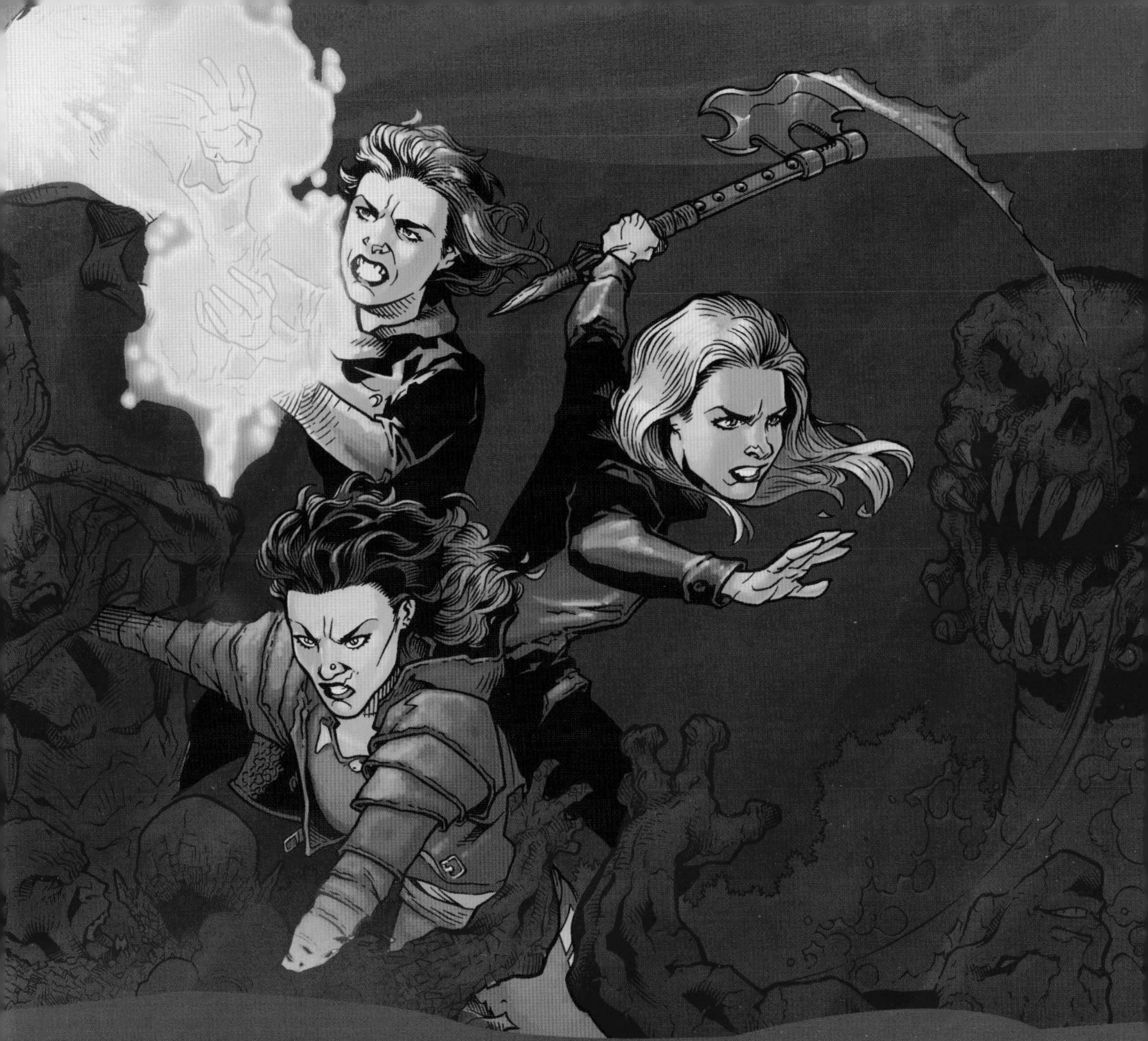

Buffy the Vampire Slayer has been saving the world from the forces of darkness since she was a teenager. Alongside vampire-with-a-soul Spike; her best friends, Wiccan Willow Rosenberg and normal guy Xander Harris; her sister Dawn; and her mentor Giles, Buffy has found nothing they can't face together.

Four years ago, Buffy journeyed to the future to team with Slayer Melaka Fray against Fray's vampire twin brother, Harth. Fray thought Buffy's knowledge of the future would change history, erasing her world . . . but it didn't.

A year has passed since rogue government forces tried to enslave magical beings and steal their power. While humanity knows the supernatural exists, it has returned to the shadows. And there have been other changes . . .

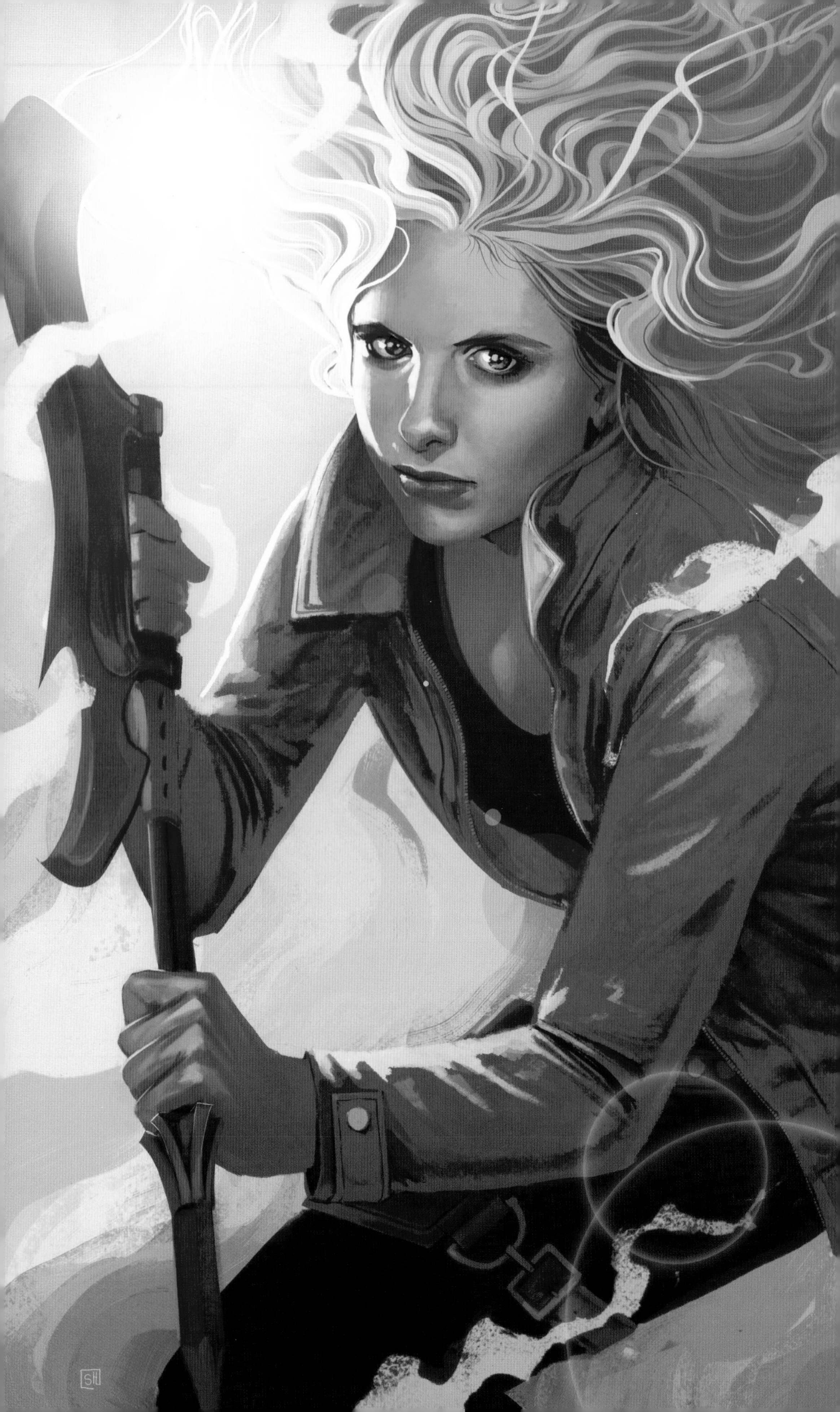

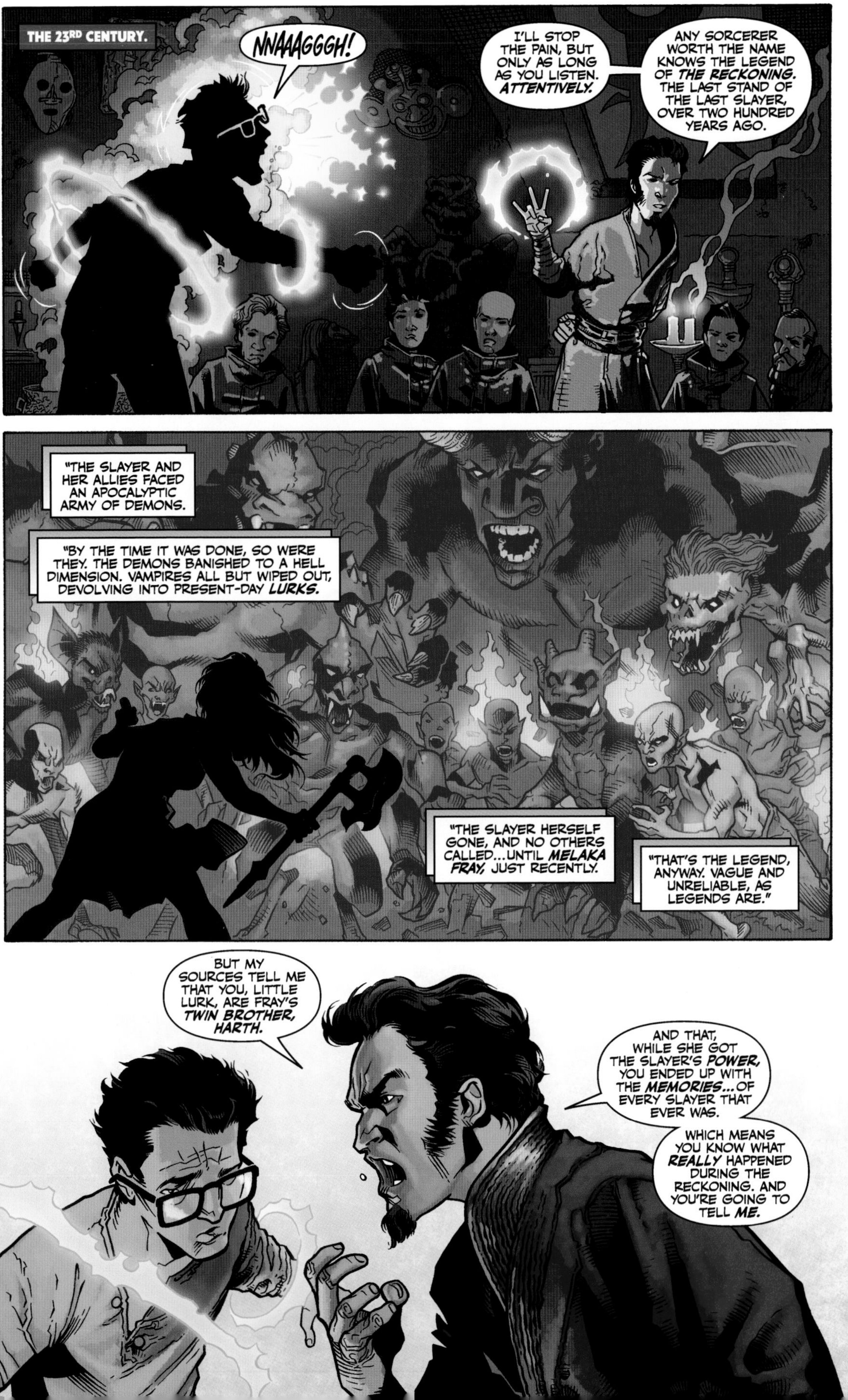
THE 23RD CENTURY.
NNAAAGGGH!
I'LL STOP THE PAIN, BUT ONLY AS LONG AS YOU LISTEN. ATTENTIVELY.
ANY SORCERER WORTH THE NAME KNOWS THE LEGEND OF THE RECKONING. THE LAST STAND OF THE LAST SLAYER, OVER TWO HUNDRED YEARS AGO.
"THE SLAYER AND HER ALLIES FACED AN APOCALYPTIC ARMY OF DEMONS.
"BY THE TIME IT WAS DONE, SO WERE THEY. THE DEMONS BANISHED TO A HELL DIMENSION. VAMPIRES ALL BUT WIPED OUT, DEVOLVING INTO PRESENT-DAY LURKS.
"THE SLAYER HERSELF GONE, AND NO OTHERS CALLED...UNTIL MELAKA FRAY, JUST RECENTLY.
"THAT'S THE LEGEND, ANYWAY. VAGUE AND UNRELIABLE, AS LEGENDS ARE."
BUT MY SOURCES TELL ME THAT YOU, LITTLE LURK, ARE FRAY'S TWIN BROTHER, HARTH.
AND THAT, WHILE SHE GOT THE SLAYER'S POWER, YOU ENDED UP WITH THE MEMORIES...OF EVERY SLAYER THAT EVER WAS.
WHICH MEANS YOU KNOW WHAT REALLY HAPPENED DURING THE RECKONING. AND YOU'RE GOING TO TELL ME.

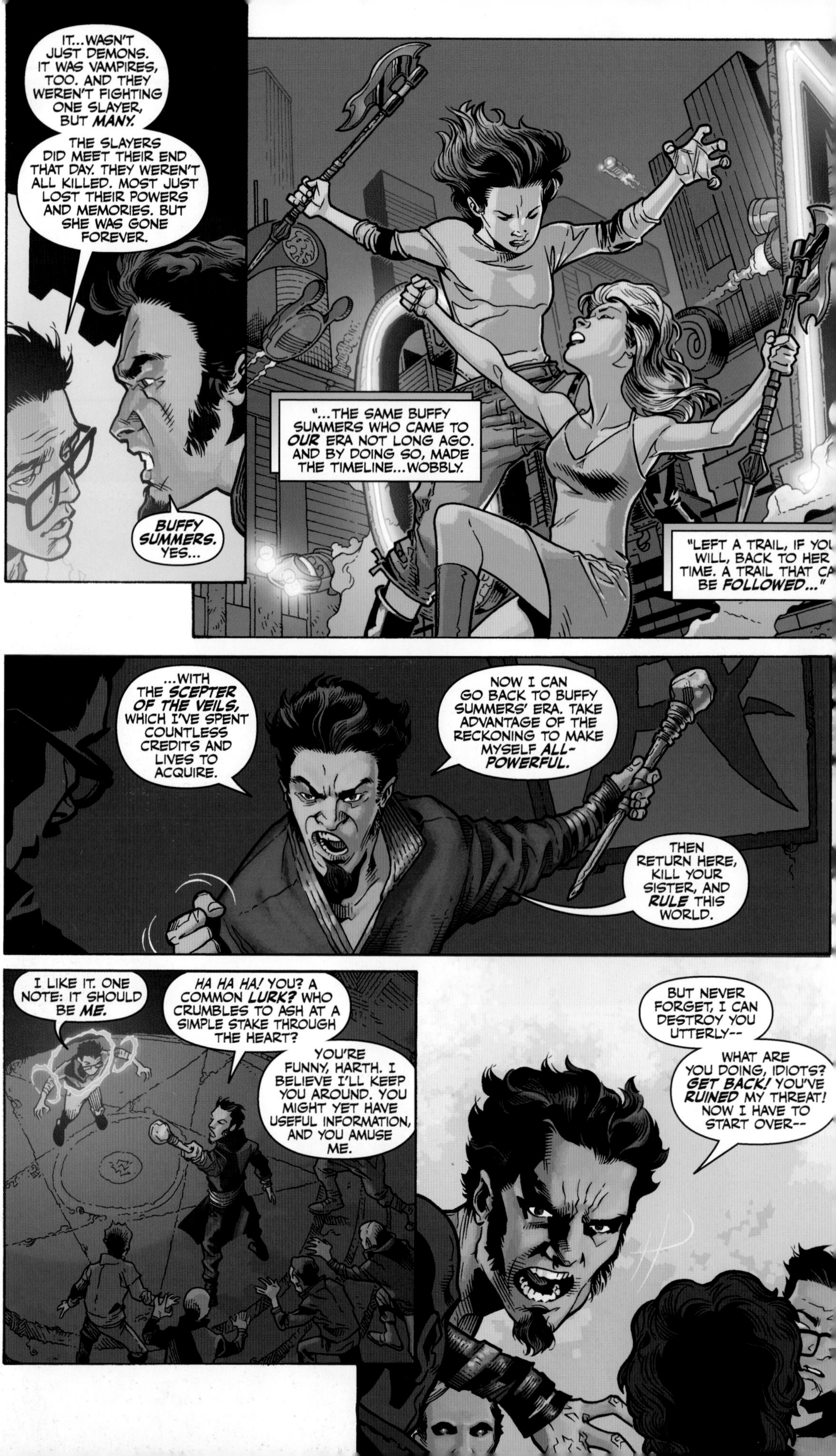

IT...WASN'T JUST DEMONS. IT WAS VAMPIRES, TOO. AND THEY WEREN'T FIGHTING ONE SLAYER, BUT *MANY.*
THE SLAYERS DID MEET THEIR END THAT DAY. THEY WEREN'T ALL KILLED. MOST JUST LOST THEIR POWERS AND MEMORIES. BUT SHE WAS GONE FOREVER.
BUFFY SUMMERS. YES...
"...THE SAME BUFFY SUMMERS WHO CAME TO *OUR* ERA NOT LONG AGO. AND BY DOING SO, MADE THE TIMELINE...WOBBLY.
"LEFT A TRAIL, IF YOU WILL, BACK TO HER TIME. A TRAIL THAT CA BE *FOLLOWED...*"
...WITH THE *SCEPTER OF THE VEILS,* WHICH I'VE SPENT COUNTLESS CREDITS AND LIVES TO ACQUIRE.
NOW I CAN GO BACK TO BUFFY SUMMERS' ERA. TAKE ADVANTAGE OF THE RECKONING TO MAKE MYSELF *ALL-POWERFUL.*
THEN RETURN HERE, KILL YOUR SISTER, AND *RULE* THIS WORLD.
I LIKE IT. ONE NOTE: IT SHOULD BE *ME.*
HA HA HA! YOU? A COMMON *LURK?* WHO CRUMBLES TO ASH AT A SIMPLE STAKE THROUGH THE HEART?
YOU'RE FUNNY, HARTH. I BELIEVE I'LL KEEP YOU AROUND. YOU MIGHT YET HAVE USEFUL INFORMATION, AND YOU AMUSE ME.
BUT NEVER FORGET, I CAN DESTROY YOU UTTERLY--
WHAT ARE YOU DOING, IDIOTS? *GET BACK!* YOU'VE *RUINED* MY THREAT! NOW I HAVE TO START OVER--

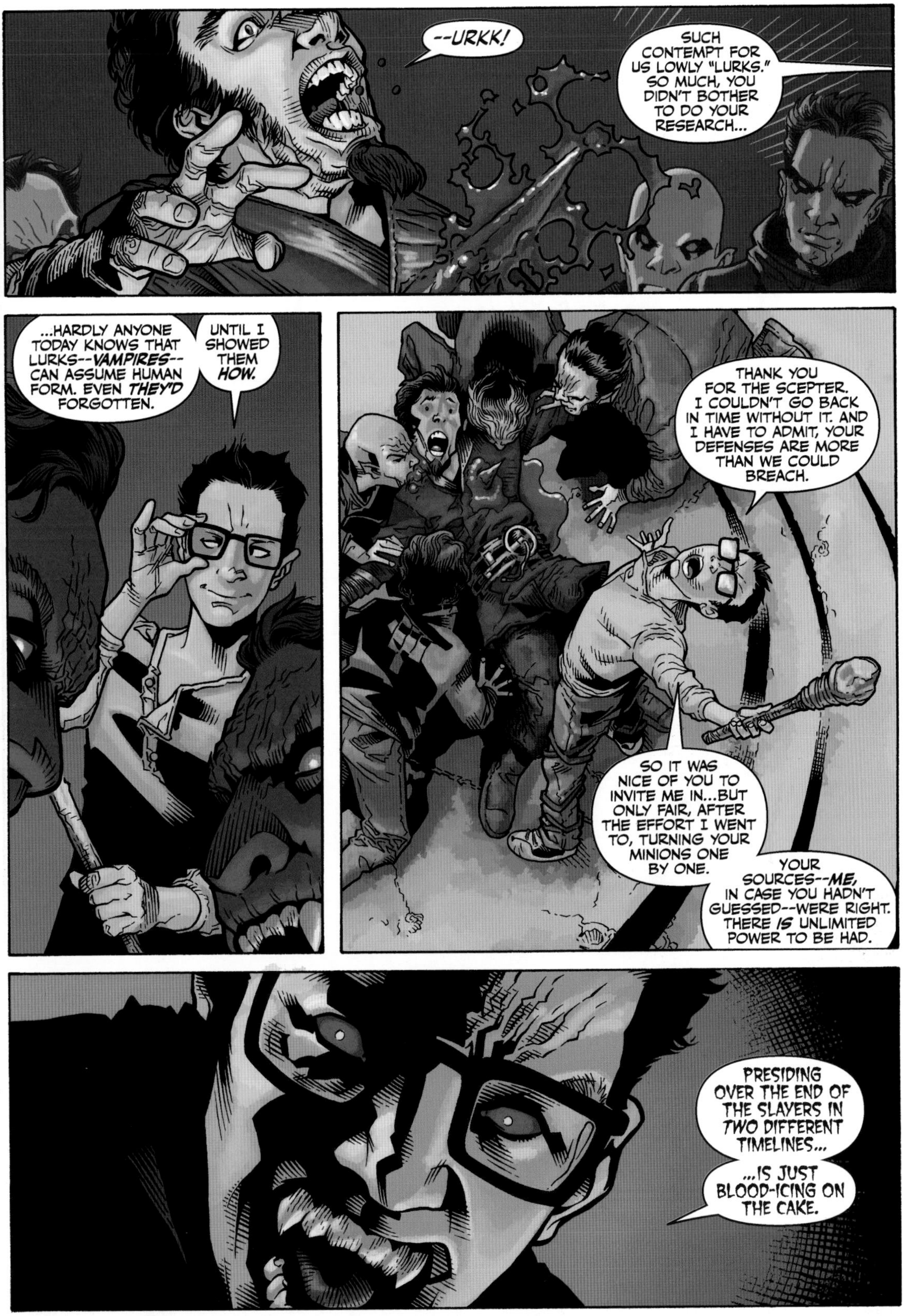
--URKK!
SUCH CONTEMPT FOR US LOWLY "LURKS." SO MUCH, YOU DIDN'T BOTHER TO DO YOUR RESEARCH...
...HARDLY ANYONE TODAY KNOWS THAT LURKS--VAMPIRES--CAN ASSUME HUMAN FORM. EVEN THEY'D FORGOTTEN.
UNTIL I SHOWED THEM HOW.
THANK YOU FOR THE SCEPTER. I COULDN'T GO BACK IN TIME WITHOUT IT. AND I HAVE TO ADMIT, YOUR DEFENSES ARE MORE THAN WE COULD BREACH.
SO IT WAS NICE OF YOU TO INVITE ME IN...BUT ONLY FAIR, AFTER THE EFFORT I WENT TO, TURNING YOUR MINIONS ONE BY ONE.
YOUR SOURCES--ME, IN CASE YOU HADN'T GUESSED--WERE RIGHT. THERE IS UNLIMITED POWER TO BE HAD.
PRESIDING OVER THE END OF THE SLAYERS IN TWO DIFFERENT TIMELINES...
...IS JUST BLOOD-ICING ON THE CAKE.

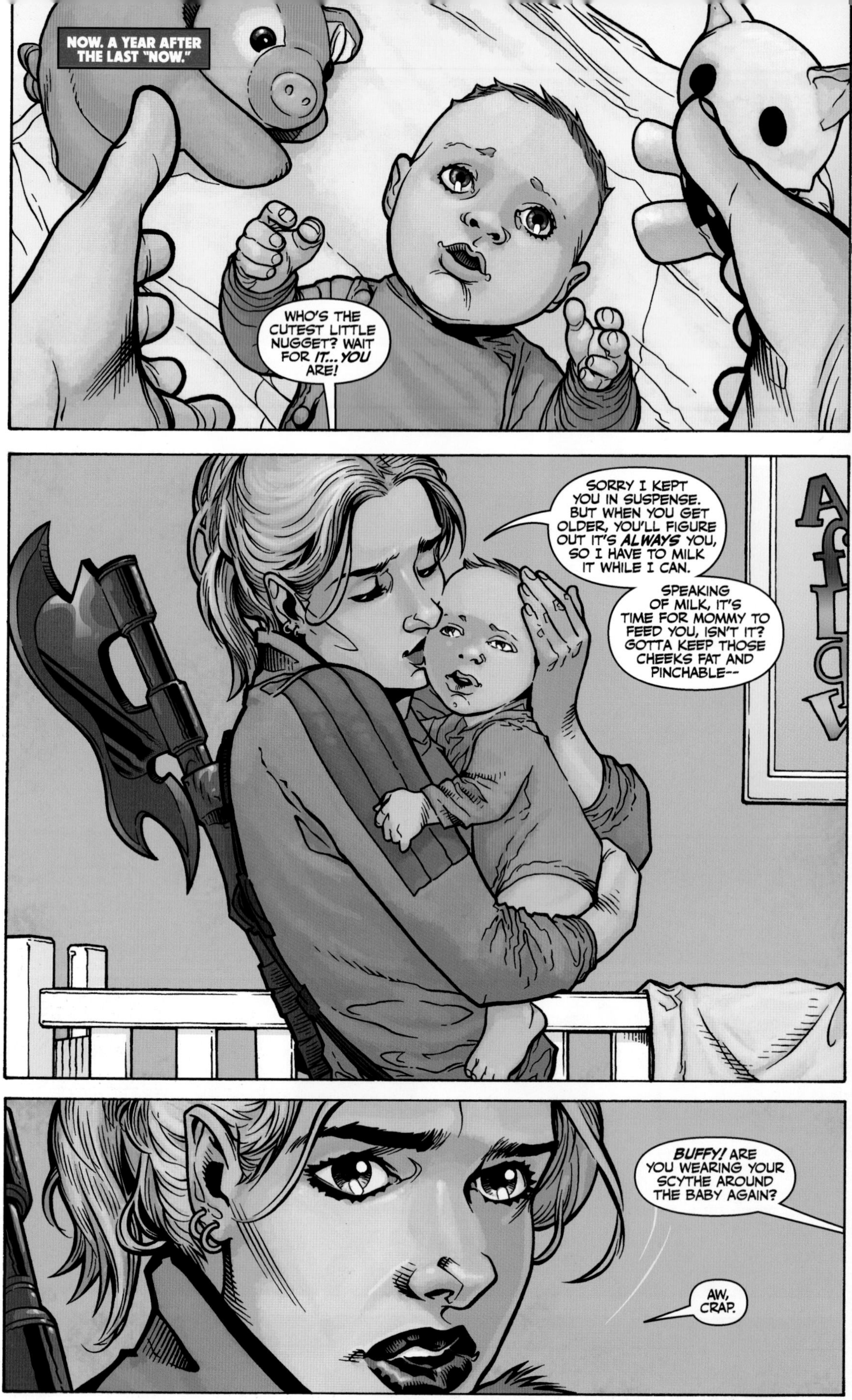
NOW. A YEAR AFTER THE LAST "NOW."
WHO'S THE CUTEST LITTLE NUGGET? WAIT FOR *IT... YOU* ARE!
SORRY I KEPT YOU IN SUSPENSE. BUT WHEN YOU GET OLDER, YOU'LL FIGURE OUT IT'S *ALWAYS* YOU, SO I HAVE TO MILK IT WHILE I CAN.
SPEAKING OF MILK, IT'S TIME FOR MOMMY TO FEED YOU, ISN'T IT? GOTTA KEEP THOSE CHEEKS FAT AND PINCHABLE--
BUFFY! ARE YOU WEARING YOUR SCYTHE AROUND THE BABY AGAIN?
AW, CRAP.

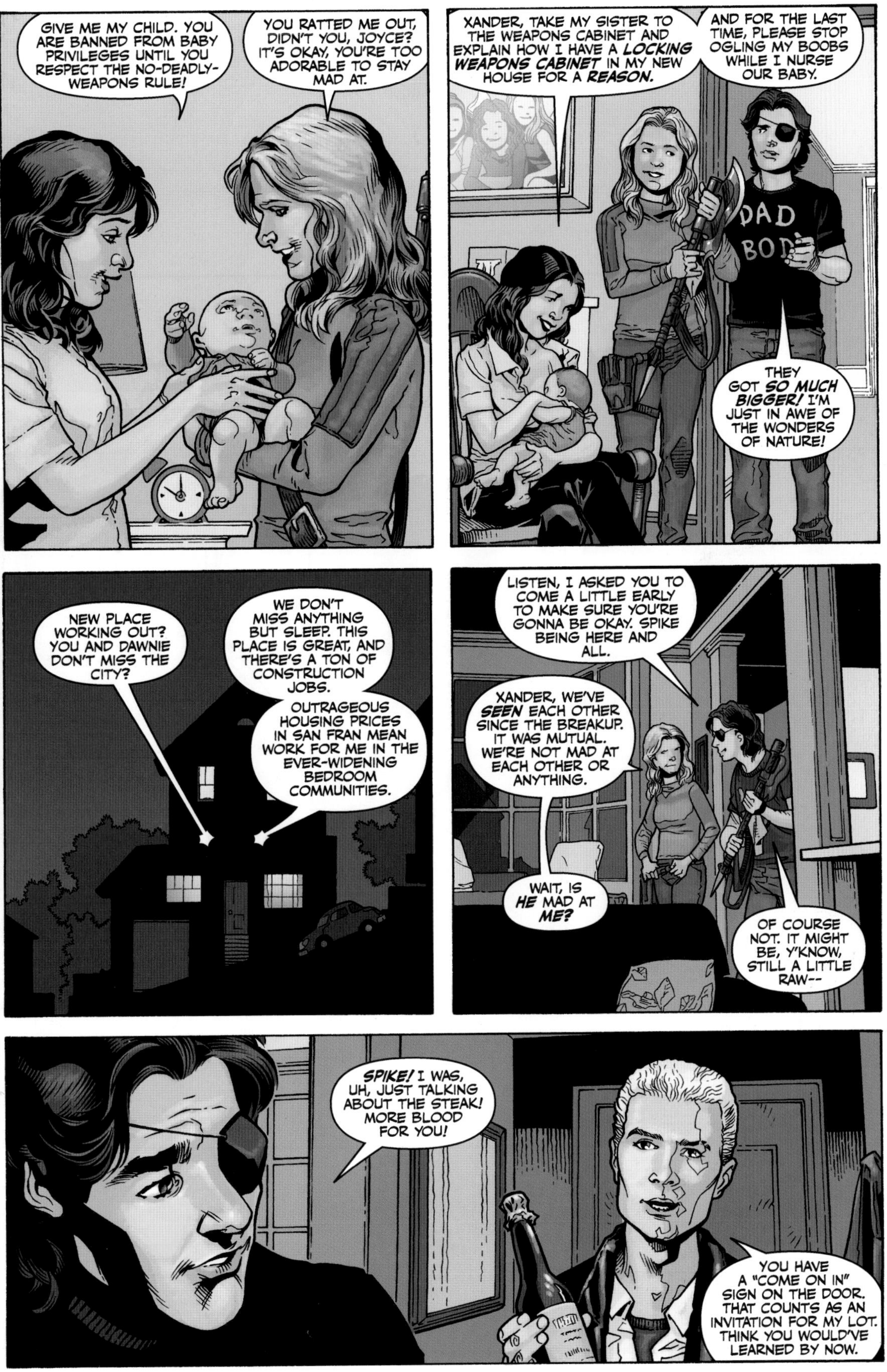
GIVE ME MY CHILD. YOU ARE BANNED FROM BABY PRIVILEGES UNTIL YOU RESPECT THE NO-DEADLY-WEAPONS RULE!
YOU RATTED ME OUT, DIDN'T YOU, JOYCE? IT'S OKAY, YOU'RE TOO ADORABLE TO STAY MAD AT.
XANDER, TAKE MY SISTER TO THE WEAPONS CABINET AND EXPLAIN HOW I HAVE A *LOCKING WEAPONS CABINET* IN MY NEW HOUSE FOR A *REASON.*
AND FOR THE LAST TIME, PLEASE STOP OGLING MY BOOBS WHILE I NURSE OUR BABY.
DAD BOD
THEY GOT *SO MUCH BIGGER!* I'M JUST IN AWE OF THE WONDERS OF NATURE!
NEW PLACE WORKING OUT? YOU AND DAWNIE DON'T MISS THE CITY?
WE DON'T MISS ANYTHING BUT SLEEP. THIS PLACE IS GREAT, AND THERE'S A TON OF CONSTRUCTION JOBS.
OUTRAGEOUS HOUSING PRICES IN SAN FRAN MEAN WORK FOR ME IN THE EVER-WIDENING BEDROOM COMMUNITIES.
LISTEN, I ASKED YOU TO COME A LITTLE EARLY TO MAKE SURE YOU'RE GONNA BE OKAY. SPIKE BEING HERE AND ALL.
XANDER, WE'VE *SEEN* EACH OTHER SINCE THE BREAKUP. IT WAS MUTUAL. WE'RE NOT MAD AT EACH OTHER OR ANYTHING.
WAIT, IS *HE* MAD AT *ME?*
OF COURSE NOT. IT MIGHT BE, Y'KNOW, STILL A LITTLE RAW--
SPIKE! I WAS, UH, JUST TALKING ABOUT THE STEAK! MORE BLOOD FOR YOU!
YOU HAVE A "COME ON IN" SIGN ON THE DOOR. THAT COUNTS AS AN INVITATION FOR MY LOT. THINK YOU WOULD'VE LEARNED BY NOW.

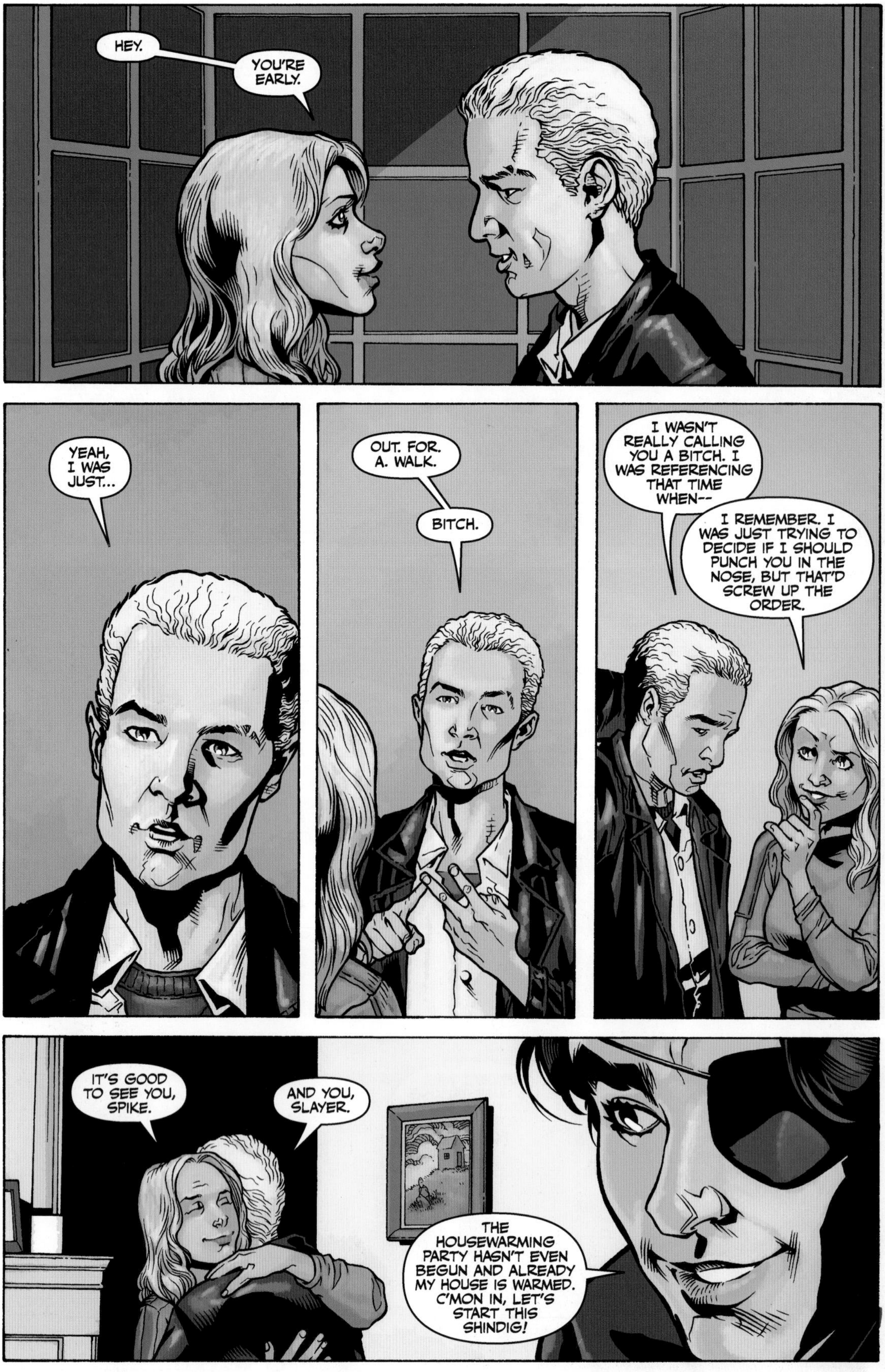
HEY.
YOU'RE EARLY.
YEAH, I WAS JUST...
OUT. FOR. A. WALK.
BITCH.
I WASN'T REALLY CALLING YOU A BITCH. I WAS REFERENCING THAT TIME WHEN--
I REMEMBER. I WAS JUST TRYING TO DECIDE IF I SHOULD PUNCH YOU IN THE NOSE, BUT THAT'D SCREW UP THE ORDER.
IT'S GOOD TO SEE YOU, SPIKE.
AND YOU, SLAYER.
THE HOUSEWARMING PARTY HASN'T EVEN BEGUN AND ALREADY MY HOUSE IS WARMED. C'MON IN, LET'S START THIS SHINDIG!

LATER...

IT'S PERMANENT THEN, GILES? YOU WON'T BE CHANGING INTO, SAY, A NINETY-YEAR-OLD CAT LADY? ON THE *OUTSIDE*, I MEAN.

YES, ALL DONE AND DUSTED. THE SPELL COULD ONLY RESTORE ME TO MY TRUE AGE. PITY THAT, I'D HAVE LOVED TO SHAVE OFF A FEW YEARS.

HEY, YOU KEPT YOUR HAIR, EVERYTHING ELSE IS GRAVY. I THINK YOU LOOK DISTINGUISHED.

"DISTINGUISHED" MEANS "ANCIENT," YOU REALIZE...

WILLOW, THAT NATURAL MOISTURIZER RECIPE--*SO GOOD!* I TURNED EVERYONE AT "MOMMY AND ME" ON TO IT.

YOU'RE LIKE A WICCAN VERSION OF THAT ACTRESS'S LIFESTYLE BLOG. BUT, LIKE, WITH *GOOD* ADVICE, NOT "GET STUNG BY BEES ON PURPOSE."

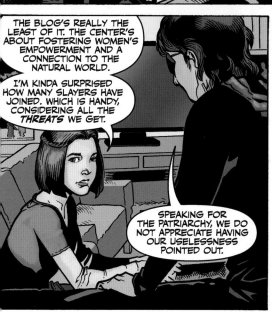

THE BLOG'S REALLY THE LEAST OF IT. THE CENTER'S ABOUT FOSTERING WOMEN'S EMPOWERMENT AND A CONNECTION TO THE NATURAL WORLD.

I'M KINDA SURPRISED HOW MANY SLAYERS HAVE JOINED. WHICH IS HANDY, CONSIDERING ALL THE *THREATS* WE GET.

SPEAKING FOR THE PATRIARCHY, WE DO NOT APPRECIATE HAVING OUR USELESSNESS POINTED OUT.

WE CAN HANDLE TROLLS. I'M WORRIED THE *GOVERNMENT* WILL SEE US AS A THREAT, LIKE WHEN WE HAD THE SLAYER ARMY GOING.

BUT RILEY ASSURES ME HE'S NOT LETTING THAT HAPPEN. AND THE DAYS OF LETTING OTHER PEOPLE'S PREJUDICES STOP ME FROM DOING WHAT FEELS RIGHT ARE *LONG* GONE.

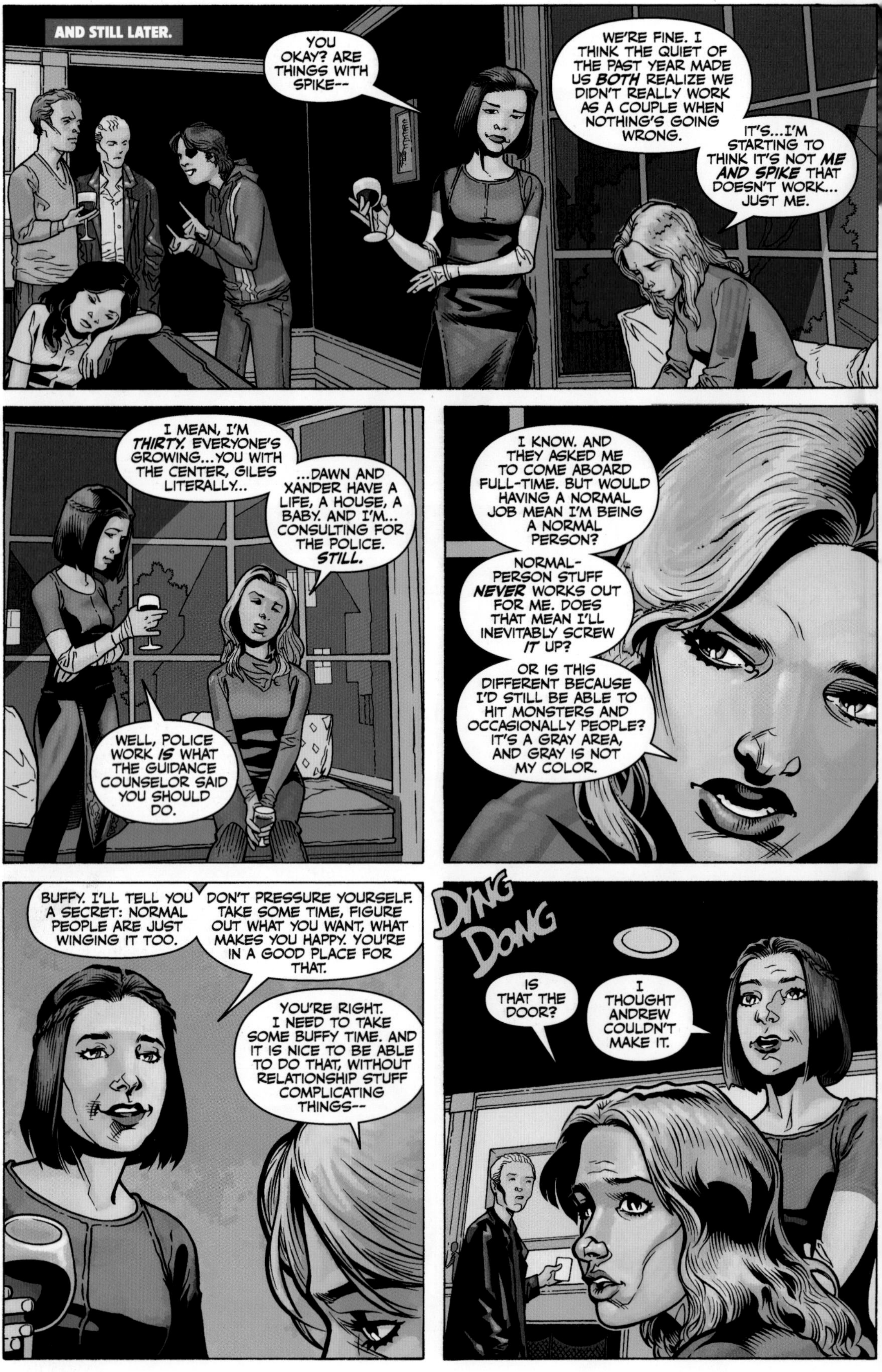
AND STILL LATER.
YOU OKAY? ARE THINGS WITH SPIKE--
WE'RE FINE. I THINK THE QUIET OF THE PAST YEAR MADE US BOTH REALIZE WE DIDN'T REALLY WORK AS A COUPLE WHEN NOTHING'S GOING WRONG.
IT'S...I'M STARTING TO THINK IT'S NOT ME AND SPIKE THAT DOESN'T WORK... JUST ME.
I MEAN, I'M THIRTY. EVERYONE'S GROWING...YOU WITH THE CENTER, GILES LITERALLY...
...DAWN AND XANDER HAVE A LIFE, A HOUSE, A BABY. AND I'M... CONSULTING FOR THE POLICE. STILL.
WELL, POLICE WORK IS WHAT THE GUIDANCE COUNSELOR SAID YOU SHOULD DO.
I KNOW. AND THEY ASKED ME TO COME ABOARD FULL-TIME. BUT WOULD HAVING A NORMAL JOB MEAN I'M BEING A NORMAL PERSON?
NORMAL-PERSON STUFF NEVER WORKS OUT FOR ME. DOES THAT MEAN I'LL INEVITABLY SCREW IT UP?
OR IS THIS DIFFERENT BECAUSE I'D STILL BE ABLE TO HIT MONSTERS AND OCCASIONALLY PEOPLE? IT'S A GRAY AREA, AND GRAY IS NOT MY COLOR.
BUFFY. I'LL TELL YOU A SECRET: NORMAL PEOPLE ARE JUST WINGING IT TOO.
DON'T PRESSURE YOURSELF. TAKE SOME TIME, FIGURE OUT WHAT YOU WANT, WHAT MAKES YOU HAPPY. YOU'RE IN A GOOD PLACE FOR THAT.
YOU'RE RIGHT. I NEED TO TAKE SOME BUFFY TIME. AND IT IS NICE TO BE ABLE TO DO THAT, WITHOUT RELATIONSHIP STUFF COMPLICATING THINGS--
DING DONG
IS THAT THE DOOR?
I THOUGHT ANDREW COULDN'T MAKE IT.

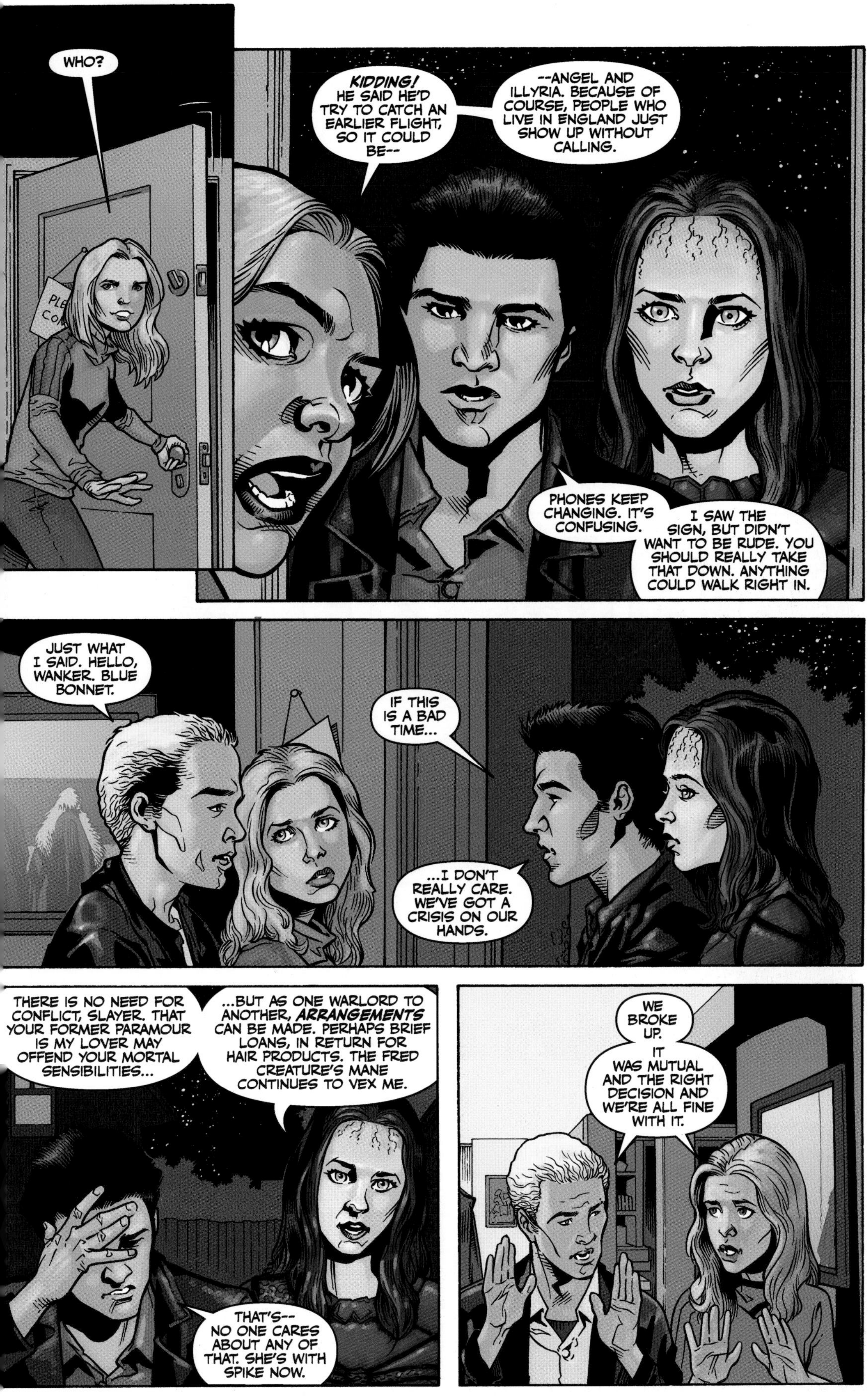
WHO?
KIDDING! HE SAID HE'D TRY TO CATCH AN EARLIER FLIGHT, SO IT COULD BE--
--ANGEL AND ILLYRIA. BECAUSE OF COURSE, PEOPLE WHO LIVE IN ENGLAND JUST SHOW UP WITHOUT CALLING.
PHONES KEEP CHANGING. IT'S CONFUSING.
I SAW THE SIGN, BUT DIDN'T WANT TO BE RUDE. YOU SHOULD REALLY TAKE THAT DOWN. ANYTHING COULD WALK RIGHT IN.
JUST WHAT I SAID. HELLO, WANKER. BLUE BONNET.
IF THIS IS A BAD TIME...
...I DON'T REALLY CARE. WE'VE GOT A CRISIS ON OUR HANDS.
THERE IS NO NEED FOR CONFLICT, SLAYER. THAT YOUR FORMER PARAMOUR IS MY LOVER MAY OFFEND YOUR MORTAL SENSIBILITIES...
...BUT AS ONE WARLORD TO ANOTHER, ARRANGEMENTS CAN BE MADE. PERHAPS BRIEF LOANS, IN RETURN FOR HAIR PRODUCTS. THE FRED CREATURE'S MANE CONTINUES TO VEX ME.
THAT'S-- NO ONE CARES ABOUT ANY OF THAT. SHE'S WITH SPIKE NOW.
WE BROKE UP.
IT WAS MUTUAL AND THE RIGHT DECISION AND WE'RE ALL FINE WITH IT.

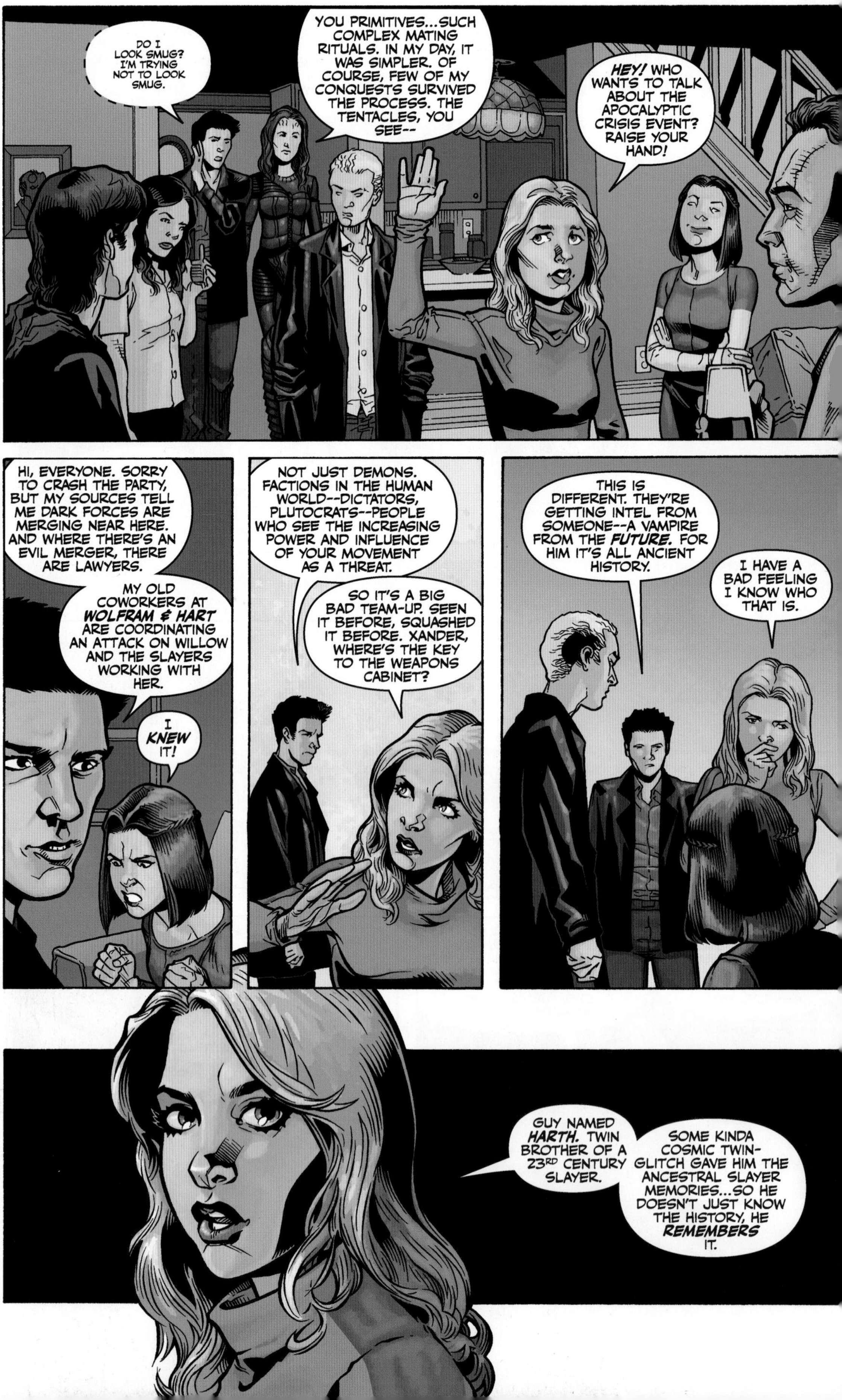

DO I LOOK SMUG? I'M TRYING NOT TO LOOK SMUG.
YOU PRIMITIVES...SUCH COMPLEX MATING RITUALS. IN MY DAY, IT WAS SIMPLER. OF COURSE, FEW OF MY CONQUESTS SURVIVED THE PROCESS. THE TENTACLES, YOU SEE--
HEY! WHO WANTS TO TALK ABOUT THE APOCALYPTIC CRISIS EVENT? RAISE YOUR HAND!
HI, EVERYONE. SORRY TO CRASH THE PARTY, BUT MY SOURCES TELL ME DARK FORCES ARE MERGING NEAR HERE. AND WHERE THERE'S AN EVIL MERGER, THERE ARE LAWYERS.
MY OLD COWORKERS AT WOLFRAM & HART ARE COORDINATING AN ATTACK ON WILLOW AND THE SLAYERS WORKING WITH HER.
I KNEW IT!
NOT JUST DEMONS. FACTIONS IN THE HUMAN WORLD--DICTATORS, PLUTOCRATS--PEOPLE WHO SEE THE INCREASING POWER AND INFLUENCE OF YOUR MOVEMENT AS A THREAT.
SO IT'S A BIG BAD TEAM-UP. SEEN IT BEFORE, SQUASHED IT BEFORE. XANDER, WHERE'S THE KEY TO THE WEAPONS CABINET?
THIS IS DIFFERENT. THEY'RE GETTING INTEL FROM SOMEONE--A VAMPIRE FROM THE FUTURE. FOR HIM IT'S ALL ANCIENT HISTORY.
I HAVE A BAD FEELING I KNOW WHO THAT IS.
GUY NAMED HARTH. TWIN BROTHER OF A 23RD CENTURY SLAYER.
SOME KINDA COSMIC TWIN-GLITCH GAVE HIM THE ANCESTRAL SLAYER MEMORIES...SO HE DOESN'T JUST KNOW THE HISTORY, HE REMEMBERS IT.

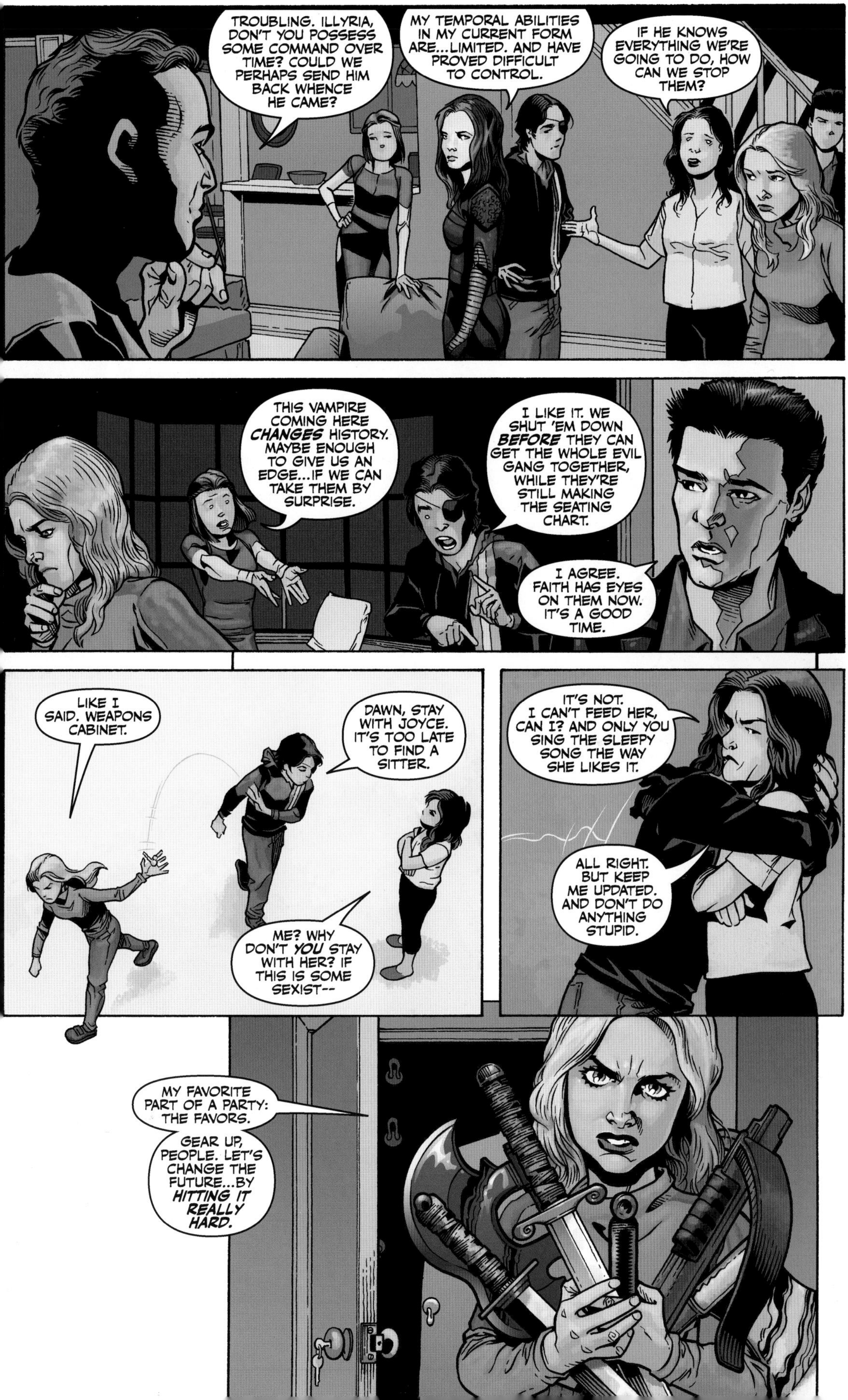
TROUBLING. ILLYRIA, DON'T YOU POSSESS SOME COMMAND OVER TIME? COULD WE PERHAPS SEND HIM BACK WHENCE HE CAME?
MY TEMPORAL ABILITIES IN MY CURRENT FORM ARE...LIMITED. AND HAVE PROVED DIFFICULT TO CONTROL.
IF HE KNOWS EVERYTHING WE'RE GOING TO DO, HOW CAN WE STOP THEM?
THIS VAMPIRE COMING HERE *CHANGES* HISTORY. MAYBE ENOUGH TO GIVE US AN EDGE...IF WE CAN TAKE THEM BY SURPRISE.
I LIKE IT. WE SHUT 'EM DOWN *BEFORE* THEY CAN GET THE WHOLE EVIL GANG TOGETHER, WHILE THEY'RE STILL MAKING THE SEATING CHART.
I AGREE. FAITH HAS EYES ON THEM NOW. IT'S A GOOD TIME.
LIKE I SAID. WEAPONS CABINET.
DAWN, STAY WITH JOYCE. IT'S TOO LATE TO FIND A SITTER.
ME? WHY DON'T *YOU* STAY WITH HER? IF THIS IS SOME SEXIST--
IT'S NOT. I CAN'T FEED HER, CAN I? AND ONLY YOU SING THE SLEEPY SONG THE WAY SHE LIKES IT.
ALL RIGHT. BUT KEEP ME UPDATED. AND DON'T DO ANYTHING STUPID.
MY FAVORITE PART OF A PARTY: THE FAVORS.
GEAR UP, PEOPLE. LET'S CHANGE THE FUTURE...BY *HITTING IT REALLY HARD.*

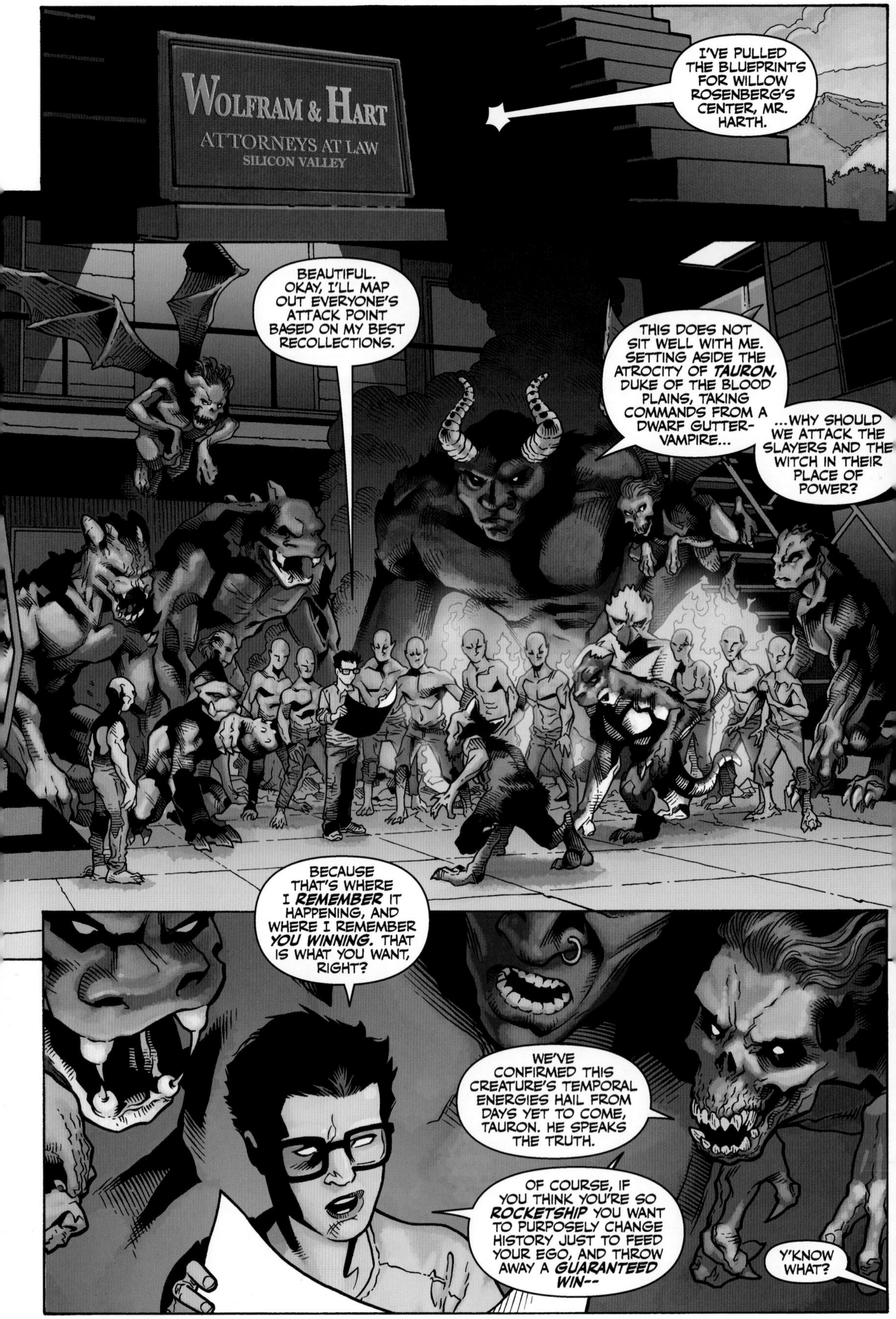
WOLFRAM & HART
ATTORNEYS AT LAW
SILICON VALLEY
I'VE PULLED THE BLUEPRINTS FOR WILLOW ROSENBERG'S CENTER, MR. HARTH.
BEAUTIFUL. OKAY, I'LL MAP OUT EVERYONE'S ATTACK POINT BASED ON MY BEST RECOLLECTIONS.
THIS DOES NOT SIT WELL WITH ME. SETTING ASIDE THE ATROCITY OF *TAURON,* DUKE OF THE BLOOD PLAINS, TAKING COMMANDS FROM A DWARF GUTTER-VAMPIRE...
...WHY SHOULD WE ATTACK THE SLAYERS AND THE WITCH IN THEIR PLACE OF POWER?
BECAUSE THAT'S WHERE I ***REMEMBER*** IT HAPPENING, AND WHERE I REMEMBER ***YOU WINNING.*** THAT IS WHAT YOU WANT, RIGHT?
WE'VE CONFIRMED THIS CREATURE'S TEMPORAL ENERGIES HAIL FROM DAYS YET TO COME, TAURON. HE SPEAKS THE TRUTH.
OF COURSE, IF YOU THINK YOU'RE SO ***ROCKETSHIP*** YOU WANT TO PURPOSELY CHANGE HISTORY JUST TO FEED YOUR EGO, AND THROW AWAY A ***GUARANTEED WIN--***
Y'KNOW WHAT?

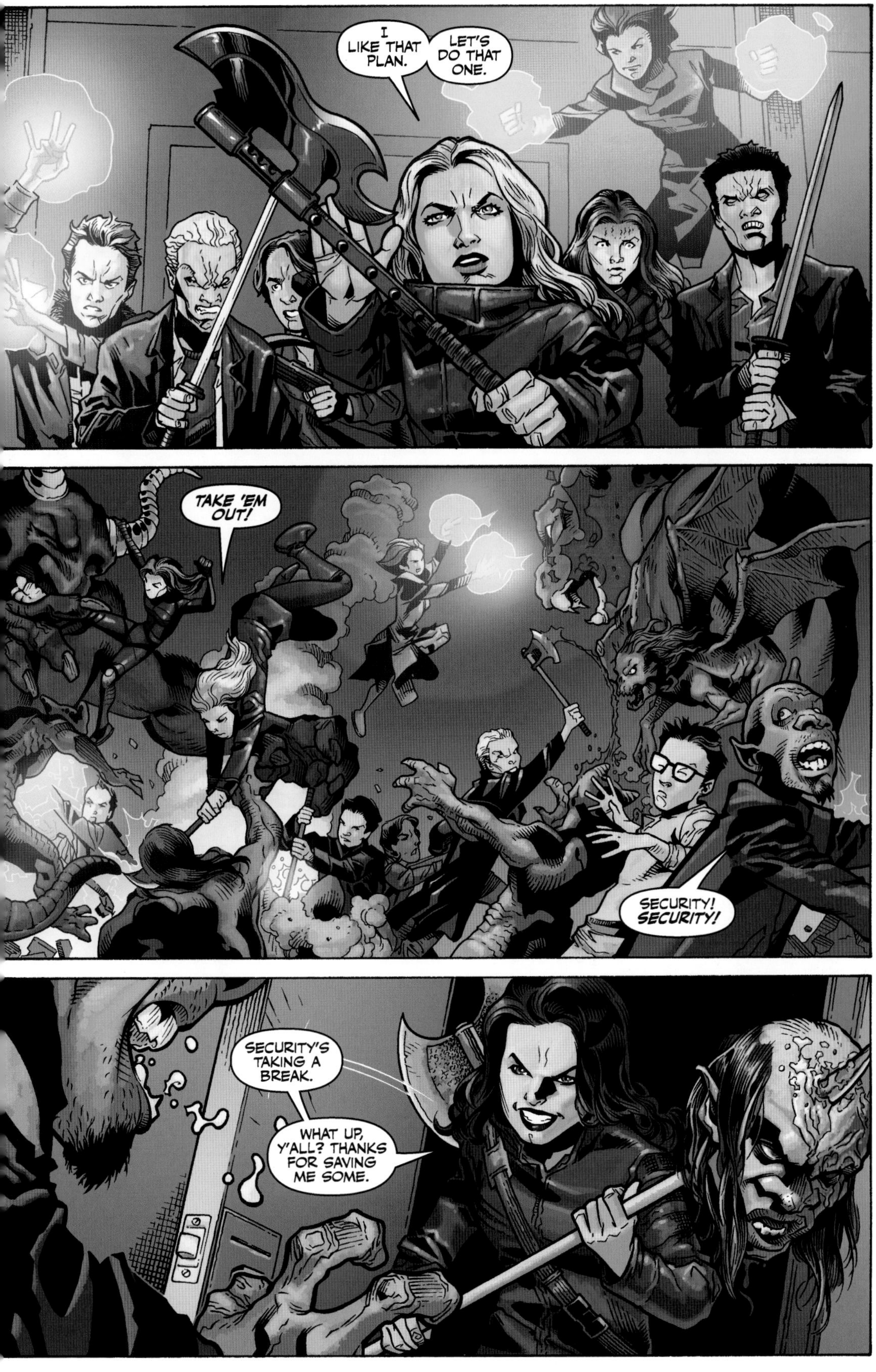
I LIKE THAT PLAN.
LET'S DO THAT ONE.
TAKE 'EM OUT!
SECURITY! SECURITY!
SECURITY'S TAKING A BREAK.
WHAT UP, Y'ALL? THANKS FOR SAVING ME SOME.

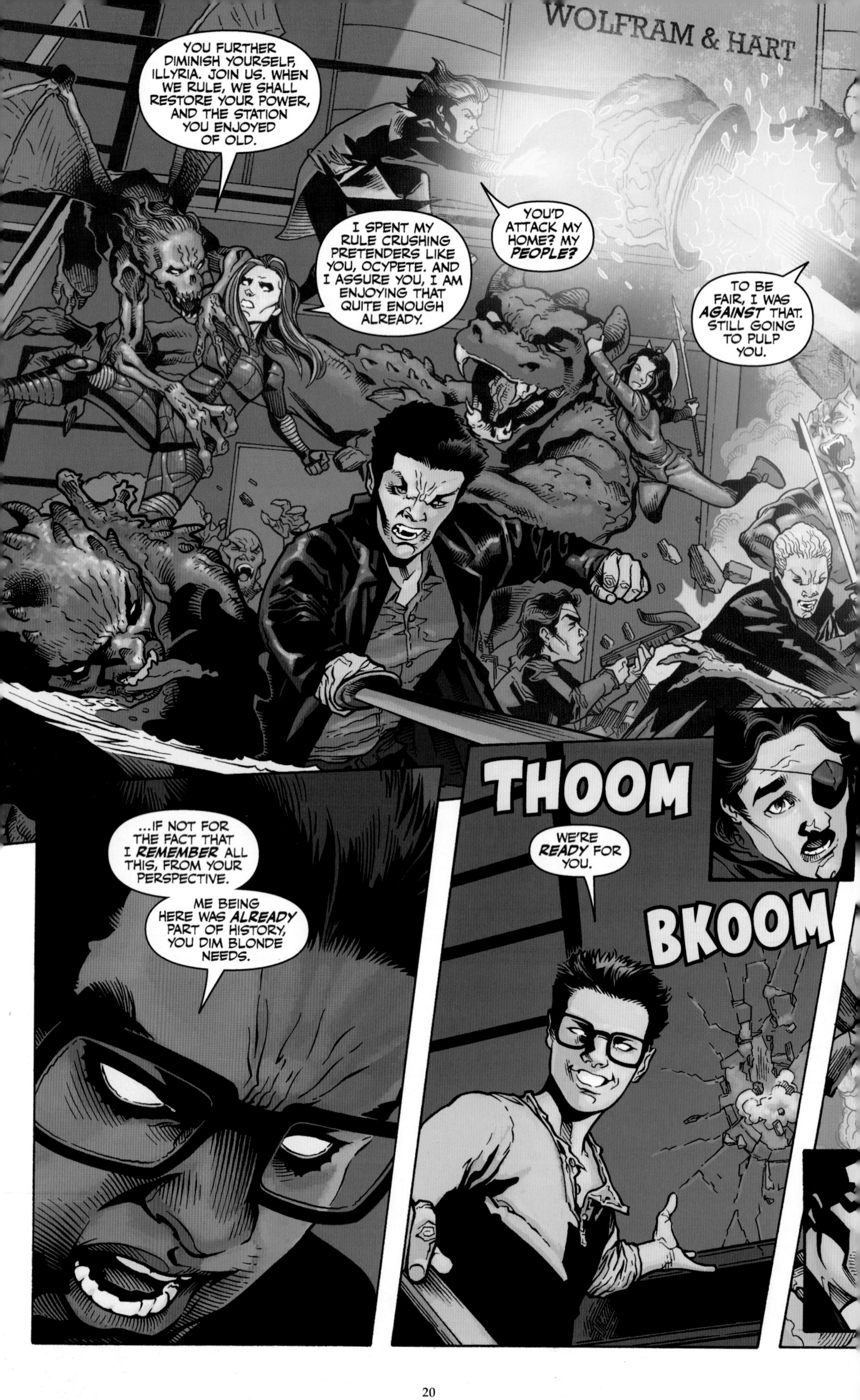
WOLFRAM & HART
YOU FURTHER DIMINISH YOURSELF, ILLYRIA. JOIN US. WHEN WE RULE, WE SHALL RESTORE YOUR POWER, AND THE STATION YOU ENJOYED OF OLD.
I SPENT MY RULE CRUSHING PRETENDERS LIKE YOU, OCYPETE. AND I ASSURE YOU, I AM ENJOYING THAT QUITE ENOUGH ALREADY.
YOU'D ATTACK MY HOME? MY PEOPLE?
TO BE FAIR, I WAS AGAINST THAT. STILL GOING TO PULP YOU.
...IF NOT FOR THE FACT THAT I REMEMBER ALL THIS, FROM YOUR PERSPECTIVE.
ME BEING HERE WAS ALREADY PART OF HISTORY, YOU DIM BLONDE NEEDS.
THOOM
WE'RE READY FOR YOU.
BKOOM

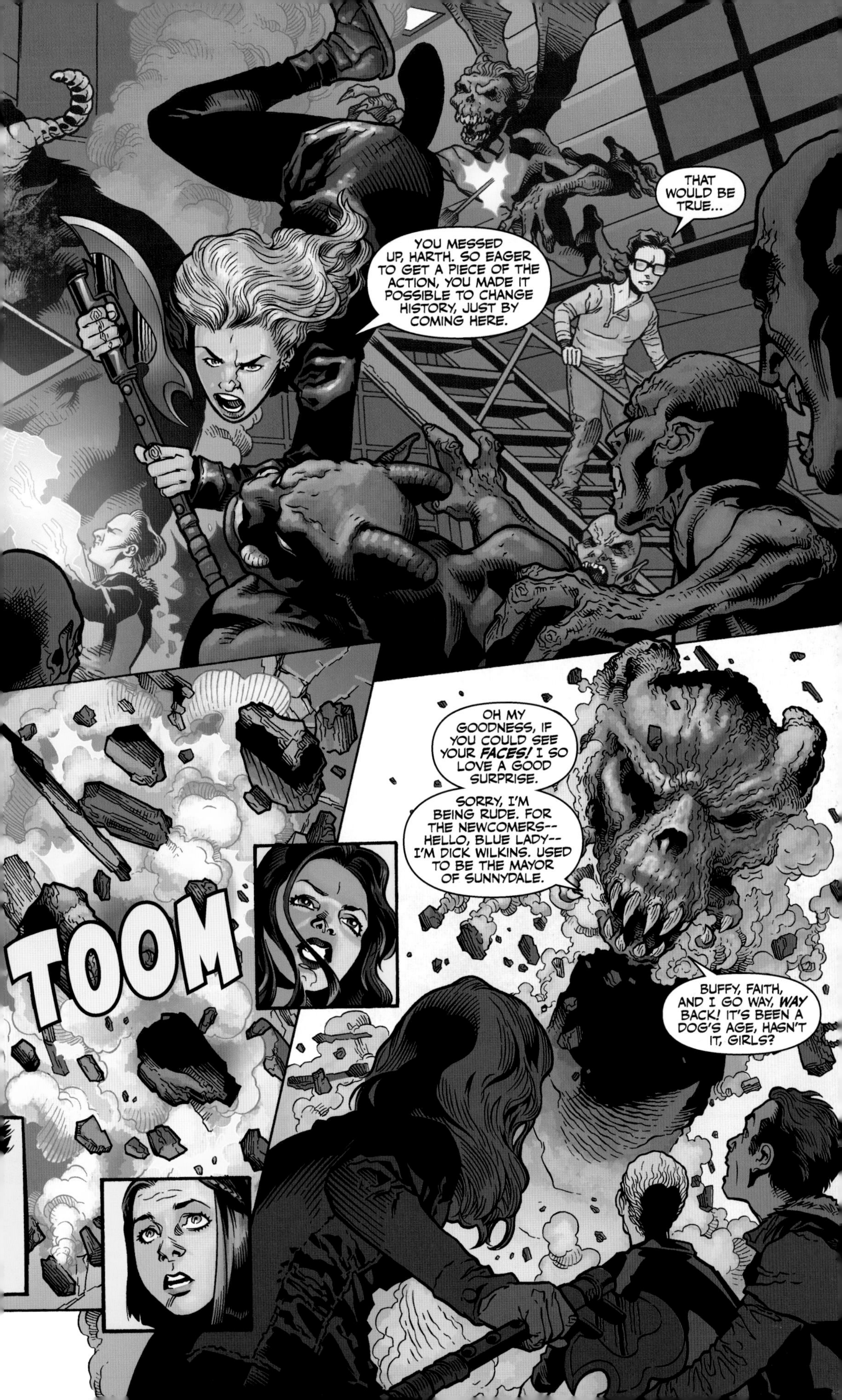
YOU MESSED UP, HARTH. SO EAGER TO GET A PIECE OF THE ACTION, YOU MADE IT POSSIBLE TO CHANGE HISTORY, JUST BY COMING HERE.
THAT WOULD BE TRUE...
TOOM
OH MY GOODNESS, IF YOU COULD SEE YOUR *FACES!* I SO LOVE A GOOD SURPRISE.
SORRY, I'M BEING RUDE. FOR THE NEWCOMERS-- HELLO, BLUE LADY-- I'M DICK WILKINS. USED TO BE THE MAYOR OF SUNNYDALE.
BUFFY, FAITH, AND I GO WAY, *WAY* BACK! IT'S BEEN A DOG'S AGE, HASN'T IT, GIRLS?

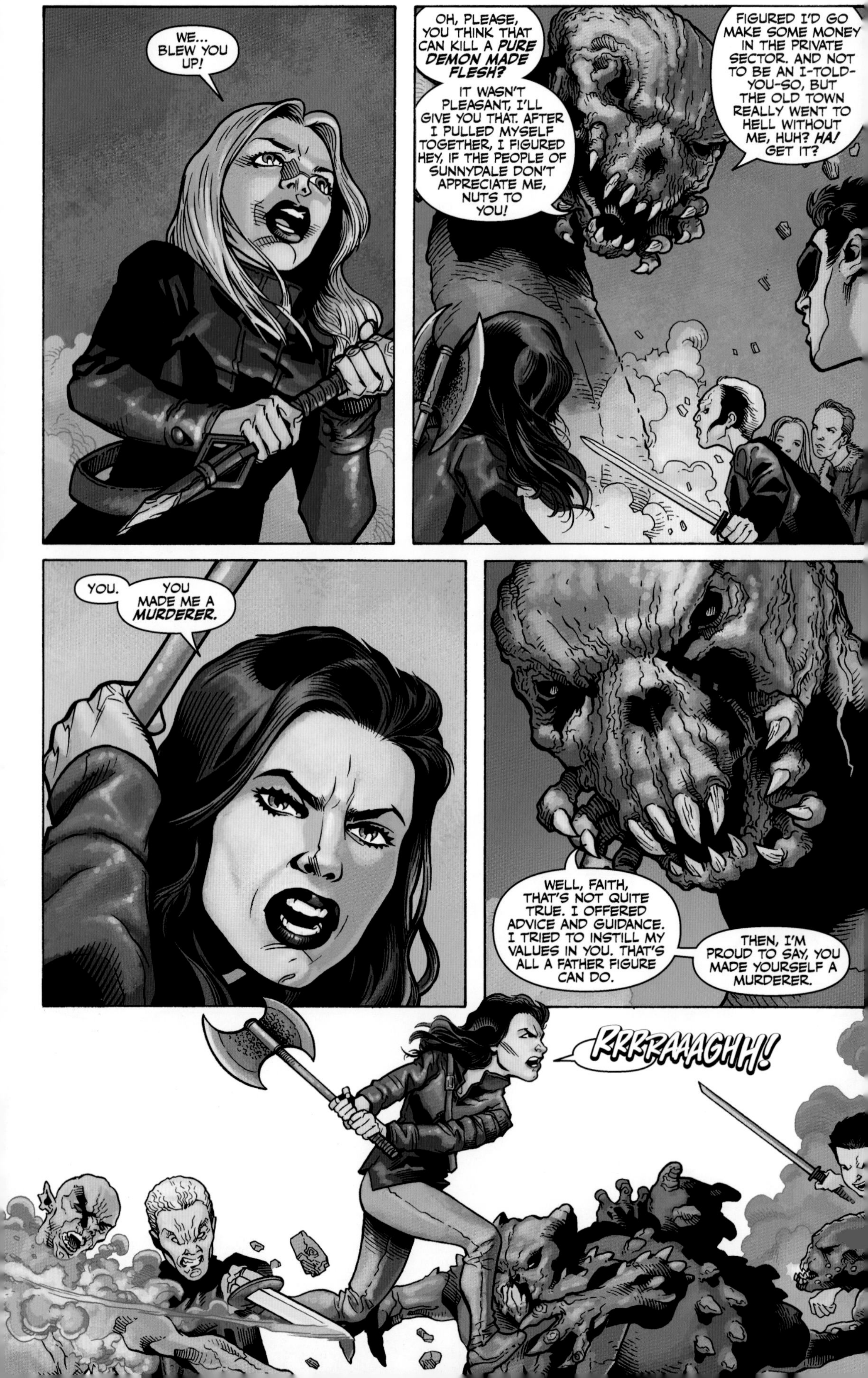

WE... BLEW YOU UP!
OH, PLEASE, YOU THINK THAT CAN KILL A PURE DEMON MADE FLESH?
IT WASN'T PLEASANT, I'LL GIVE YOU THAT. AFTER I PULLED MYSELF TOGETHER, I FIGURED HEY, IF THE PEOPLE OF SUNNYDALE DON'T APPRECIATE ME, NUTS TO YOU!
FIGURED I'D GO MAKE SOME MONEY IN THE PRIVATE SECTOR. AND NOT TO BE AN I-TOLD-YOU-SO, BUT THE OLD TOWN REALLY WENT TO HELL WITHOUT ME, HUH? HA! GET IT?
YOU.
YOU MADE ME A MURDERER.
WELL, FAITH, THAT'S NOT QUITE TRUE. I OFFERED ADVICE AND GUIDANCE. I TRIED TO INSTILL MY VALUES IN YOU. THAT'S ALL A FATHER FIGURE CAN DO.
THEN, I'M PROUD TO SAY, YOU MADE YOURSELF A MURDERER.
RRRRAAAGHH!

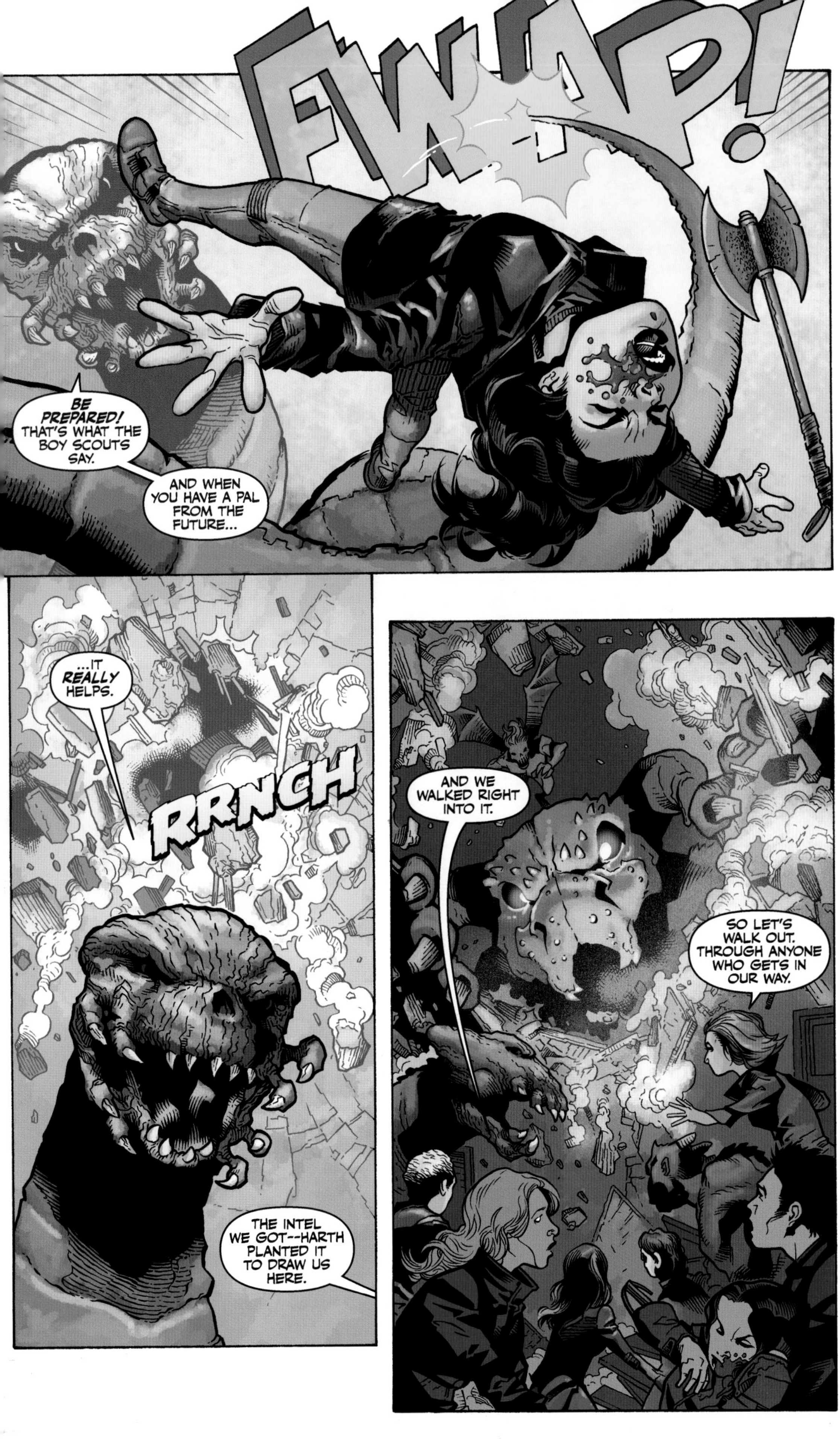
FWAP!
BE PREPARED! THAT'S WHAT THE BOY SCOUTS SAY.
AND WHEN YOU HAVE A PAL FROM THE FUTURE...
...IT REALLY HELPS.
RRNCH
THE INTEL WE GOT--HARTH PLANTED IT TO DRAW US HERE.
AND WE WALKED RIGHT INTO IT.
SO LET'S WALK OUT. THROUGH ANYONE WHO GETS IN OUR WAY.

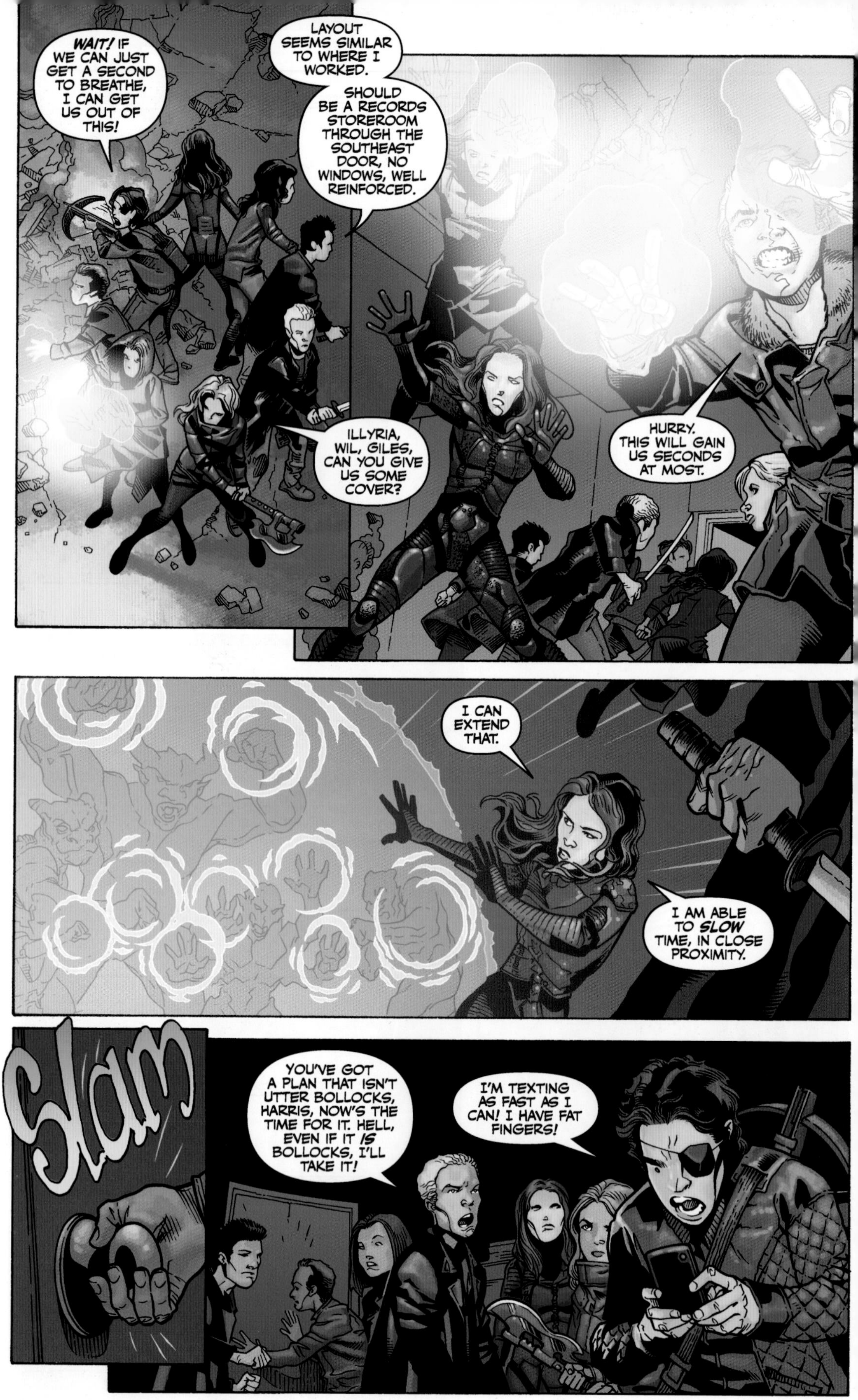
WAIT! IF WE CAN JUST GET A SECOND TO BREATHE, I CAN GET US OUT OF THIS!
LAYOUT SEEMS SIMILAR TO WHERE I WORKED.
SHOULD BE A RECORDS STOREROOM THROUGH THE SOUTHEAST DOOR, NO WINDOWS, WELL REINFORCED.
ILLYRIA, WIL, GILES, CAN YOU GIVE US SOME COVER?
HURRY. THIS WILL GAIN US SECONDS AT MOST.
I CAN EXTEND THAT.
I AM ABLE TO SLOW TIME, IN CLOSE PROXIMITY.
Slam
YOU'VE GOT A PLAN THAT ISN'T UTTER BOLLOCKS, HARRIS, NOW'S THE TIME FOR IT. HELL, EVEN IF IT IS BOLLOCKS, I'LL TAKE IT!
I'M TEXTING AS FAST AS I CAN! I HAVE FAT FINGERS!

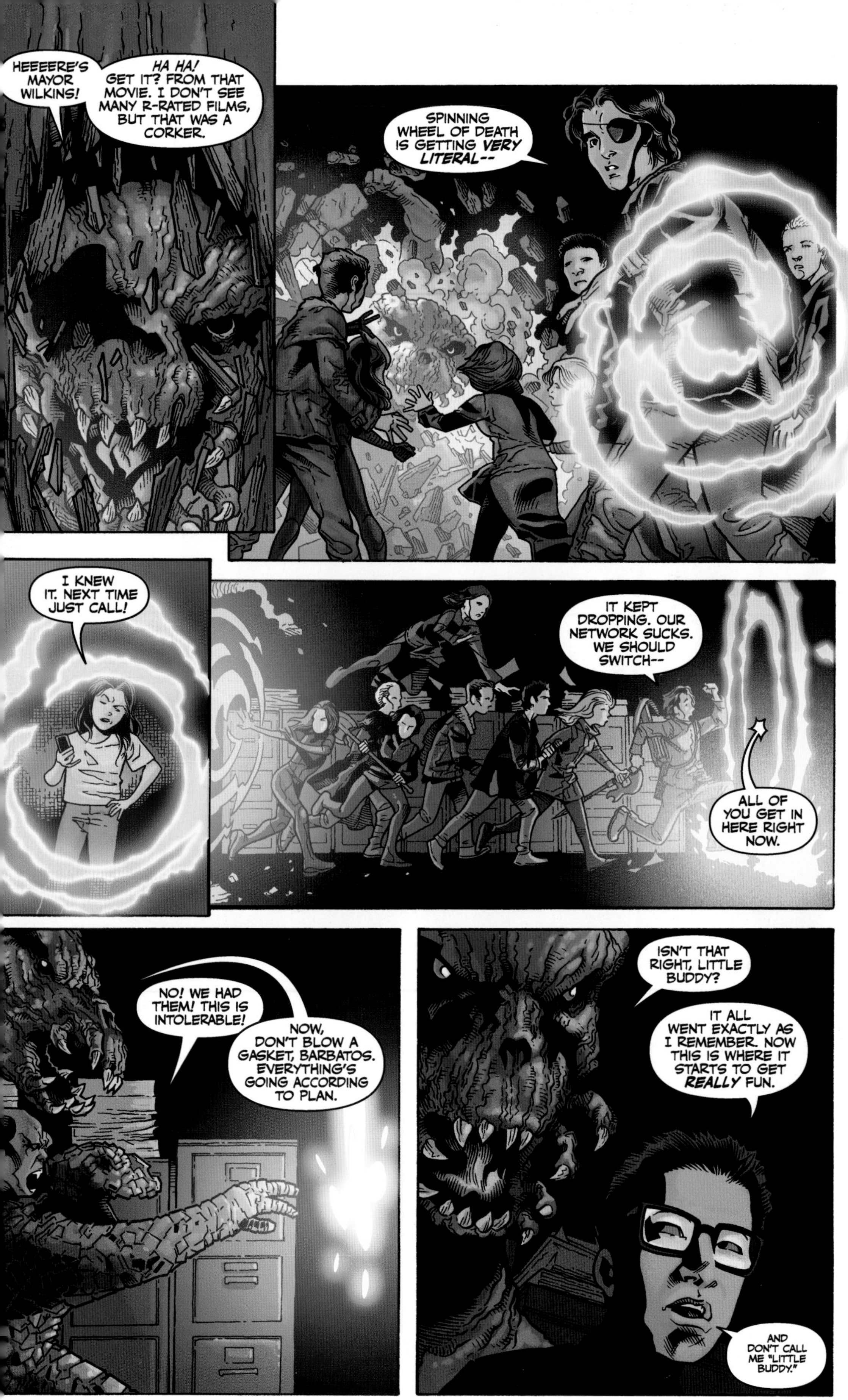
HEEEERE'S MAYOR WILKINS!
HA HA! GET IT? FROM THAT MOVIE. I DON'T SEE MANY R-RATED FILMS, BUT THAT WAS A CORKER.
SPINNING WHEEL OF DEATH IS GETTING VERY LITERAL--
I KNEW IT. NEXT TIME JUST CALL!
IT KEPT DROPPING. OUR NETWORK SUCKS. WE SHOULD SWITCH--
ALL OF YOU GET IN HERE RIGHT NOW.
NO! WE HAD THEM! THIS IS INTOLERABLE!
NOW, DON'T BLOW A GASKET, BARBATOS. EVERYTHING'S GOING ACCORDING TO PLAN.
ISN'T THAT RIGHT, LITTLE BUDDY?
IT ALL WENT EXACTLY AS I REMEMBER. NOW THIS IS WHERE IT STARTS TO GET REALLY FUN.
AND DON'T CALL ME "LITTLE BUDDY."

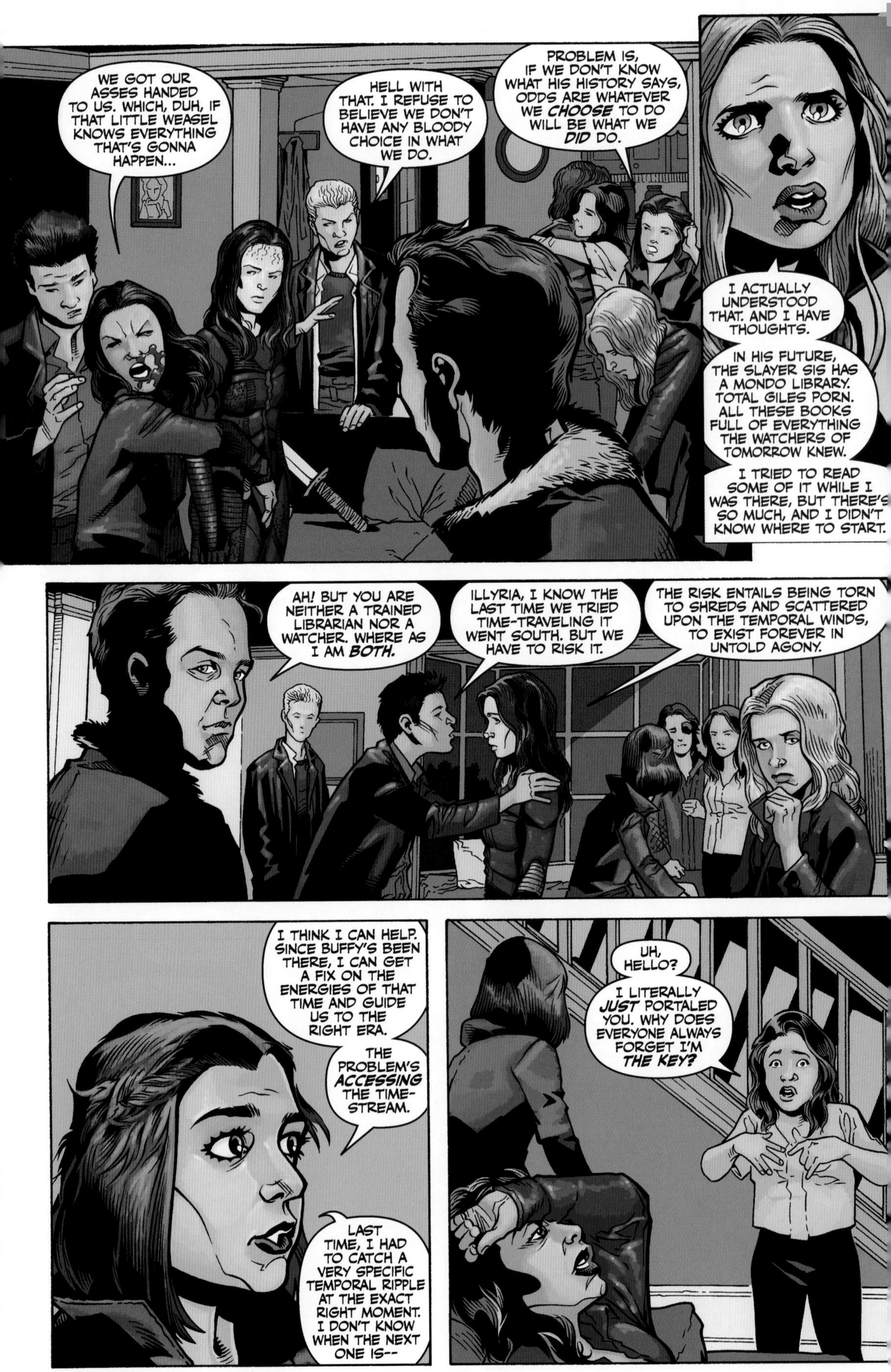
WE GOT OUR ASSES HANDED TO US. WHICH, DUH, IF THAT LITTLE WEASEL KNOWS EVERYTHING THAT'S GONNA HAPPEN...
HELL WITH THAT. I REFUSE TO BELIEVE WE DON'T HAVE ANY BLOODY CHOICE IN WHAT WE DO.
PROBLEM IS, IF WE DON'T KNOW WHAT HIS HISTORY SAYS, ODDS ARE WHATEVER WE *CHOOSE* TO DO WILL BE WHAT WE *DID* DO.
I ACTUALLY UNDERSTOOD THAT. AND I HAVE THOUGHTS.
IN HIS FUTURE, THE SLAYER SIS HAS A MONDO LIBRARY. TOTAL GILES PORN. ALL THESE BOOKS FULL OF EVERYTHING THE WATCHERS OF TOMORROW KNEW.
I TRIED TO READ SOME OF IT WHILE I WAS THERE, BUT THERE'S SO MUCH, AND I DIDN'T KNOW WHERE TO START.
AH! BUT YOU ARE NEITHER A TRAINED LIBRARIAN NOR A WATCHER. WHERE AS I AM *BOTH.*
ILLYRIA, I KNOW THE LAST TIME WE TRIED TIME-TRAVELING IT WENT SOUTH. BUT WE HAVE TO RISK IT.
THE RISK ENTAILS BEING TORN TO SHREDS AND SCATTERED UPON THE TEMPORAL WINDS, TO EXIST FOREVER IN UNTOLD AGONY.
I THINK I CAN HELP. SINCE BUFFY'S BEEN THERE, I CAN GET A FIX ON THE ENERGIES OF THAT TIME AND GUIDE US TO THE RIGHT ERA.
THE PROBLEM'S *ACCESSING* THE TIME-STREAM.
LAST TIME, I HAD TO CATCH A VERY SPECIFIC TEMPORAL RIPPLE AT THE EXACT RIGHT MOMENT. I DON'T KNOW WHEN THE NEXT ONE IS--
UH, HELLO?
I LITERALLY *JUST* PORTALED YOU. WHY DOES EVERYONE ALWAYS FORGET I'M *THE KEY?*

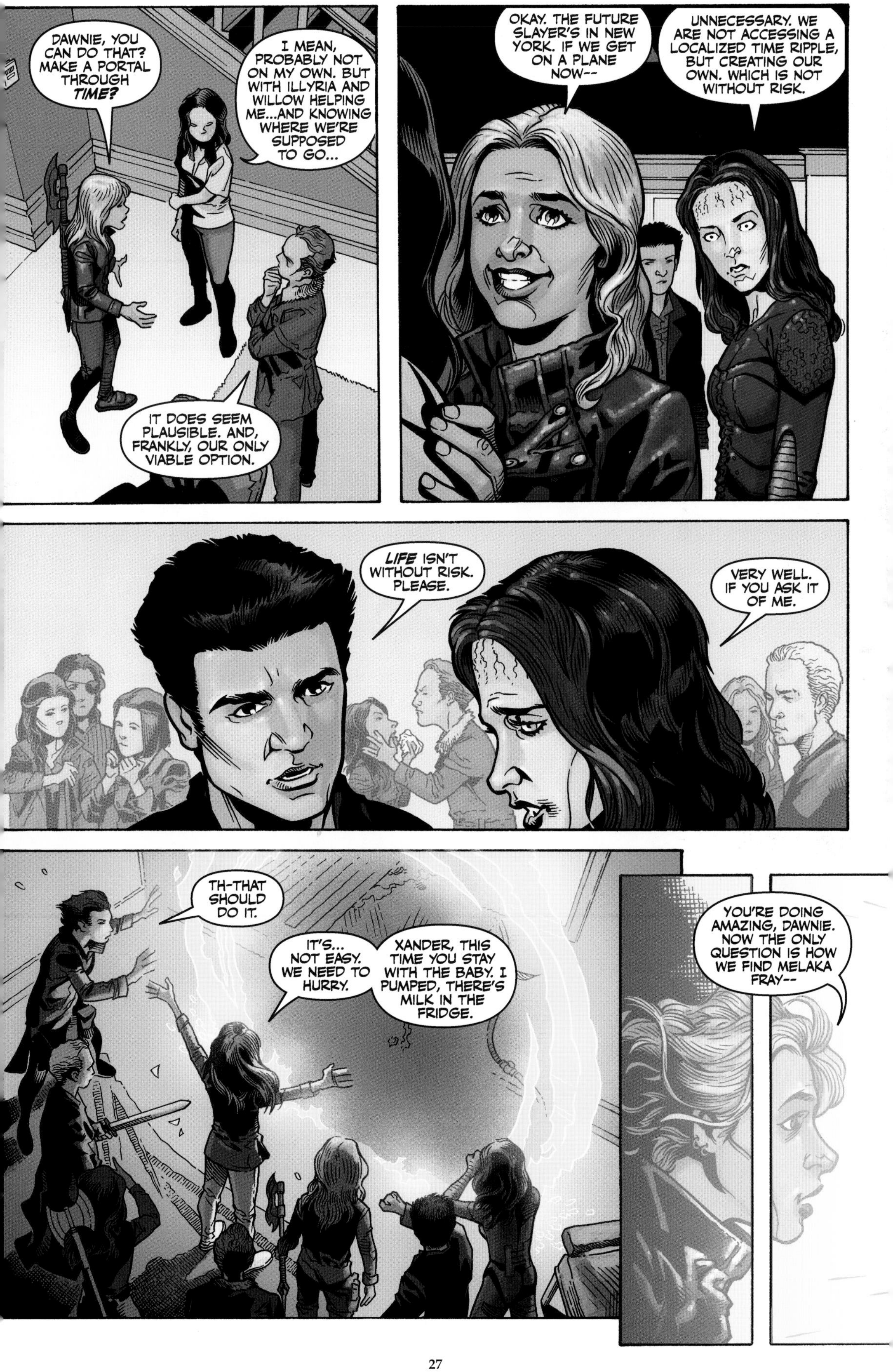
DAWNIE, YOU CAN DO THAT? MAKE A PORTAL THROUGH *TIME?*
I MEAN, PROBABLY NOT ON MY OWN. BUT WITH ILLYRIA AND WILLOW HELPING ME...AND KNOWING WHERE WE'RE SUPPOSED TO GO...
IT DOES SEEM PLAUSIBLE. AND, FRANKLY, OUR ONLY VIABLE OPTION.
OKAY. THE FUTURE SLAYER'S IN NEW YORK. IF WE GET ON A PLANE NOW--
UNNECESSARY. WE ARE NOT ACCESSING A LOCALIZED TIME RIPPLE, BUT CREATING OUR OWN. WHICH IS NOT WITHOUT RISK.
LIFE ISN'T WITHOUT RISK. PLEASE.
VERY WELL. IF YOU ASK IT OF ME.
TH-THAT SHOULD DO IT.
IT'S... NOT EASY. WE NEED TO HURRY.
XANDER, THIS TIME YOU STAY WITH THE BABY. I PUMPED, THERE'S MILK IN THE FRIDGE.
YOU'RE DOING AMAZING, DAWNIE. NOW THE ONLY QUESTION IS HOW WE FIND MELAKA FRAY--

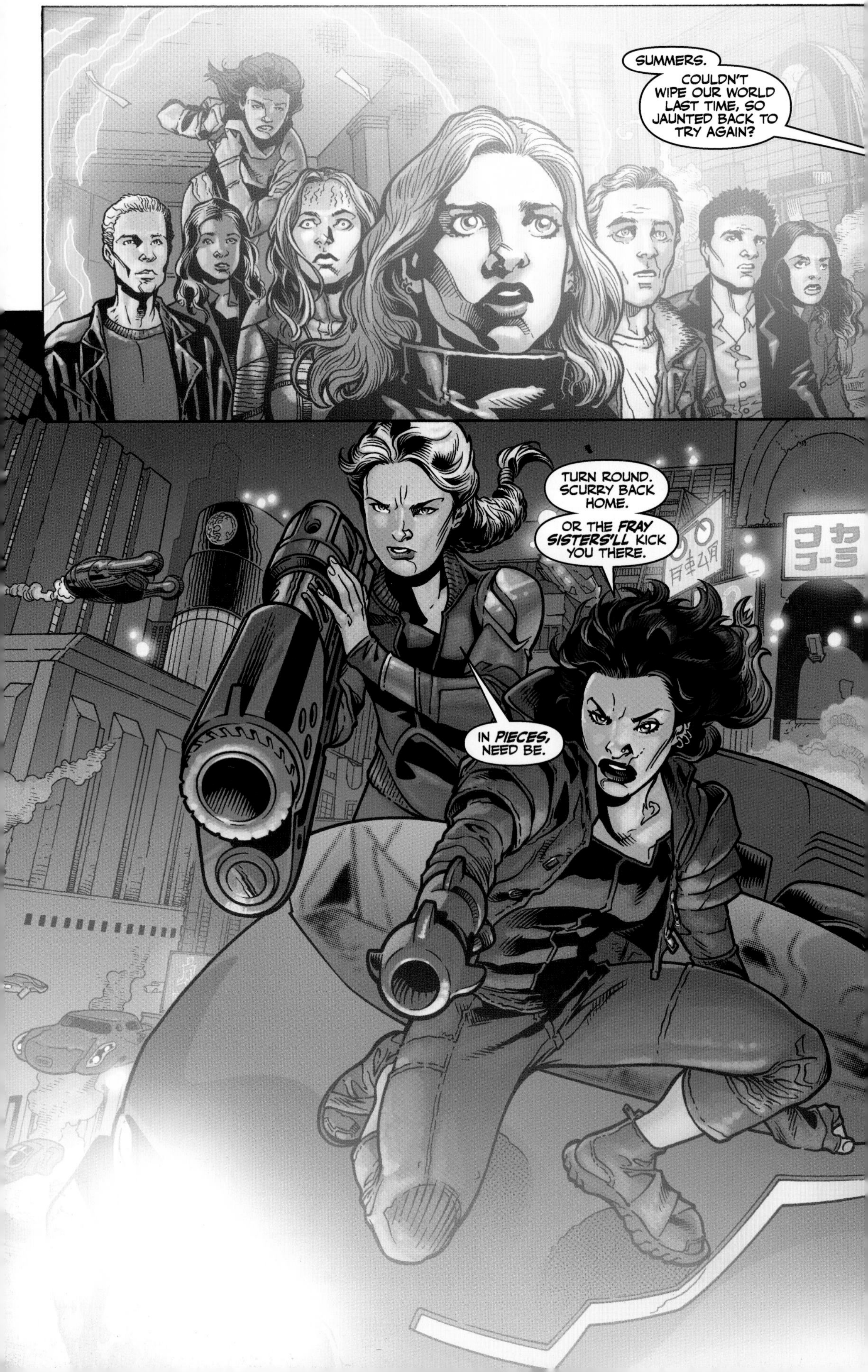
SUMMERS.
COULDN'T WIPE OUR WORLD LAST TIME, SO JAUNTED BACK TO TRY AGAIN?
TURN ROUND. SCURRY BACK HOME.
OR THE *FRAY SISTERS'LL* KICK YOU THERE.
IN *PIECES,* NEED BE.

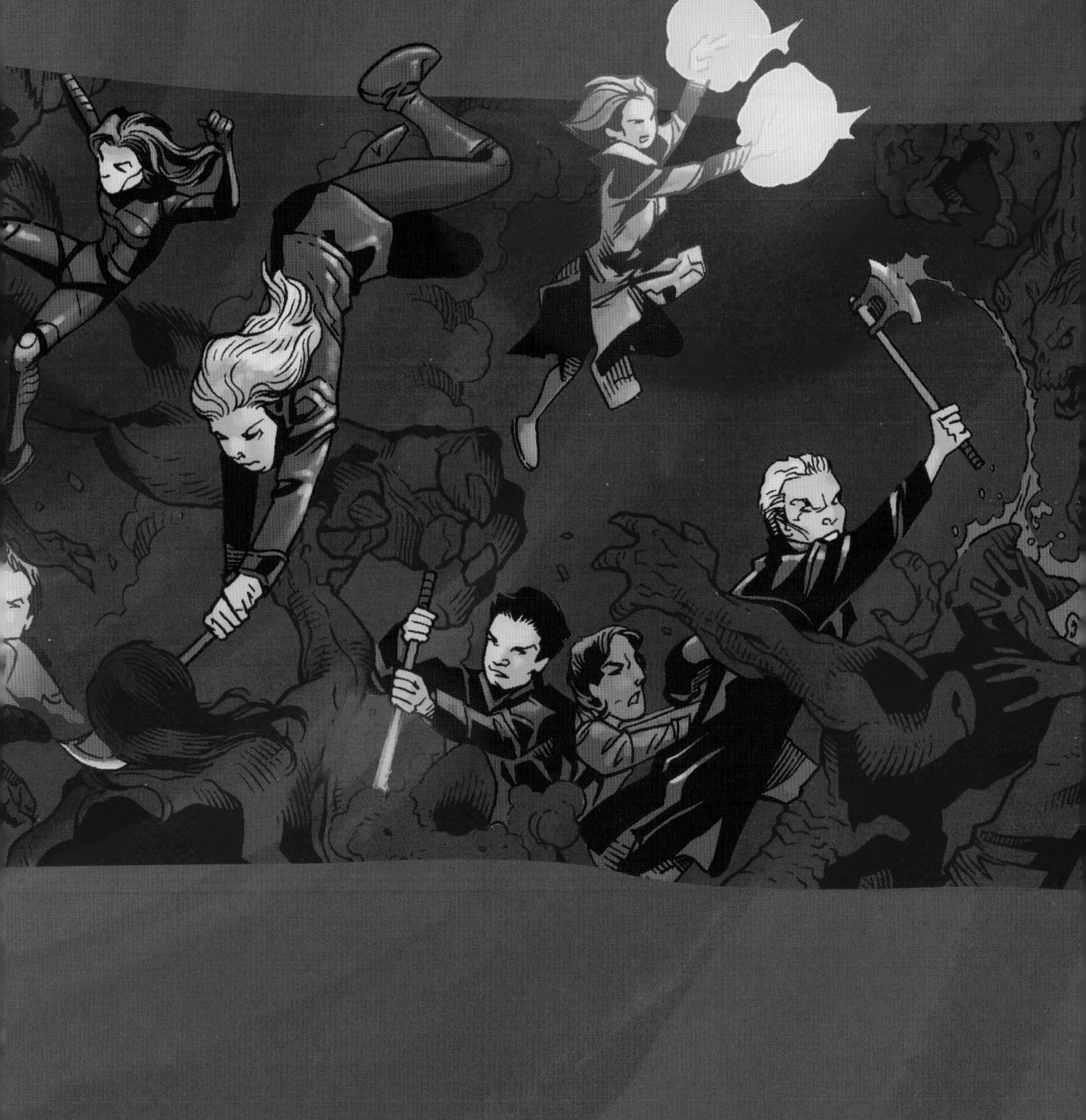

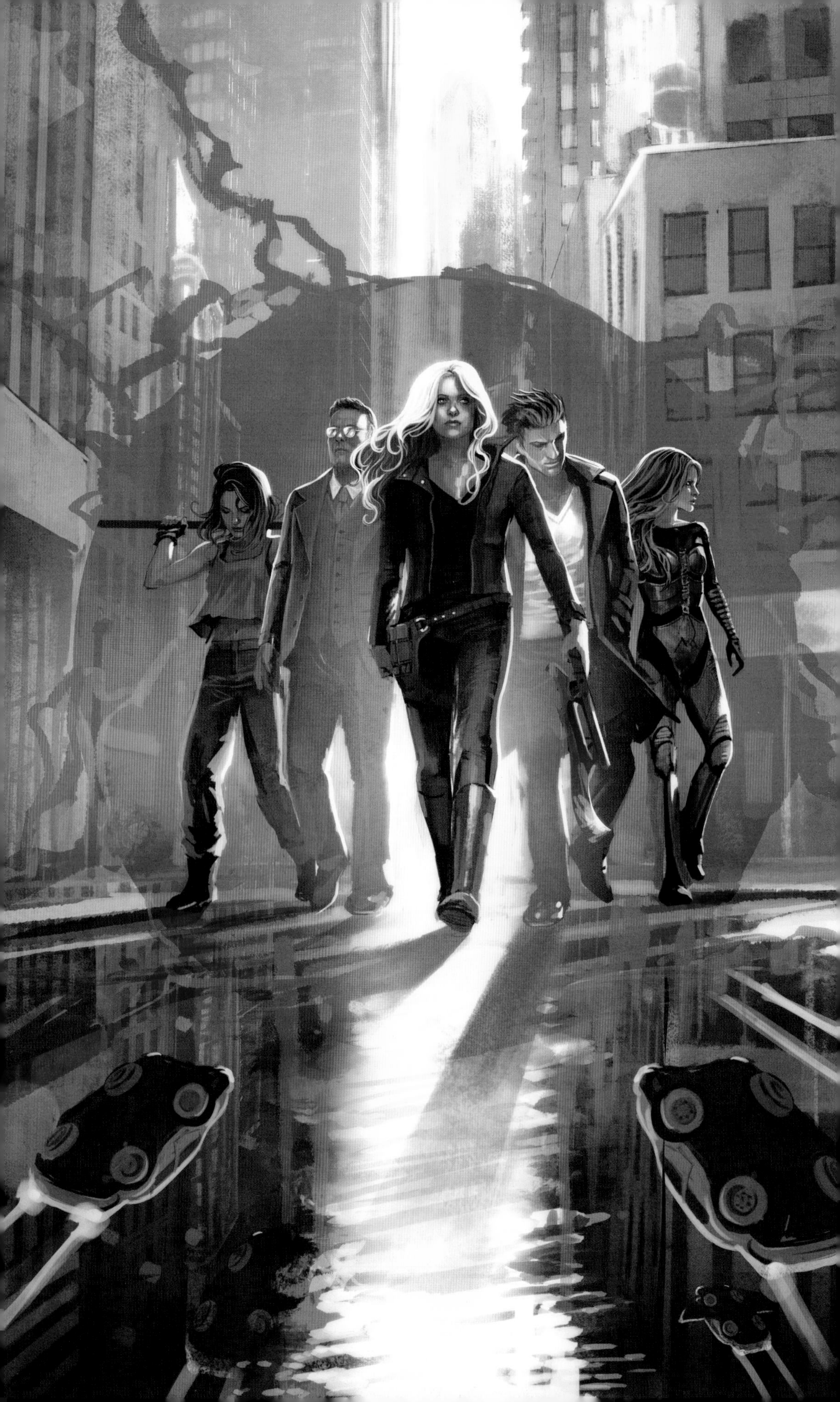

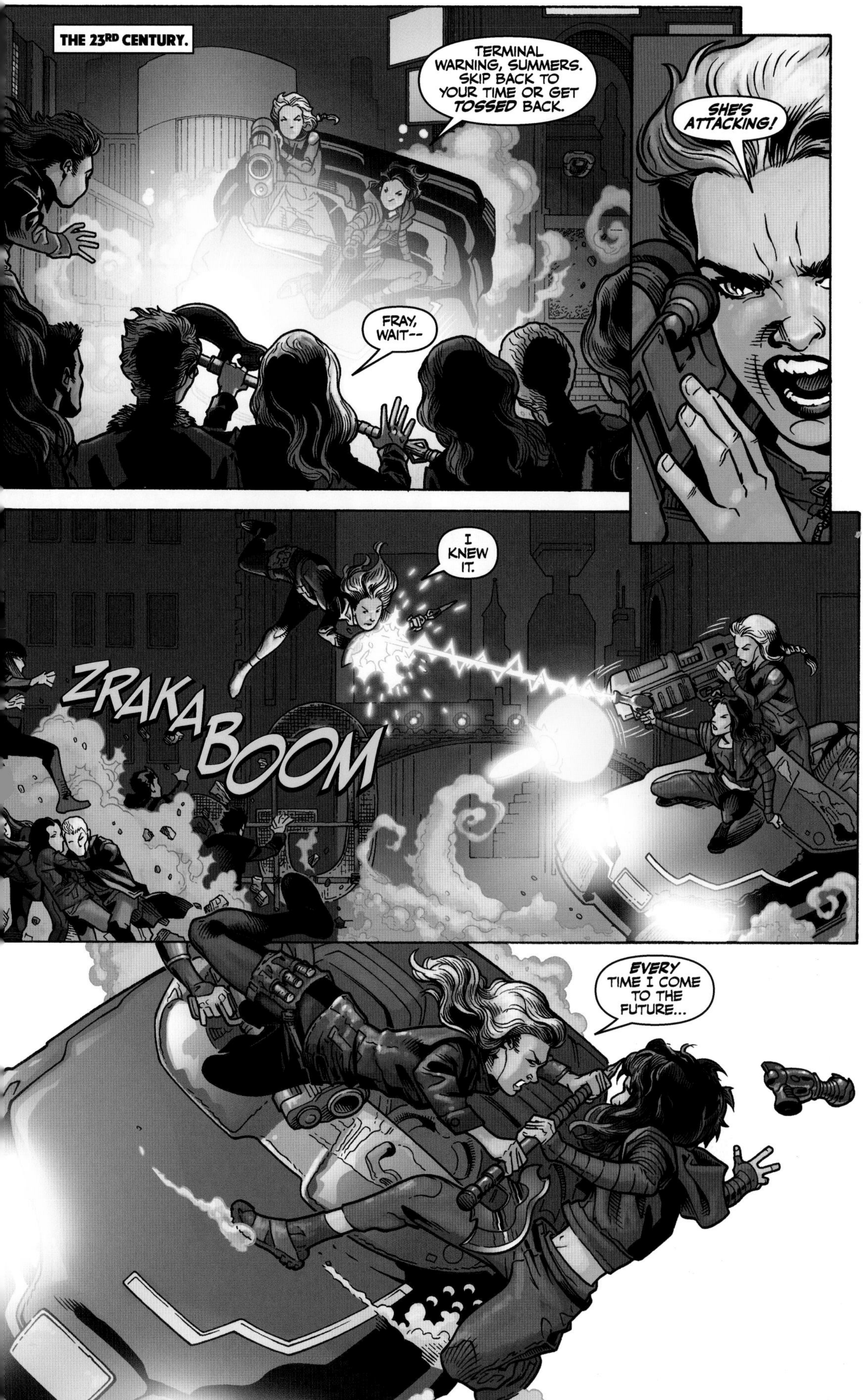
THE 23RD CENTURY.
TERMINAL WARNING, SUMMERS. SKIP BACK TO YOUR TIME OR GET TOSSED BACK.
SHE'S ATTACKING!
FRAY, WAIT--
I KNEW IT.
ZRAKABOOM
EVERY TIME I COME TO THE FUTURE...

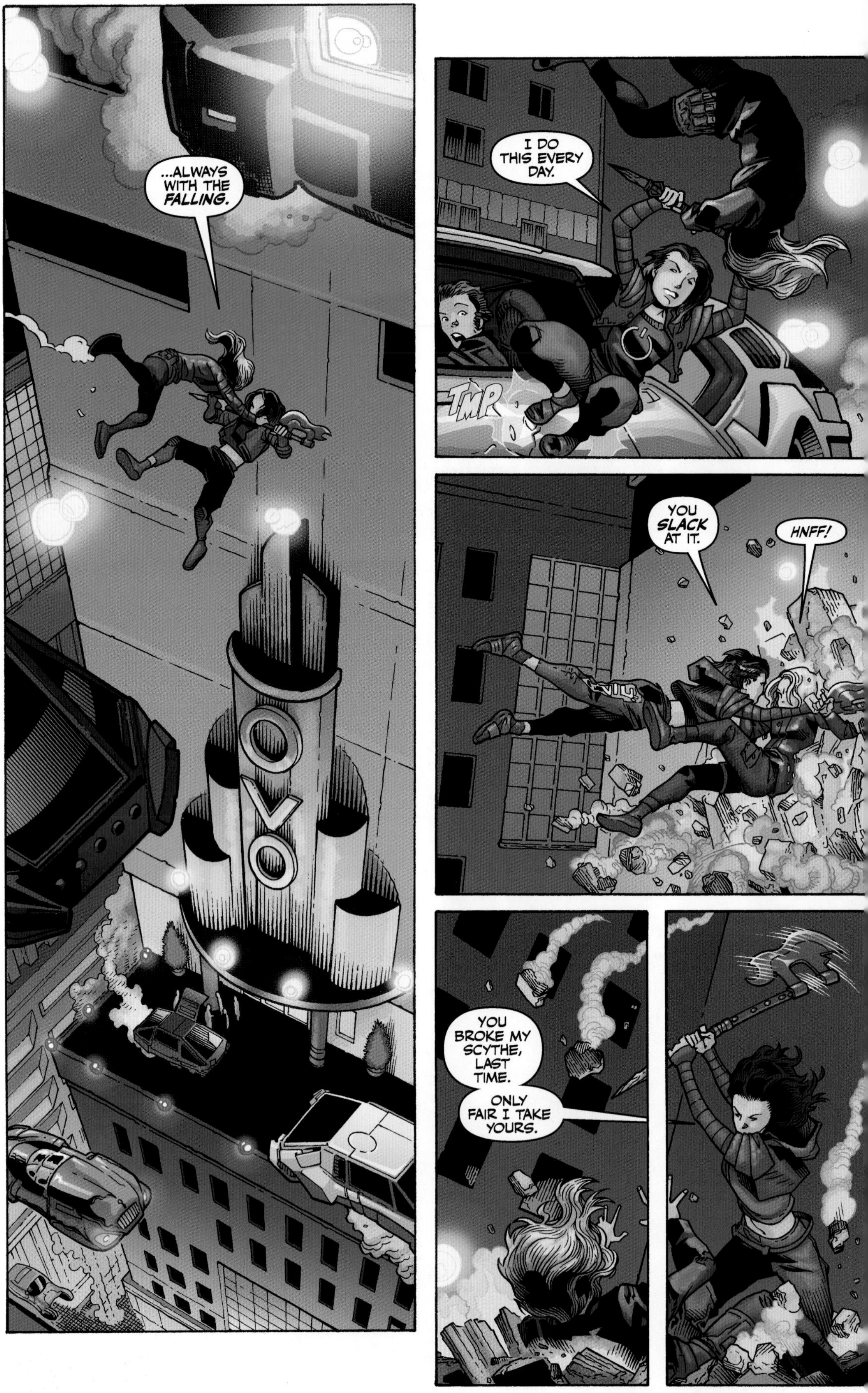
...ALWAYS WITH THE FALLING.
I DO THIS EVERY DAY.
TMP
YOU SLACK AT IT.
HNFF!
YOU BROKE MY SCYTHE, LAST TIME.
ONLY FAIR I TAKE YOURS.

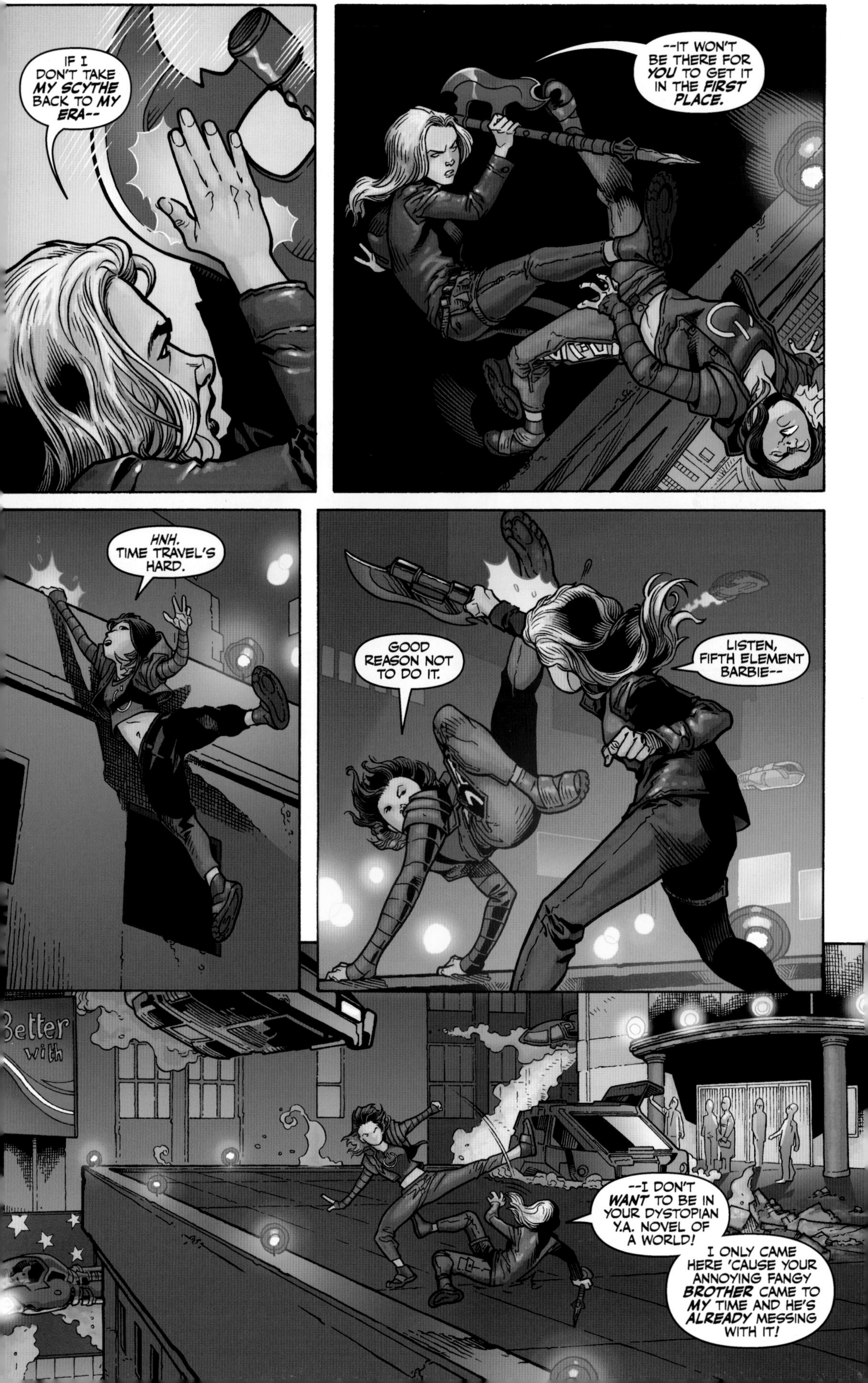
IF I DON'T TAKE MY SCYTHE BACK TO MY ERA--
--IT WON'T BE THERE FOR YOU TO GET IT IN THE FIRST PLACE.
HNH. TIME TRAVEL'S HARD.
GOOD REASON NOT TO DO IT.
LISTEN, FIFTH ELEMENT BARBIE--
Better with
--I DON'T WANT TO BE IN YOUR DYSTOPIAN Y.A. NOVEL OF A WORLD!
I ONLY CAME HERE 'CAUSE YOUR ANNOYING FANGY BROTHER CAME TO MY TIME AND HE'S ALREADY MESSING WITH IT!

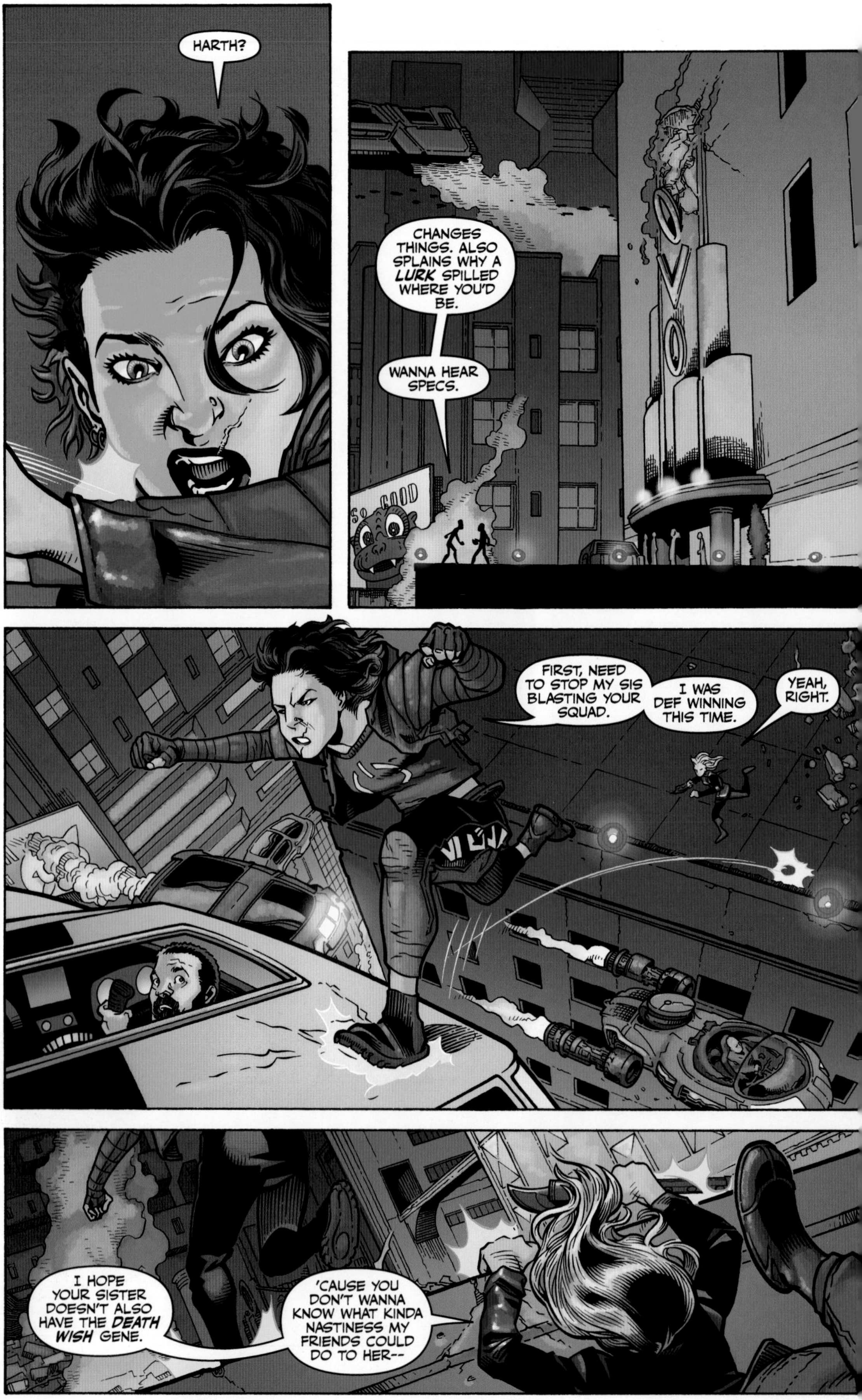
HARTH?
CHANGES THINGS. ALSO SPLAINS WHY A LURK SPILLED WHERE YOU'D BE.
WANNA HEAR SPECS.
SO GOOD
FIRST, NEED TO STOP MY SIS BLASTING YOUR SQUAD.
I WAS DEF WINNING THIS TIME.
YEAH, RIGHT.
I HOPE YOUR SISTER DOESN'T ALSO HAVE THE DEATH WISH GENE.
'CAUSE YOU DON'T WANNA KNOW WHAT KINDA NASTINESS MY FRIENDS COULD DO TO HER--

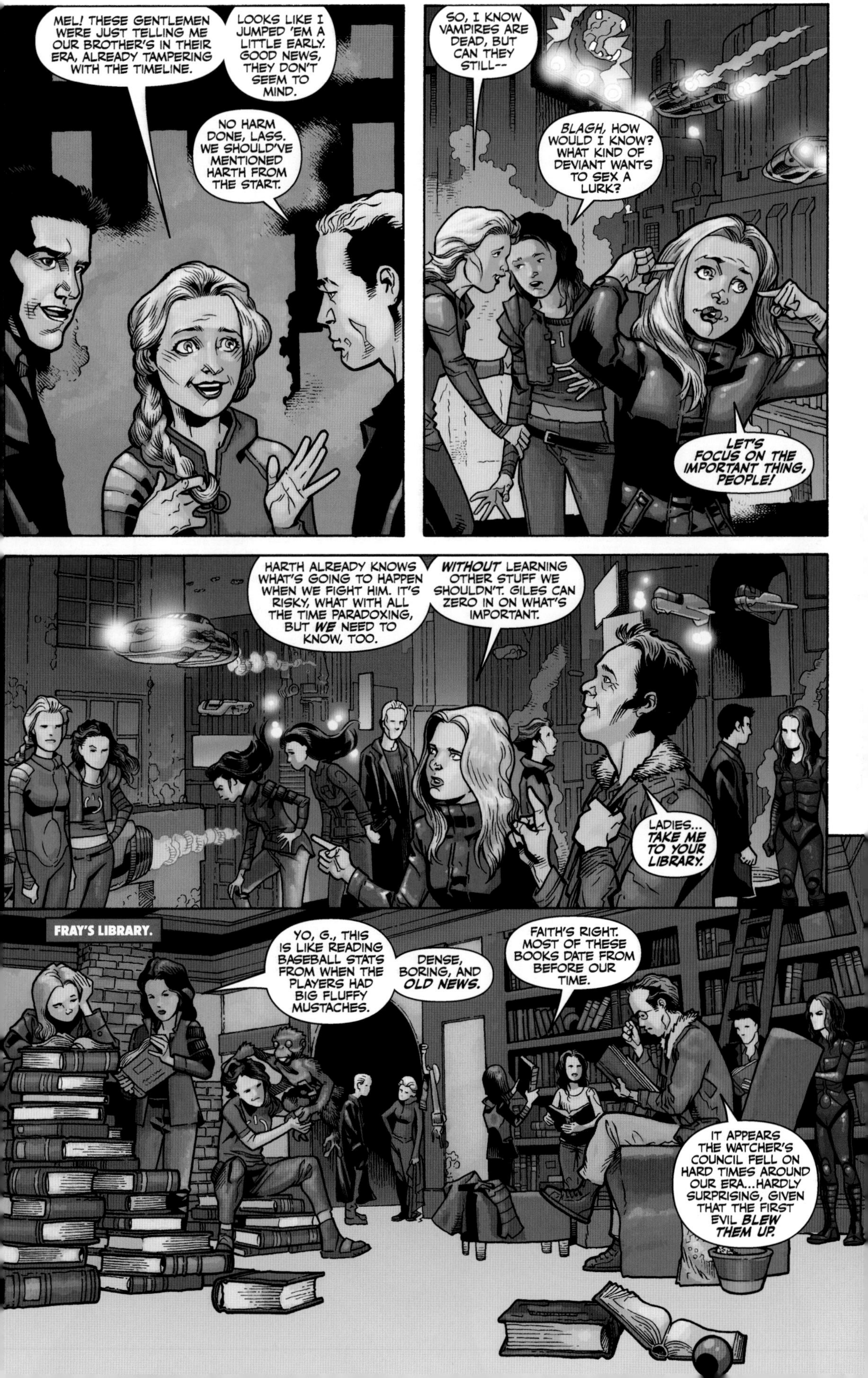

MEL! THESE GENTLEMEN WERE JUST TELLING ME OUR BROTHER'S IN THEIR ERA, ALREADY TAMPERING WITH THE TIMELINE.
LOOKS LIKE I JUMPED 'EM A LITTLE EARLY. GOOD NEWS, THEY DON'T SEEM TO MIND.
NO HARM DONE, LASS. WE SHOULD'VE MENTIONED HARTH FROM THE START.
SO, I KNOW VAMPIRES ARE DEAD, BUT CAN THEY STILL--
BLAGH, HOW WOULD I KNOW? WHAT KIND OF DEVIANT WANTS TO SEX A LURK?
LET'S FOCUS ON THE IMPORTANT THING, PEOPLE!
HARTH ALREADY KNOWS WHAT'S GOING TO HAPPEN WHEN WE FIGHT HIM. IT'S RISKY, WHAT WITH ALL THE TIME PARADOXING, BUT WE NEED TO KNOW, TOO.
WITHOUT LEARNING OTHER STUFF WE SHOULDN'T. GILES CAN ZERO IN ON WHAT'S IMPORTANT.
LADIES... TAKE ME TO YOUR LIBRARY.
FRAY'S LIBRARY.
YO, G., THIS IS LIKE READING BASEBALL STATS FROM WHEN THE PLAYERS HAD BIG FLUFFY MUSTACHES.
DENSE, BORING, AND OLD NEWS.
FAITH'S RIGHT. MOST OF THESE BOOKS DATE FROM BEFORE OUR TIME.
IT APPEARS THE WATCHER'S COUNCIL FELL ON HARD TIMES AROUND OUR ERA...HARDLY SURPRISING, GIVEN THAT THE FIRST EVIL BLEW THEM UP.

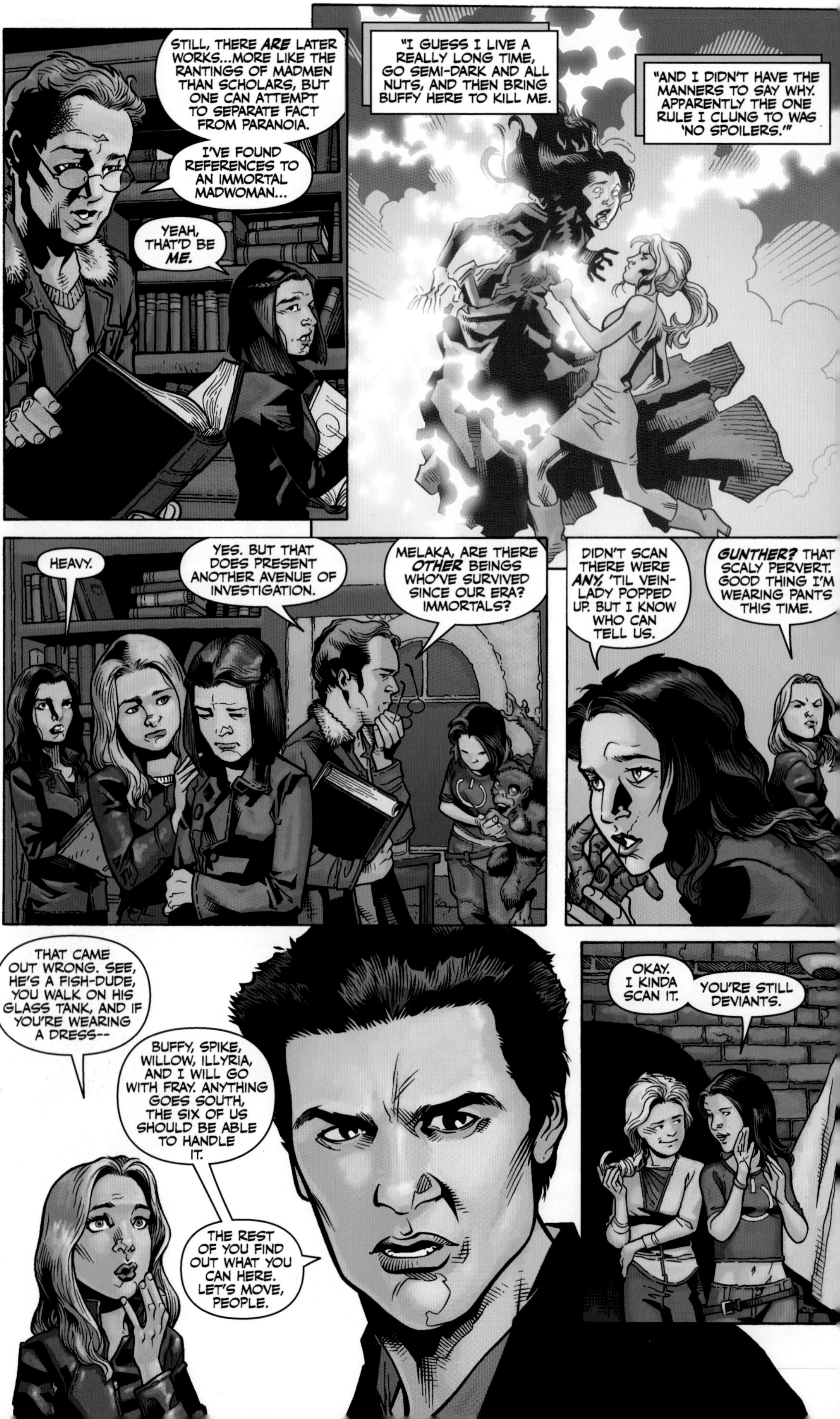

STILL, THERE ARE LATER WORKS...MORE LIKE THE RANTINGS OF MADMEN THAN SCHOLARS, BUT ONE CAN ATTEMPT TO SEPARATE FACT FROM PARANOIA.
I'VE FOUND REFERENCES TO AN IMMORTAL MADWOMAN...
YEAH, THAT'D BE ME.
"I GUESS I LIVE A REALLY LONG TIME, GO SEMI-DARK AND ALL NUTS, AND THEN BRING BUFFY HERE TO KILL ME.
"AND I DIDN'T HAVE THE MANNERS TO SAY WHY. APPARENTLY THE ONE RULE I CLUNG TO WAS 'NO SPOILERS.'"
HEAVY.
YES. BUT THAT DOES PRESENT ANOTHER AVENUE OF INVESTIGATION.
MELAKA, ARE THERE OTHER BEINGS WHO'VE SURVIVED SINCE OUR ERA? IMMORTALS?
DIDN'T SCAN THERE WERE ANY, 'TIL VEIN-LADY POPPED UP. BUT I KNOW WHO CAN TELL US.
GUNTHER? THAT SCALY PERVERT. GOOD THING I'M WEARING PANTS THIS TIME.
THAT CAME OUT WRONG. SEE, HE'S A FISH-DUDE, YOU WALK ON HIS GLASS TANK, AND IF YOU'RE WEARING A DRESS--
BUFFY, SPIKE, WILLOW, ILLYRIA, AND I WILL GO WITH FRAY. ANYTHING GOES SOUTH, THE SIX OF US SHOULD BE ABLE TO HANDLE IT.
THE REST OF YOU FIND OUT WHAT YOU CAN HERE. LET'S MOVE, PEOPLE.
OKAY. I KINDA SCAN IT.
YOU'RE STILL DEVIANTS.

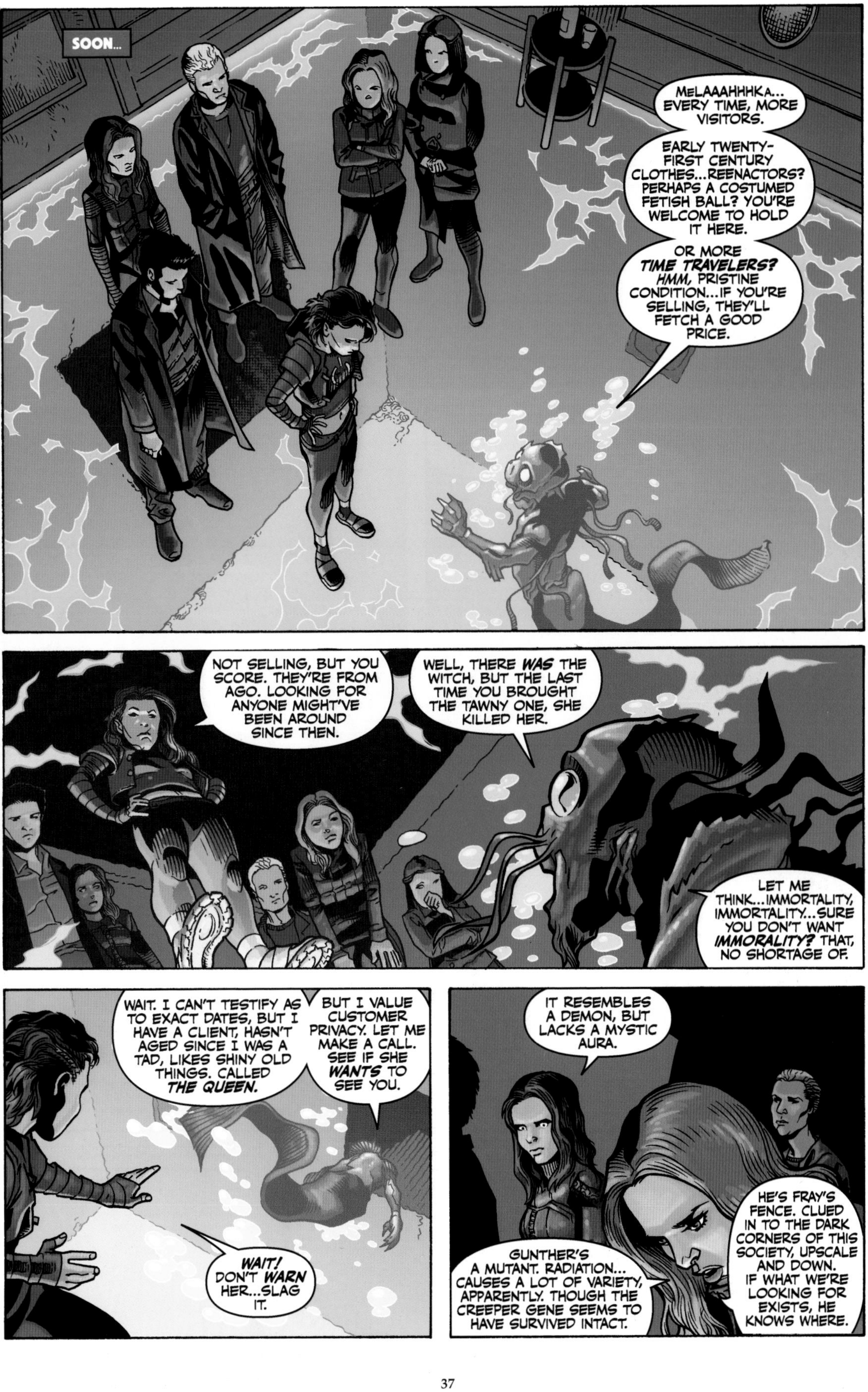
SOON...
MELAAAHHHKA... EVERY TIME, MORE VISITORS.
EARLY TWENTY-FIRST CENTURY CLOTHES...REENACTORS? PERHAPS A COSTUMED FETISH BALL? YOU'RE WELCOME TO HOLD IT HERE.
OR MORE TIME TRAVELERS? HMM, PRISTINE CONDITION...IF YOU'RE SELLING, THEY'LL FETCH A GOOD PRICE.
NOT SELLING, BUT YOU SCORE. THEY'RE FROM AGO. LOOKING FOR ANYONE MIGHT'VE BEEN AROUND SINCE THEN.
WELL, THERE WAS THE WITCH, BUT THE LAST TIME YOU BROUGHT THE TAWNY ONE, SHE KILLED HER.
LET ME THINK...IMMORTALITY, IMMORTALITY...SURE YOU DON'T WANT IMMORALITY? THAT, NO SHORTAGE OF.
WAIT. I CAN'T TESTIFY AS TO EXACT DATES, BUT I HAVE A CLIENT, HASN'T AGED SINCE I WAS A TAD, LIKES SHINY OLD THINGS. CALLED THE QUEEN.
BUT I VALUE CUSTOMER PRIVACY. LET ME MAKE A CALL. SEE IF SHE WANTS TO SEE YOU.
WAIT! DON'T WARN HER...SLAG IT.
IT RESEMBLES A DEMON, BUT LACKS A MYSTIC AURA.
GUNTHER'S A MUTANT. RADIATION... CAUSES A LOT OF VARIETY, APPARENTLY. THOUGH THE CREEPER GENE SEEMS TO HAVE SURVIVED INTACT.
HE'S FRAY'S FENCE. CLUED IN TO THE DARK CORNERS OF THIS SOCIETY, UPSCALE AND DOWN. IF WHAT WE'RE LOOKING FOR EXISTS, HE KNOWS WHERE.

YOU'RE IMMORTAL. MAYBE THIS "QUEEN" IS YOU.

WERE I PRESENT ON THIS PLANE, I WOULD SENSE IT. I AM NOT. CLEARLY THE BANISHMENT OF MAGICAL THINGS DURING THE RECKONING ENCOMPASSED ME.

GOOD TO SEE YOU BACK, BLUE THUNDER. I'D MISSED YOUR SUNNY OUTLOOK.

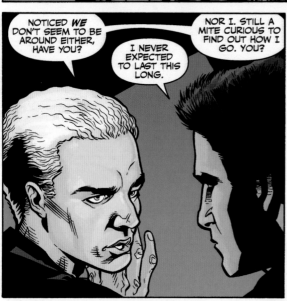

NOTICED WE DON'T SEEM TO BE AROUND EITHER, HAVE YOU?

I NEVER EXPECTED TO LAST THIS LONG.

NOR I. STILL A MITE CURIOUS TO FIND OUT HOW I GO. YOU?

NO.

WHATEVER IT IS, I'VE GOT IT COMING.

SPLENDID NEWS! THE QUEEN WILL SEE YOU. SEEMS SHE DOES GO BACK TO YOUR TIME.

IN FACT...

...SHE SAYS SHE KNOWS YOU.

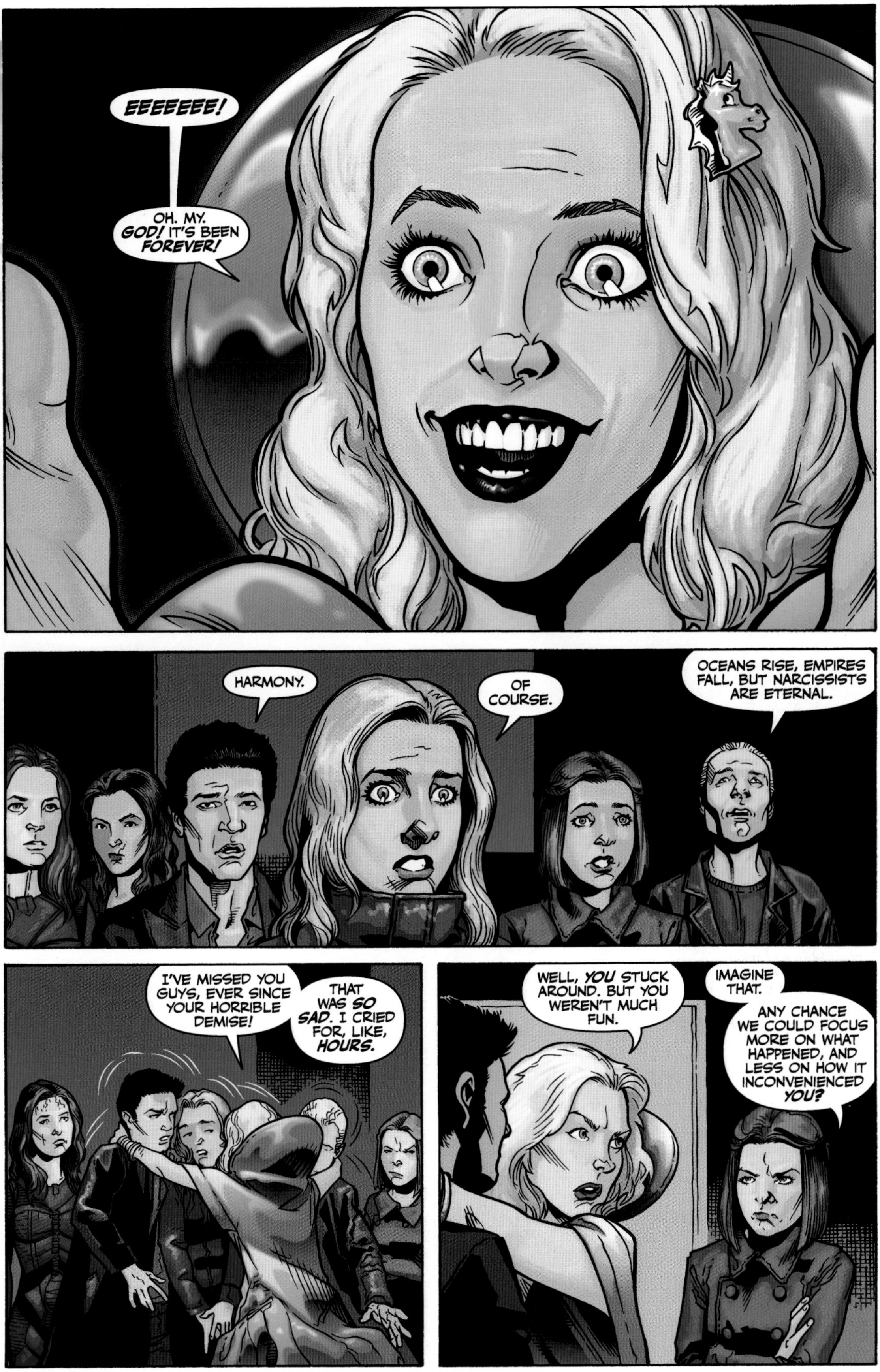
EEEEEEE!
OH. MY. GOD! IT'S BEEN FOREVER!
HARMONY.
OF COURSE.
OCEANS RISE, EMPIRES FALL, BUT NARCISSISTS ARE ETERNAL.
I'VE MISSED YOU GUYS, EVER SINCE YOUR HORRIBLE DEMISE!
THAT WAS SO SAD. I CRIED FOR, LIKE, HOURS.
WELL, YOU STUCK AROUND. BUT YOU WEREN'T MUCH FUN.
IMAGINE THAT.
ANY CHANCE WE COULD FOCUS MORE ON WHAT HAPPENED, AND LESS ON HOW IT INCONVENIENCED YOU?

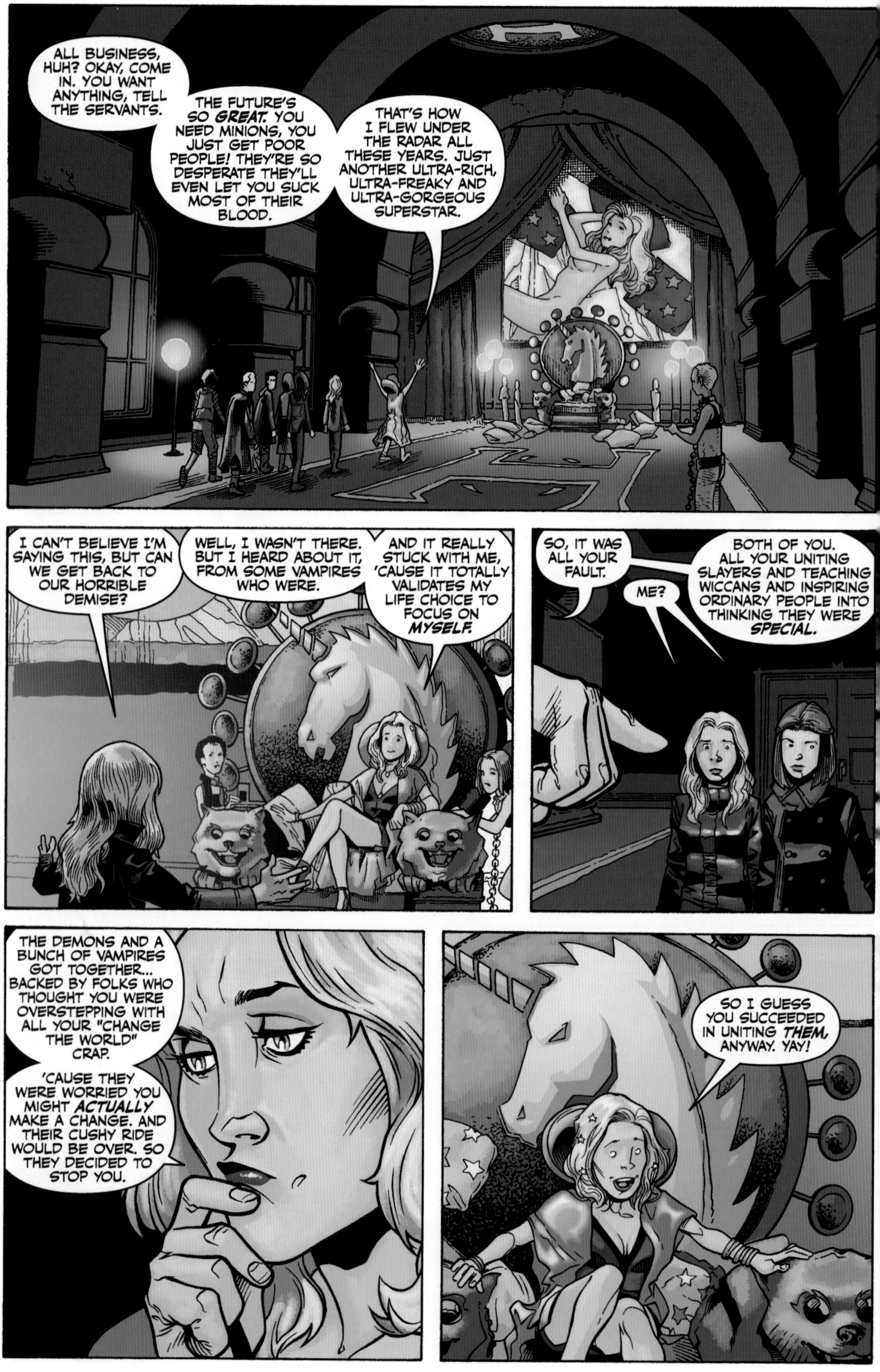
ALL BUSINESS, HUH? OKAY, COME IN. YOU WANT ANYTHING, TELL THE SERVANTS.
THE FUTURE'S SO **GREAT.** YOU NEED MINIONS, YOU JUST GET POOR PEOPLE! THEY'RE SO DESPERATE THEY'LL EVEN LET YOU SUCK MOST OF THEIR BLOOD.
THAT'S HOW I FLEW UNDER THE RADAR ALL THESE YEARS. JUST ANOTHER ULTRA-RICH, ULTRA-FREAKY AND ULTRA-GORGEOUS SUPERSTAR.
I CAN'T BELIEVE I'M SAYING THIS, BUT CAN WE GET BACK TO OUR HORRIBLE DEMISE?
WELL, I WASN'T THERE. BUT I HEARD ABOUT IT, FROM SOME VAMPIRES WHO WERE.
AND IT REALLY STUCK WITH ME, 'CAUSE IT TOTALLY VALIDATES MY LIFE CHOICE TO FOCUS ON ***MYSELF.***
SO, IT WAS ALL YOUR FAULT.
ME?
BOTH OF YOU. ALL YOUR UNITING SLAYERS AND TEACHING WICCANS AND INSPIRING ORDINARY PEOPLE INTO THINKING THEY WERE ***SPECIAL.***
THE DEMONS AND A BUNCH OF VAMPIRES GOT TOGETHER... BACKED BY FOLKS WHO THOUGHT YOU WERE OVERSTEPPING WITH ALL YOUR "CHANGE THE WORLD" CRAP.
'CAUSE THEY WERE WORRIED YOU MIGHT ***ACTUALLY*** MAKE A CHANGE. AND THEIR CUSHY RIDE WOULD BE OVER. SO THEY DECIDED TO STOP YOU.
SO I GUESS YOU SUCCEEDED IN UNITING ***THEM,*** ANYWAY. YAY!

"SO THERE WAS, LIKE, A MONDO FIGHT. AT THAT NEW AGE CENTER WILLOW HAD WHERE SHE HELPED WOMEN FIND THEIR VOICE AND BLAH BLAH.

"IT. WAS. *HORRIBLE!* BLOOD AND GUTS AND DEAD EVERYBODY ALL OVER.

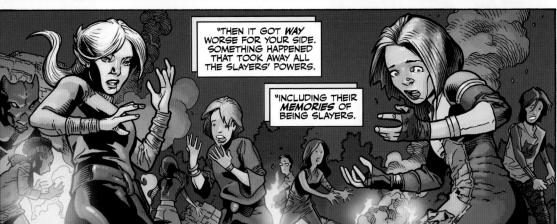

"THEN IT GOT *WAY* WORSE FOR YOUR SIDE. SOMETHING HAPPENED THAT TOOK AWAY ALL THE SLAYERS' POWERS.

"INCLUDING THEIR *MEMORIES* OF BEING SLAYERS.

"BUT NOT YOURS, BUFFY. I DON'T KNOW WHY. YOU WERE STILL THERE, FIGHTING, WHILE THE EX-SLAYERS RAN AWAY.

"NO ONE EVER MENTIONED FAITH AGAIN, SO I FIGURE SHE WAS ONE OF THE LOST GENERATION. PROBABLY WENT BACK TO *BOSTON* AND *PAHKED CAHS.*

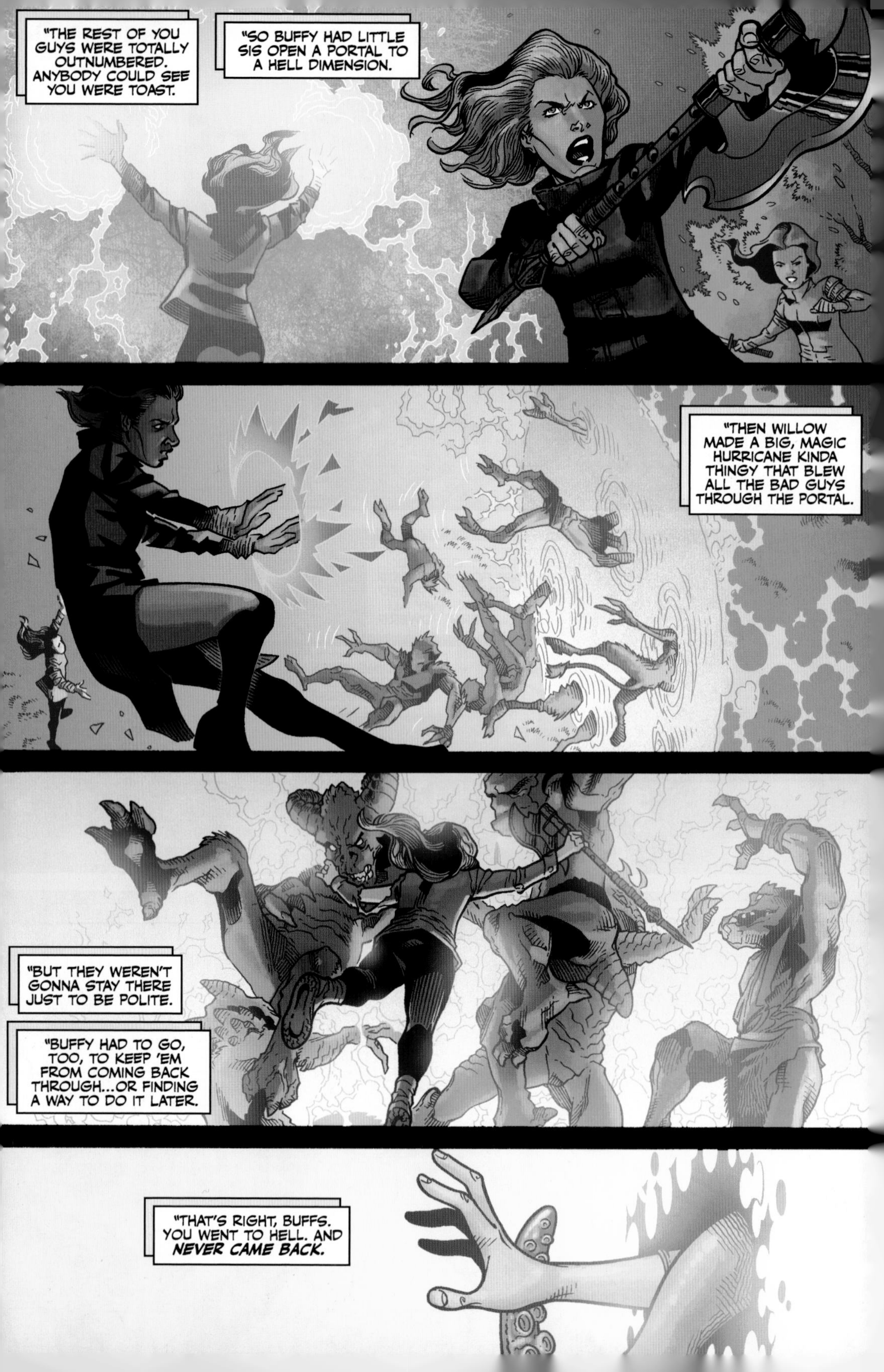
"THE REST OF YOU GUYS WERE TOTALLY OUTNUMBERED. ANYBODY COULD SEE YOU WERE TOAST.
"SO BUFFY HAD LITTLE SIS OPEN A PORTAL TO A HELL DIMENSION.
"THEN WILLOW MADE A BIG, MAGIC HURRICANE KINDA THINGY THAT BLEW ALL THE BAD GUYS THROUGH THE PORTAL.
"BUT THEY WEREN'T GONNA STAY THERE JUST TO BE POLITE.
"BUFFY HAD TO GO, TOO, TO KEEP 'EM FROM COMING BACK THROUGH...OR FINDING A WAY TO DO IT LATER.
"THAT'S RIGHT, BUFFS. YOU WENT TO HELL. AND *NEVER CAME BACK*.

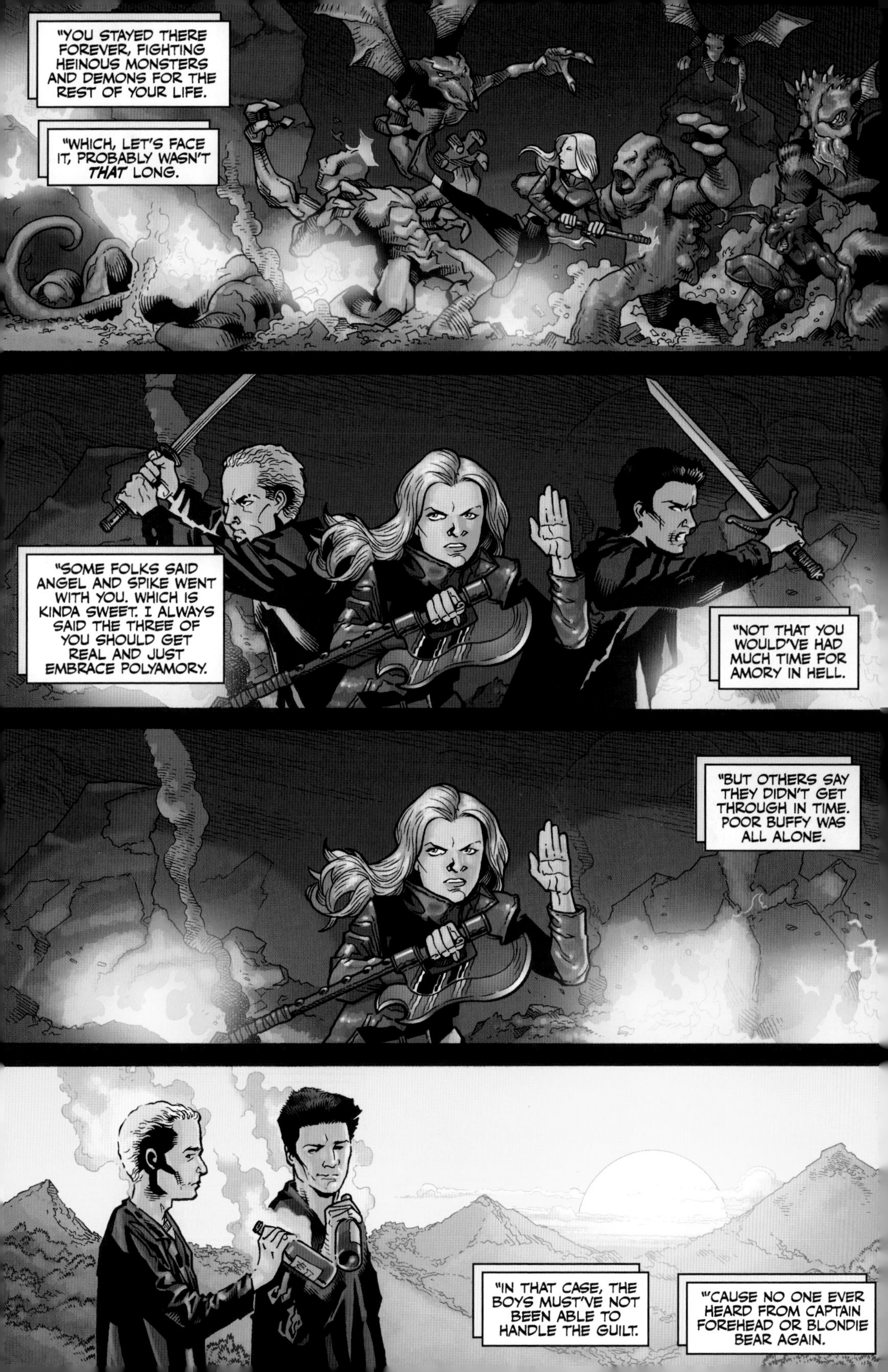
"YOU STAYED THERE FOREVER, FIGHTING HEINOUS MONSTERS AND DEMONS FOR THE REST OF YOUR LIFE.
"WHICH, LET'S FACE IT, PROBABLY WASN'T *THAT* LONG.
"SOME FOLKS SAID ANGEL AND SPIKE WENT WITH YOU. WHICH IS KINDA SWEET. I ALWAYS SAID THE THREE OF YOU SHOULD GET REAL AND JUST EMBRACE POLYAMORY.
"NOT THAT YOU WOULD'VE HAD MUCH TIME FOR AMORY IN HELL.
"BUT OTHERS SAY THEY DIDN'T GET THROUGH IN TIME. POOR BUFFY WAS ALL ALONE.
"IN THAT CASE, THE BOYS MUST'VE NOT BEEN ABLE TO HANDLE THE GUILT.
"'CAUSE NO ONE EVER HEARD FROM CAPTAIN FOREHEAD OR BLONDIE BEAR AGAIN.

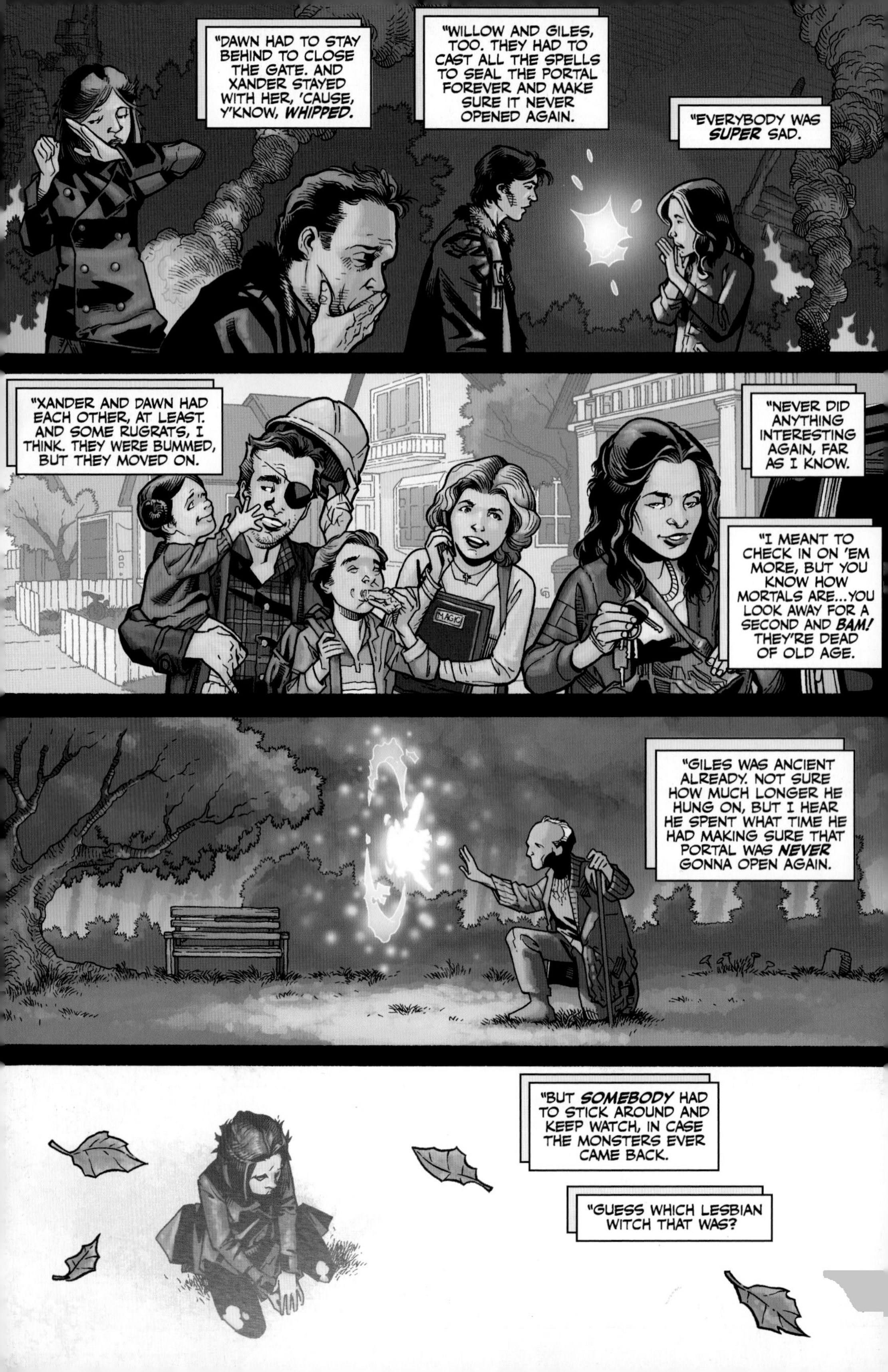
"DAWN HAD TO STAY BEHIND TO CLOSE THE GATE. AND XANDER STAYED WITH HER, 'CAUSE, Y'KNOW, *WHIPPED.*
"WILLOW AND GILES, TOO. THEY HAD TO CAST ALL THE SPELLS TO SEAL THE PORTAL FOREVER AND MAKE SURE IT NEVER OPENED AGAIN.
"EVERYBODY WAS *SUPER* SAD.
"XANDER AND DAWN HAD EACH OTHER, AT LEAST. AND SOME RUGRATS, I THINK. THEY WERE BUMMED, BUT THEY MOVED ON.
MAGIC
"NEVER DID ANYTHING INTERESTING AGAIN, FAR AS I KNOW.
"I MEANT TO CHECK IN ON 'EM MORE, BUT YOU KNOW HOW MORTALS ARE...YOU LOOK AWAY FOR A SECOND AND *BAM!* THEY'RE DEAD OF OLD AGE.
"GILES WAS ANCIENT ALREADY. NOT SURE HOW MUCH LONGER HE HUNG ON, BUT I HEAR HE SPENT WHAT TIME HE HAD MAKING SURE THAT PORTAL WAS *NEVER* GONNA OPEN AGAIN.
"BUT *SOMEBODY* HAD TO STICK AROUND AND KEEP WATCH, IN CASE THE MONSTERS EVER CAME BACK.
"GUESS WHICH LESBIAN WITCH THAT WAS?

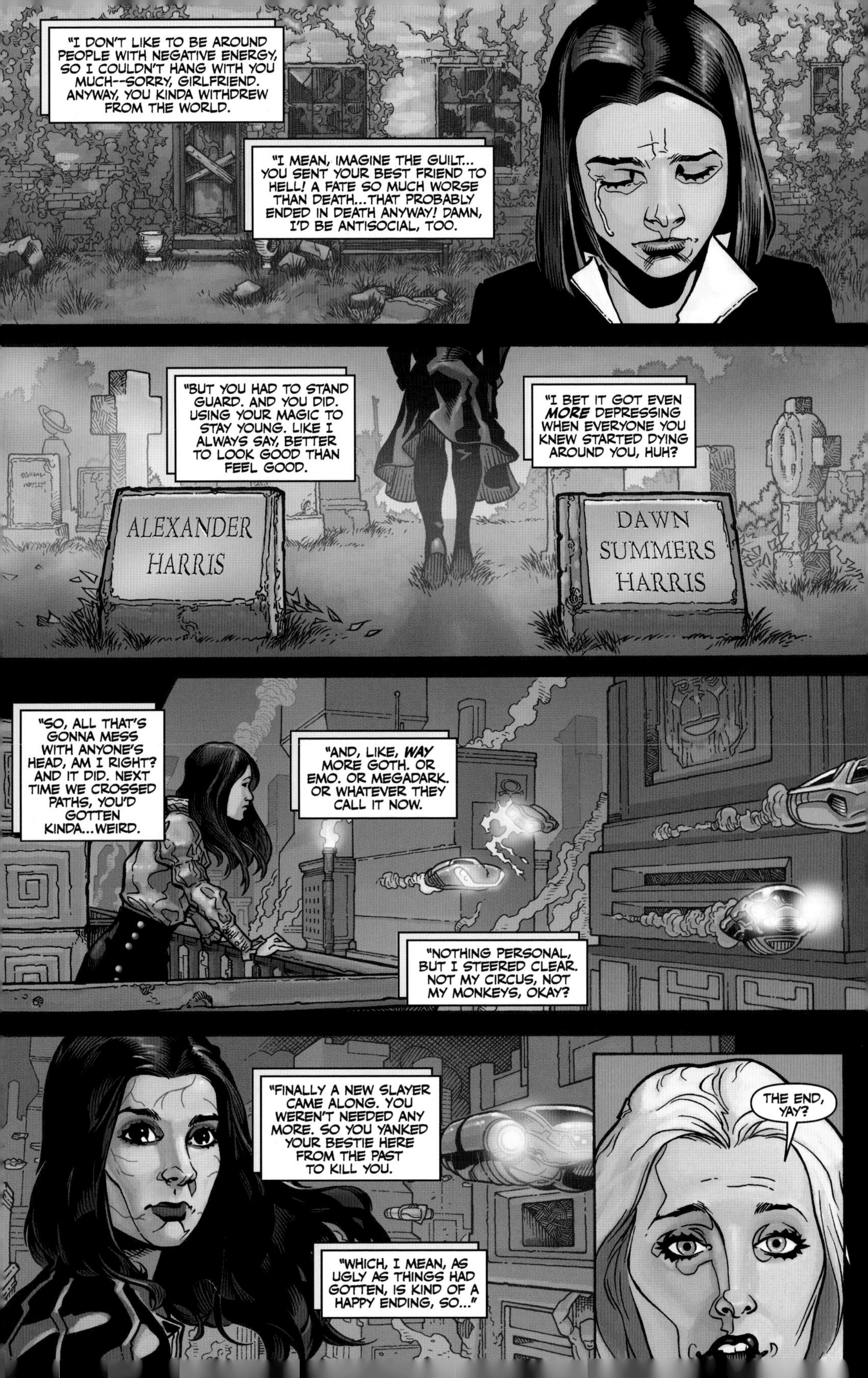
"I DON'T LIKE TO BE AROUND PEOPLE WITH NEGATIVE ENERGY, SO I COULDN'T HANG WITH YOU MUCH--SORRY, GIRLFRIEND. ANYWAY, YOU KINDA WITHDREW FROM THE WORLD.
"I MEAN, IMAGINE THE GUILT... YOU SENT YOUR BEST FRIEND TO HELL! A FATE SO MUCH WORSE THAN DEATH...THAT PROBABLY ENDED IN DEATH ANYWAY! DAMN, I'D BE ANTISOCIAL, TOO.
"BUT YOU HAD TO STAND GUARD. AND YOU DID. USING YOUR MAGIC TO STAY YOUNG. LIKE I ALWAYS SAY, BETTER TO LOOK GOOD THAN FEEL GOOD.
"I BET IT GOT EVEN *MORE* DEPRESSING WHEN EVERYONE YOU KNEW STARTED DYING AROUND YOU, HUH?
ALEXANDER HARRIS
DAWN SUMMERS HARRIS
"SO, ALL THAT'S GONNA MESS WITH ANYONE'S HEAD, AM I RIGHT? AND IT DID. NEXT TIME WE CROSSED PATHS, YOU'D GOTTEN KINDA...WEIRD.
"AND, LIKE, *WAY* MORE GOTH. OR EMO. OR MEGADARK. OR WHATEVER THEY CALL IT NOW.
"NOTHING PERSONAL, BUT I STEERED CLEAR. NOT MY CIRCUS, NOT MY MONKEYS, OKAY?
"FINALLY A NEW SLAYER CAME ALONG. YOU WEREN'T NEEDED ANY MORE. SO YOU YANKED YOUR BESTIE HERE FROM THE PAST TO KILL YOU.
"WHICH, I MEAN, AS UGLY AS THINGS HAD GOTTEN, IS KIND OF A HAPPY ENDING, SO..."
THE END, YAY?

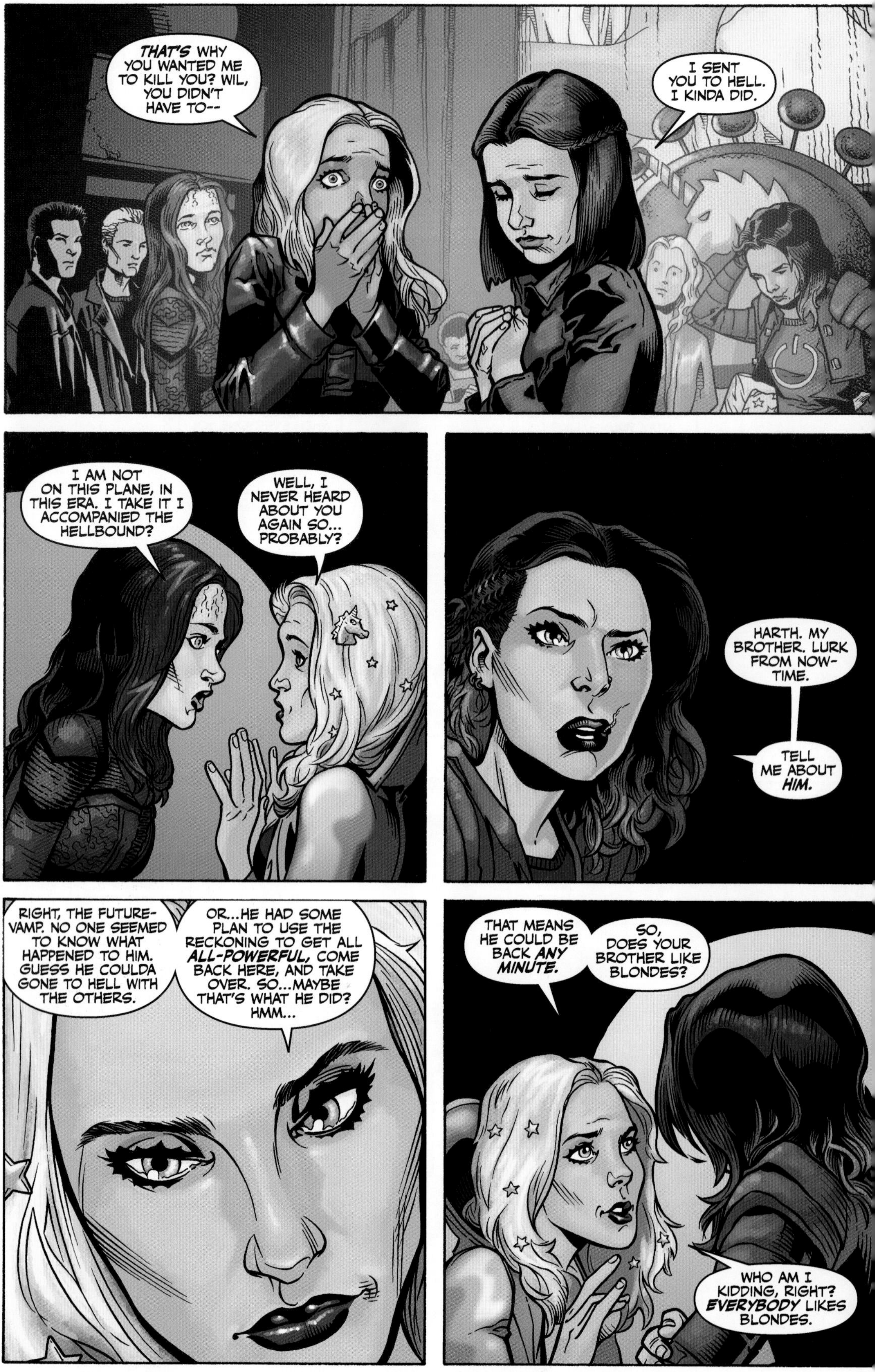
THAT'S WHY YOU WANTED ME TO KILL YOU? WIL, YOU DIDN'T HAVE TO--
I SENT YOU TO HELL. I KINDA DID.
I AM NOT ON THIS PLANE, IN THIS ERA. I TAKE IT I ACCOMPANIED THE HELLBOUND?
WELL, I NEVER HEARD ABOUT YOU AGAIN SO... PROBABLY?
HARTH. MY BROTHER. LURK FROM NOW-TIME.
TELL ME ABOUT HIM.
RIGHT, THE FUTURE-VAMP. NO ONE SEEMED TO KNOW WHAT HAPPENED TO HIM. GUESS HE COULDA GONE TO HELL WITH THE OTHERS.
OR...HE HAD SOME PLAN TO USE THE RECKONING TO GET ALL ALL-POWERFUL, COME BACK HERE, AND TAKE OVER. SO...MAYBE THAT'S WHAT HE DID? HMM...
THAT MEANS HE COULD BE BACK ANY MINUTE.
SO, DOES YOUR BROTHER LIKE BLONDES?
WHO AM I KIDDING, RIGHT? EVERYBODY LIKES BLONDES.

I...GUESS WE *DO* SAVE THE WORLD. FOR A WHILE, ANYWAY.

NOT *MY* WORLD. HARTH COMES BACK LEVELED UP, *NOTHING* CAN STOP HIM.

SO WE STAY HERE UNTIL HE COMES BACK AND FIGHT HIM. WE'RE GUARANTEED TO WIN, SINCE WE HAVE TO GO BACK TO PARTICIPATE IN THE RECKONING.

THAT'S BLOODY DAFT. HOW DO WE KNOW THAT WE WON'T CHANGE HISTORY BY STAYING HERE?

GET KILLED, CAN'T GO BACK TO THE PAST, THE BADDIES WIN THEN *AND* NOW?

I SHALL STAY. I SHALL FIGHT THE HARTH CREATURE.

MY ROLE IN THE RECKONING IS CLEARLY AN UNREMARKABLE ONE, AS HISTORY DOES NOT RECORD IT.

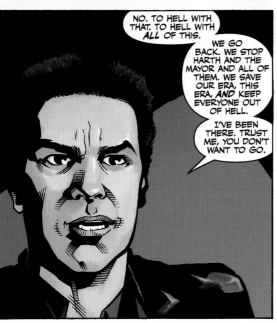

NO. TO HELL WITH THAT. TO HELL WITH *ALL* OF THIS.

WE GO BACK. WE STOP HARTH AND THE MAYOR AND ALL OF THEM. WE SAVE OUR ERA, THIS ERA, *AND* KEEP EVERYONE OUT OF HELL.

I'VE BEEN THERE. TRUST ME, YOU DON'T WANT TO GO.

THAT'S SWEET...BUT EVEN IF IT ENDS BADLY FOR US, THE WAY THINGS WENT HISTORICALLY WORKED OUT FOR THE BEST FOR EVERYONE ELSE.

WE CAN'T TAKE THE CHANCE OF MAKING IT WORSE. ILLYRIA'S RIGHT...SHE STAYS HERE, WE GO BACK. THAT'S FINAL.

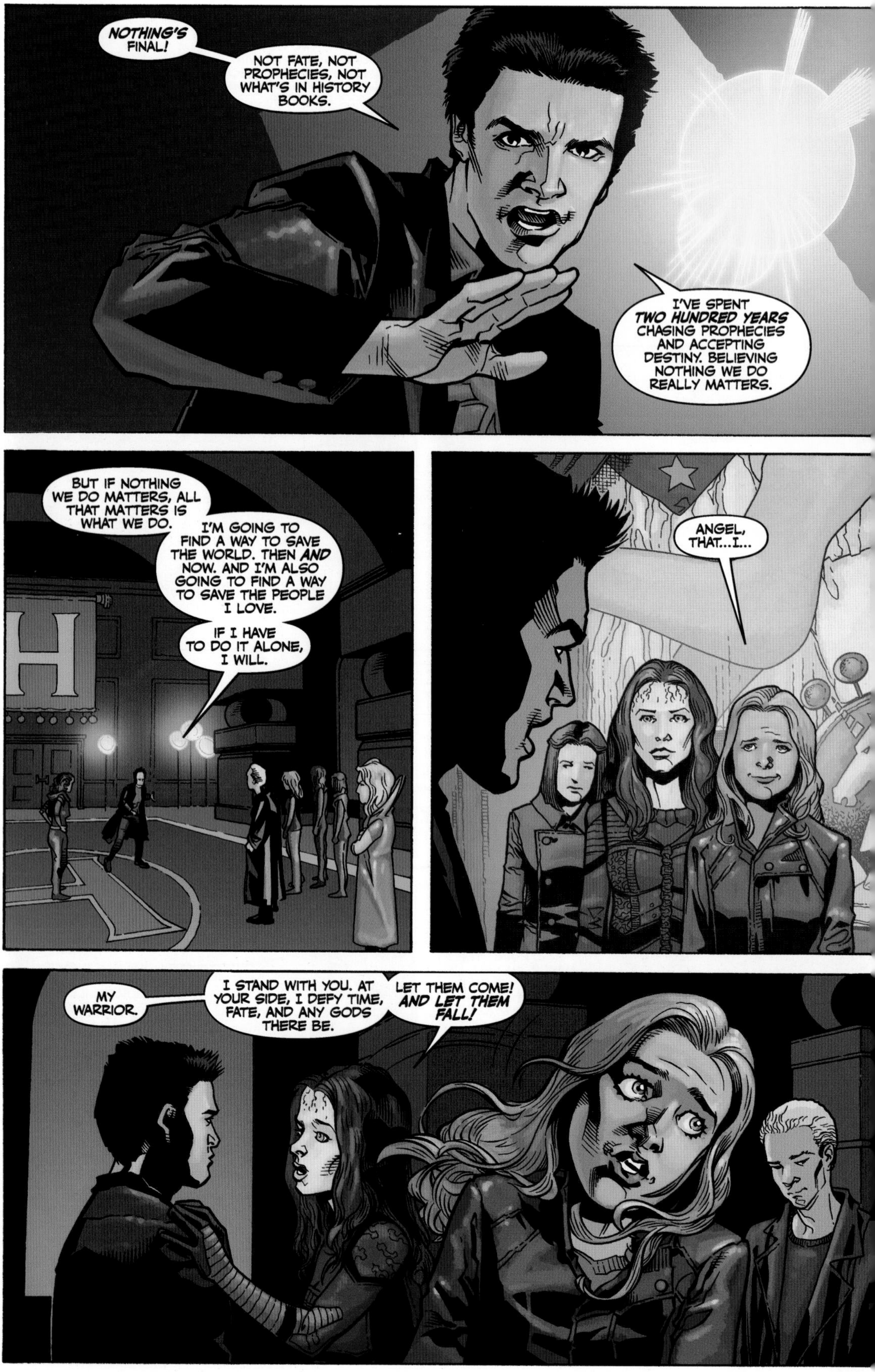
NOTHING'S FINAL!
NOT FATE, NOT PROPHECIES, NOT WHAT'S IN HISTORY BOOKS.
I'VE SPENT TWO HUNDRED YEARS CHASING PROPHECIES AND ACCEPTING DESTINY. BELIEVING NOTHING WE DO REALLY MATTERS.
BUT IF NOTHING WE DO MATTERS, ALL THAT MATTERS IS WHAT WE DO.
I'M GOING TO FIND A WAY TO SAVE THE WORLD. THEN AND NOW. AND I'M ALSO GOING TO FIND A WAY TO SAVE THE PEOPLE I LOVE.
IF I HAVE TO DO IT ALONE, I WILL.
ANGEL, THAT...I...
MY WARRIOR.
I STAND WITH YOU. AT YOUR SIDE, I DEFY TIME, FATE, AND ANY GODS THERE BE.
LET THEM COME! AND LET THEM FALL!

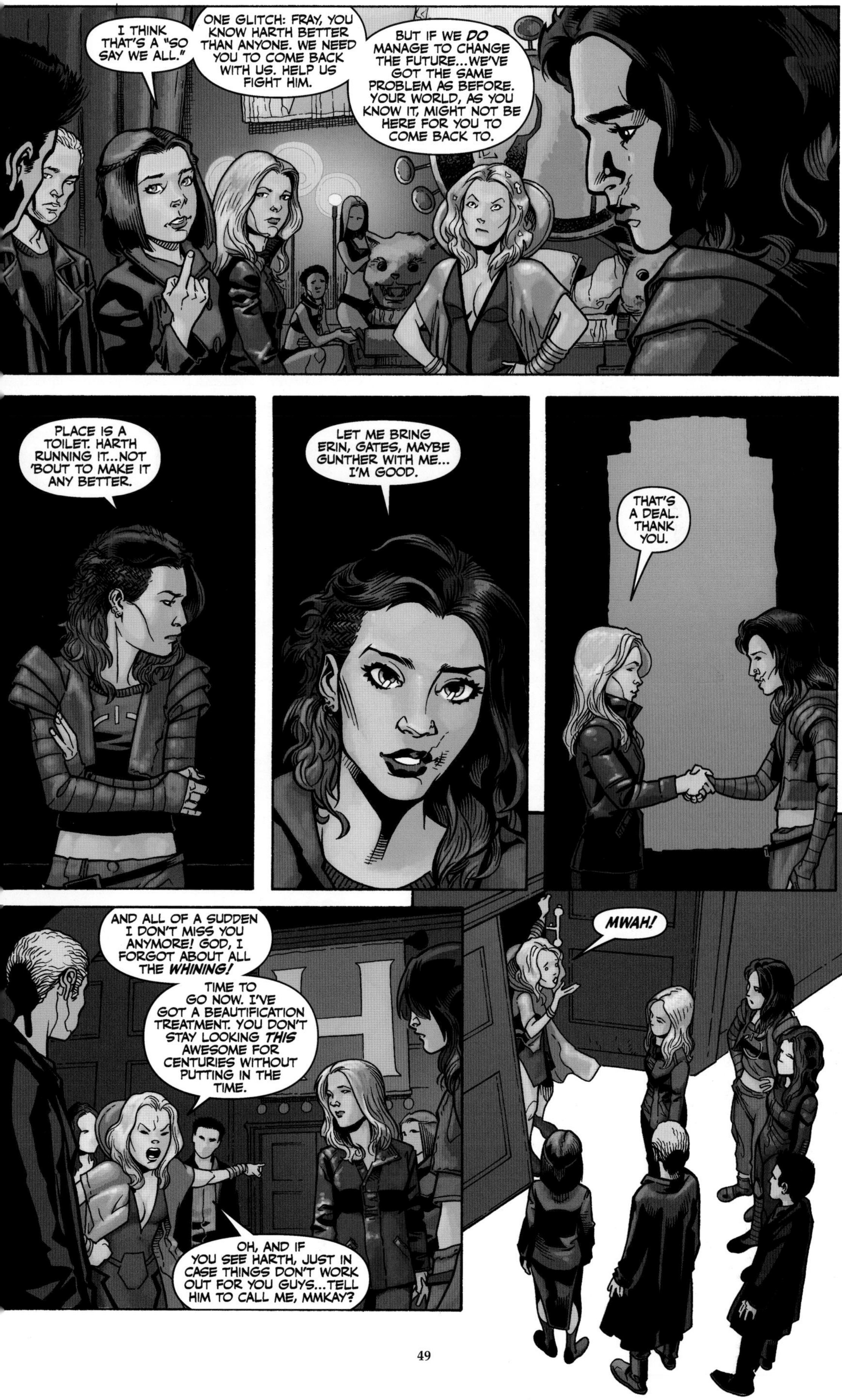

I THINK THAT'S A "SO SAY WE ALL."
ONE GLITCH: FRAY, YOU KNOW HARTH BETTER THAN ANYONE. WE NEED YOU TO COME BACK WITH US. HELP US FIGHT HIM.
BUT IF WE DO MANAGE TO CHANGE THE FUTURE...WE'VE GOT THE SAME PROBLEM AS BEFORE. YOUR WORLD, AS YOU KNOW IT, MIGHT NOT BE HERE FOR YOU TO COME BACK TO.
PLACE IS A TOILET. HARTH RUNNING IT...NOT 'BOUT TO MAKE IT ANY BETTER.
LET ME BRING ERIN, GATES, MAYBE GUNTHER WITH ME... I'M GOOD.
THAT'S A DEAL. THANK YOU.
AND ALL OF A SUDDEN I DON'T MISS YOU ANYMORE! GOD, I FORGOT ABOUT ALL THE WHINING!
TIME TO GO NOW. I'VE GOT A BEAUTIFICATION TREATMENT. YOU DON'T STAY LOOKING THIS AWESOME FOR CENTURIES WITHOUT PUTTING IN THE TIME.
OH, AND IF YOU SEE HARTH, JUST IN CASE THINGS DON'T WORK OUT FOR YOU GUYS...TELL HIM TO CALL ME, MMKAY?
MWAH!

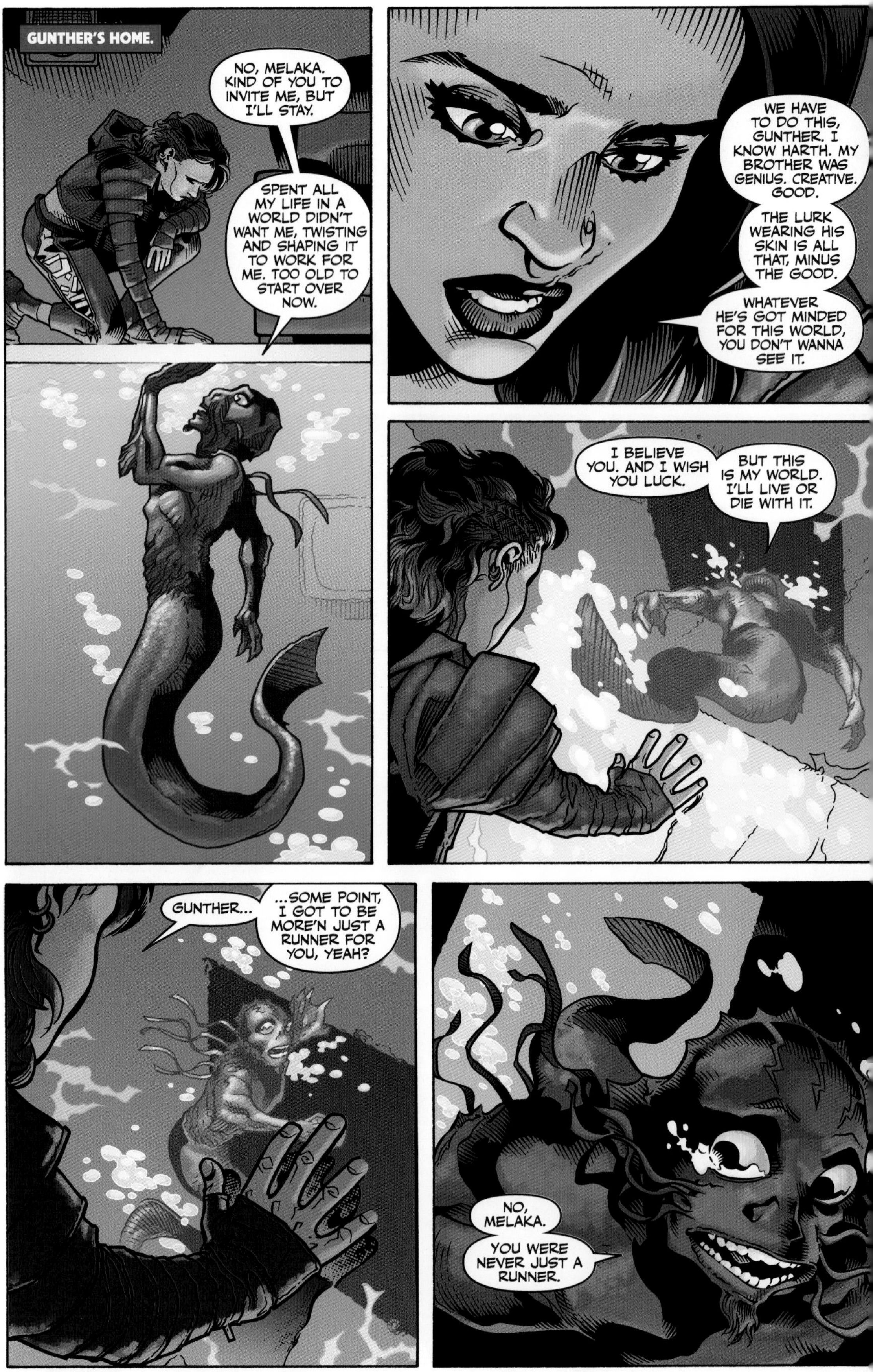
GUNTHER'S HOME.
NO, MELAKA. KIND OF YOU TO INVITE ME, BUT I'LL STAY.
SPENT ALL MY LIFE IN A WORLD DIDN'T WANT ME, TWISTING AND SHAPING IT TO WORK FOR ME. TOO OLD TO START OVER NOW.
WE HAVE TO DO THIS, GUNTHER. I KNOW HARTH. MY BROTHER WAS GENIUS. CREATIVE. GOOD.
THE LURK WEARING HIS SKIN IS ALL THAT, MINUS THE GOOD.
WHATEVER HE'S GOT MINDED FOR THIS WORLD, YOU DON'T WANNA SEE IT.
I BELIEVE YOU. AND I WISH YOU LUCK.
BUT THIS IS MY WORLD. I'LL LIVE OR DIE WITH IT.
GUNTHER...
...SOME POINT, I GOT TO BE MORE'N JUST A RUNNER FOR YOU, YEAH?
NO, MELAKA.
YOU WERE NEVER JUST A RUNNER.

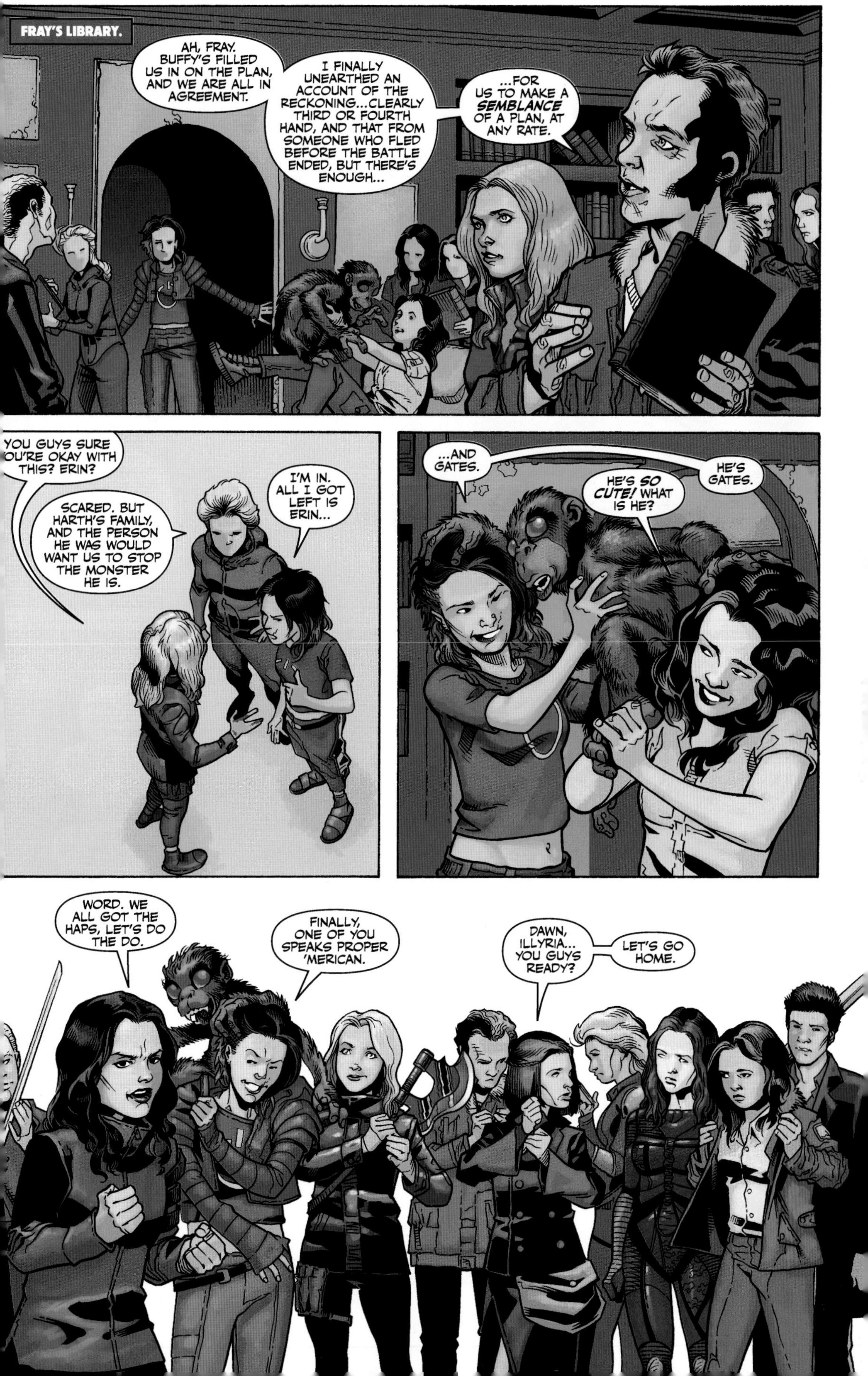

FRAY'S LIBRARY.
AH, FRAY. BUFFY'S FILLED US IN ON THE PLAN, AND WE ARE ALL IN AGREEMENT.
I FINALLY UNEARTHED AN ACCOUNT OF THE RECKONING...CLEARLY THIRD OR FOURTH HAND, AND THAT FROM SOMEONE WHO FLED BEFORE THE BATTLE ENDED, BUT THERE'S ENOUGH...
...FOR US TO MAKE A SEMBLANCE OF A PLAN, AT ANY RATE.
YOU GUYS SURE OU'RE OKAY WITH THIS? ERIN?
SCARED. BUT HARTH'S FAMILY, AND THE PERSON HE WAS WOULD WANT US TO STOP THE MONSTER HE IS.
I'M IN. ALL I GOT LEFT IS ERIN...
...AND GATES.
HE'S SO CUTE! WHAT IS HE?
HE'S GATES.
WORD. WE ALL GOT THE HAPS, LET'S DO THE DO.
FINALLY, ONE OF YOU SPEAKS PROPER 'MERICAN.
DAWN, ILLYRIA... YOU GUYS READY?
LET'S GO HOME.

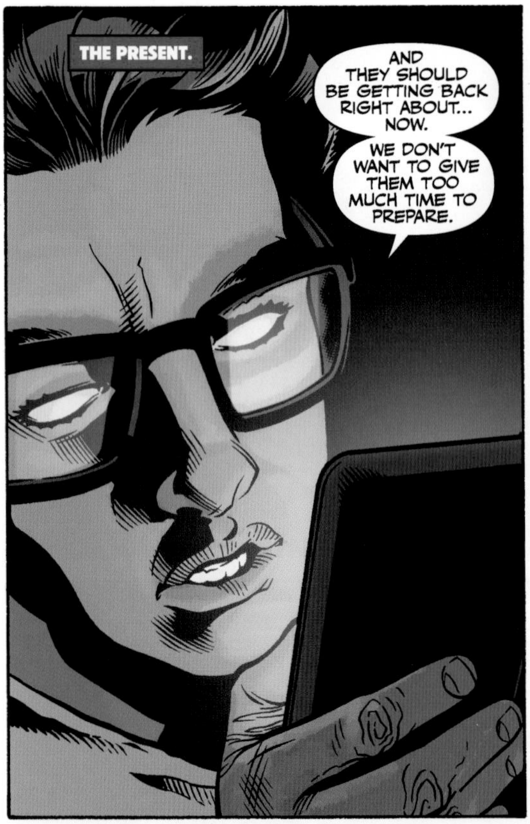
THE PRESENT.
AND THEY SHOULD BE GETTING BACK RIGHT ABOUT... NOW.
WE DON'T WANT TO GIVE THEM TOO MUCH TIME TO PREPARE.

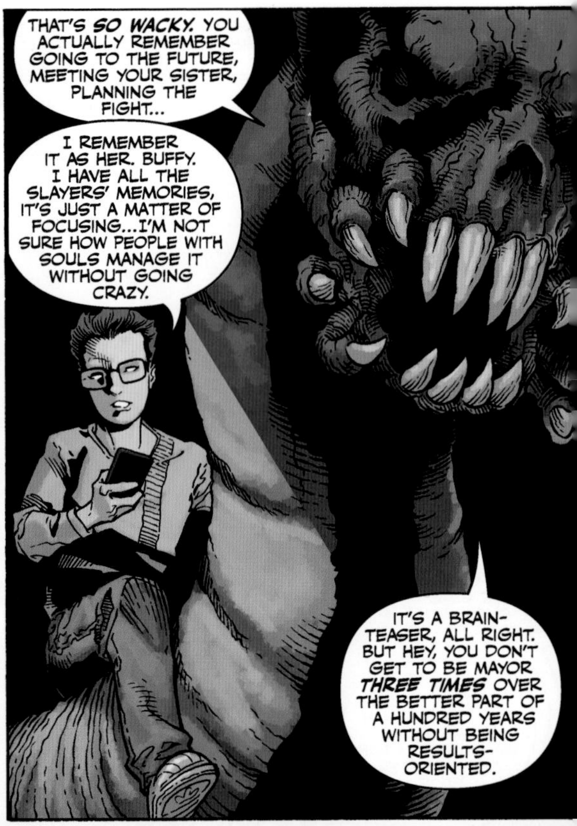
THAT'S SO WACKY. YOU ACTUALLY REMEMBER GOING TO THE FUTURE, MEETING YOUR SISTER, PLANNING THE FIGHT...
I REMEMBER IT AS HER. BUFFY. I HAVE ALL THE SLAYERS' MEMORIES, IT'S JUST A MATTER OF FOCUSING...I'M NOT SURE HOW PEOPLE WITH SOULS MANAGE IT WITHOUT GOING CRAZY.
IT'S A BRAIN-TEASER, ALL RIGHT. BUT HEY, YOU DON'T GET TO BE MAYOR THREE TIMES OVER THE BETTER PART OF A HUNDRED YEARS WITHOUT BEING RESULTS-ORIENTED.

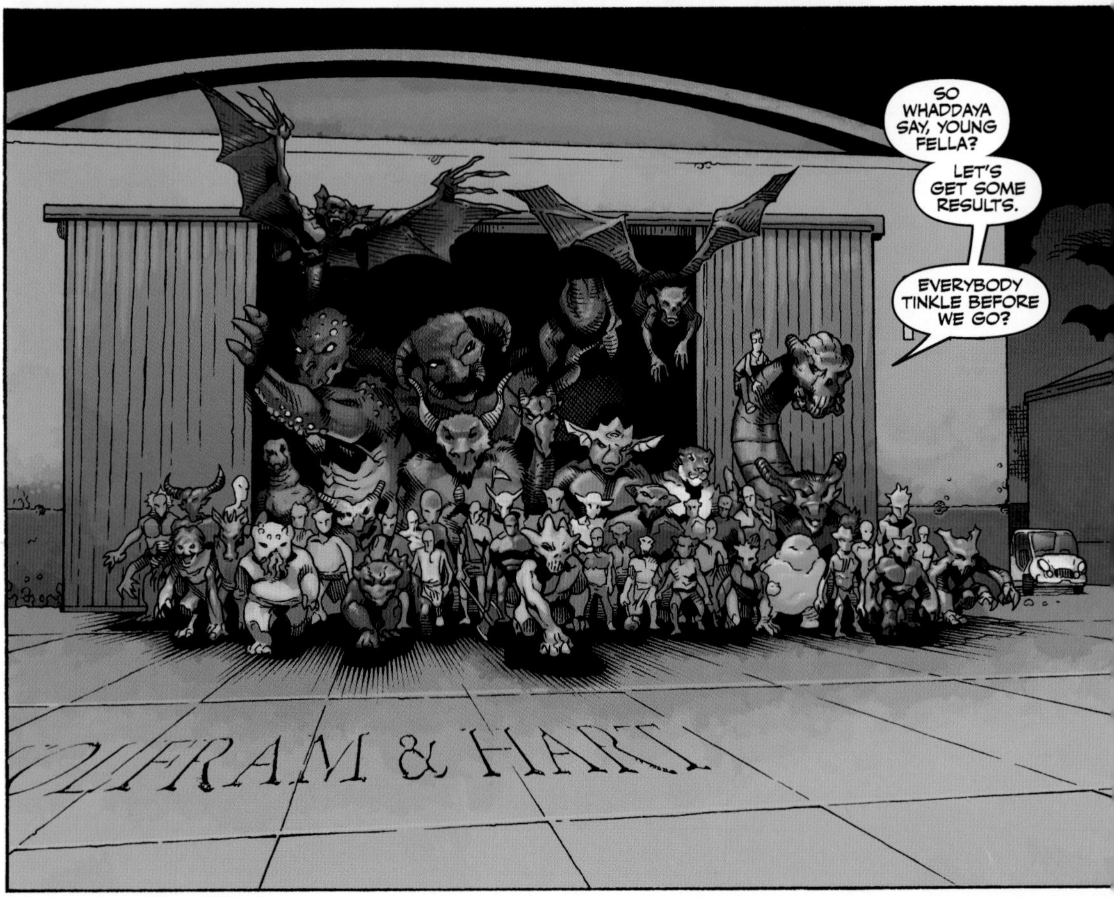
SO WHADDAYA SAY, YOUNG FELLA?
LET'S GET SOME RESULTS.
EVERYBODY TINKLE BEFORE WE GO?
OLFRAM & HART

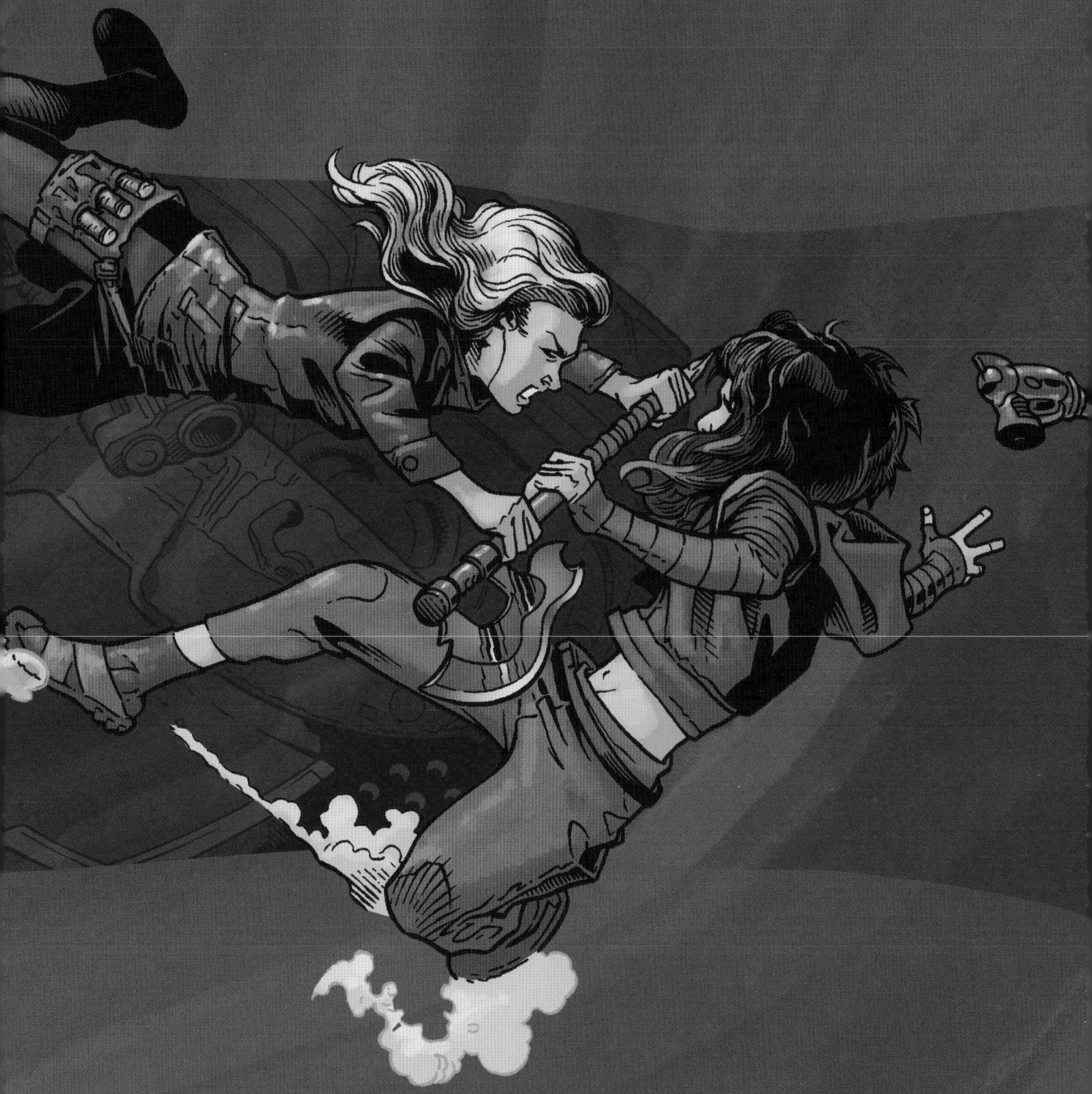

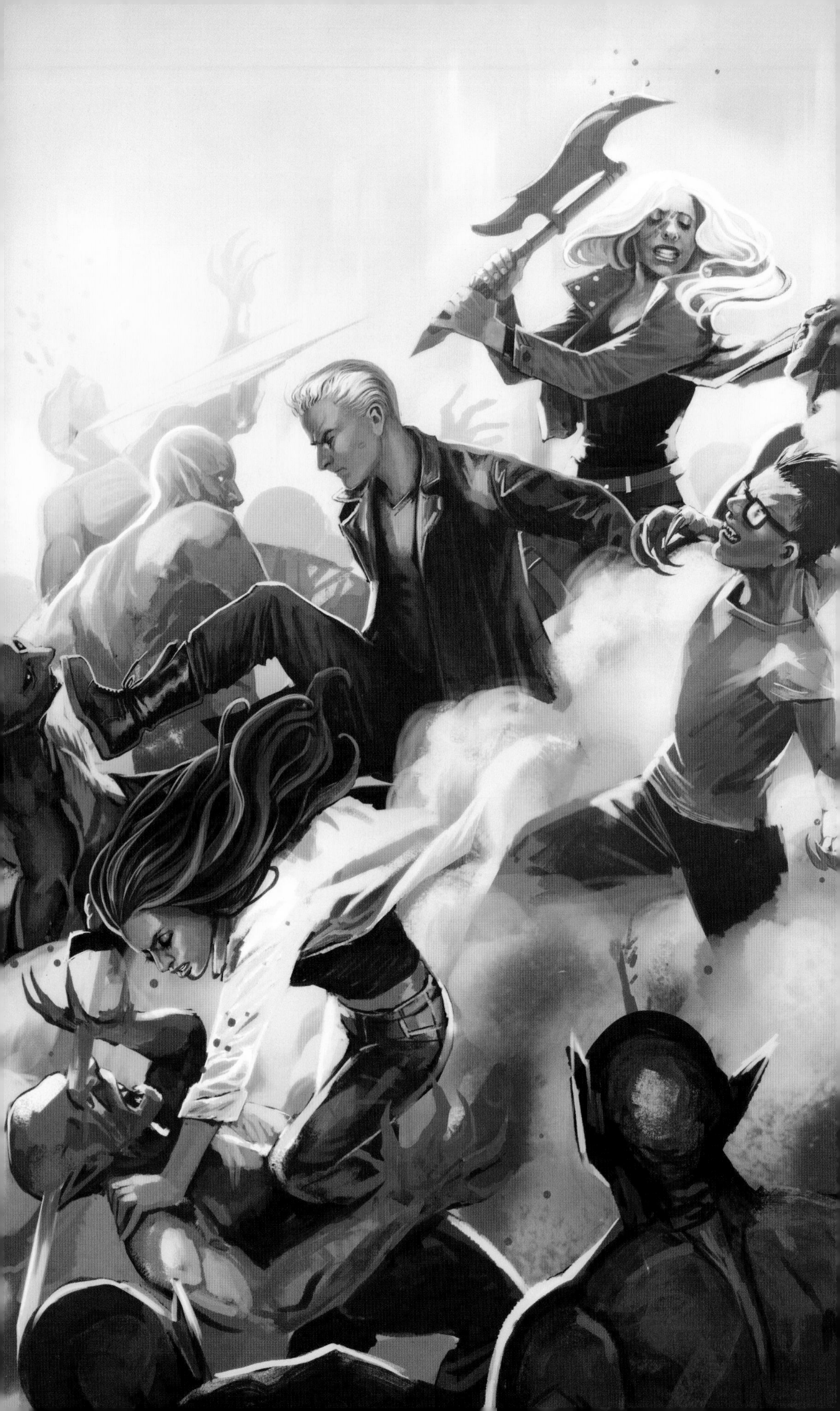

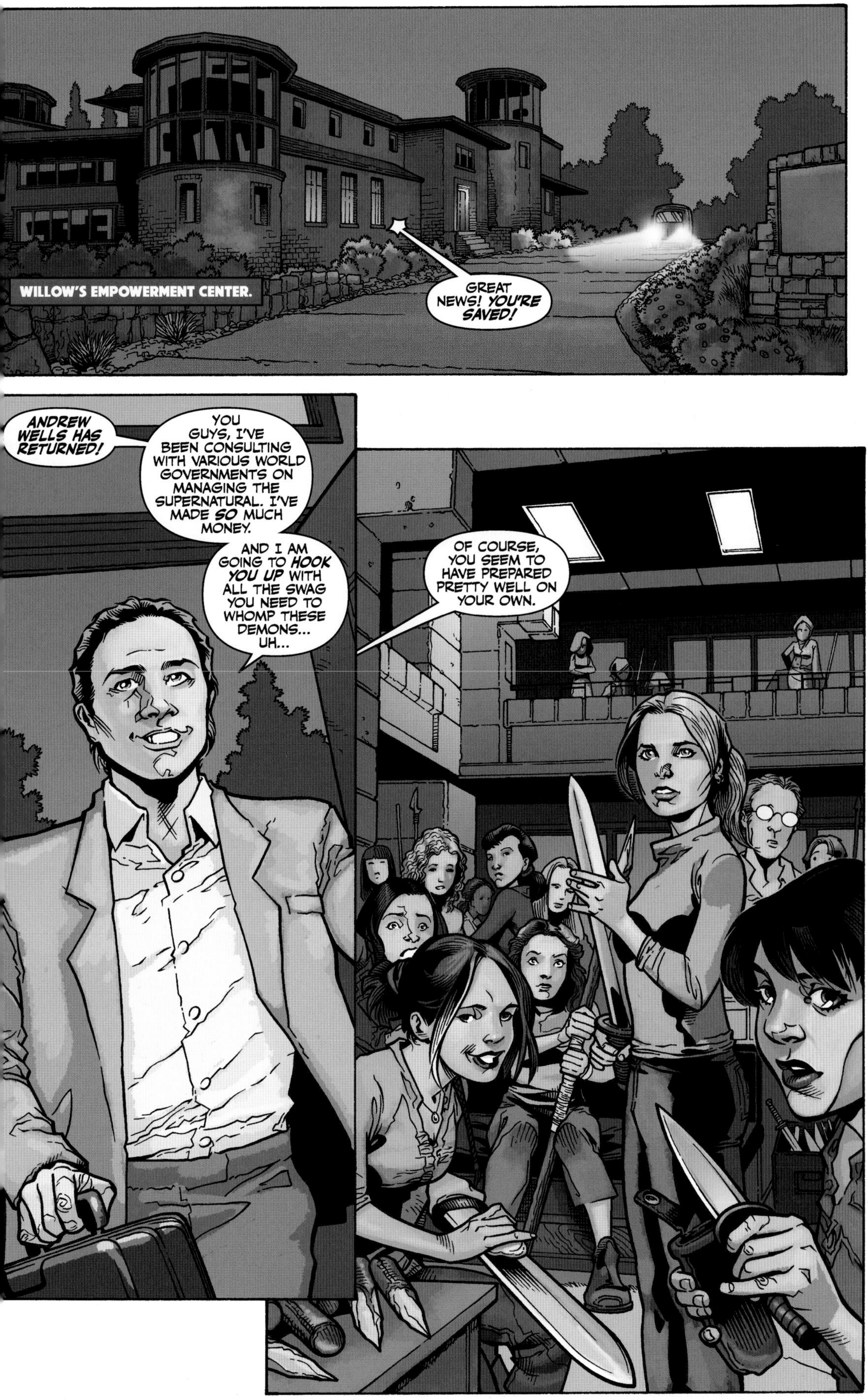
WILLOW'S EMPOWERMENT CENTER.
GREAT NEWS! YOU'RE SAVED!
ANDREW WELLS HAS RETURNED!
YOU GUYS, I'VE BEEN CONSULTING WITH VARIOUS WORLD GOVERNMENTS ON MANAGING THE SUPERNATURAL. I'VE MADE SO MUCH MONEY.
AND I AM GOING TO HOOK YOU UP WITH ALL THE SWAG YOU NEED TO WHOMP THESE DEMONS... UH...
OF COURSE, YOU SEEM TO HAVE PREPARED PRETTY WELL ON YOUR OWN.

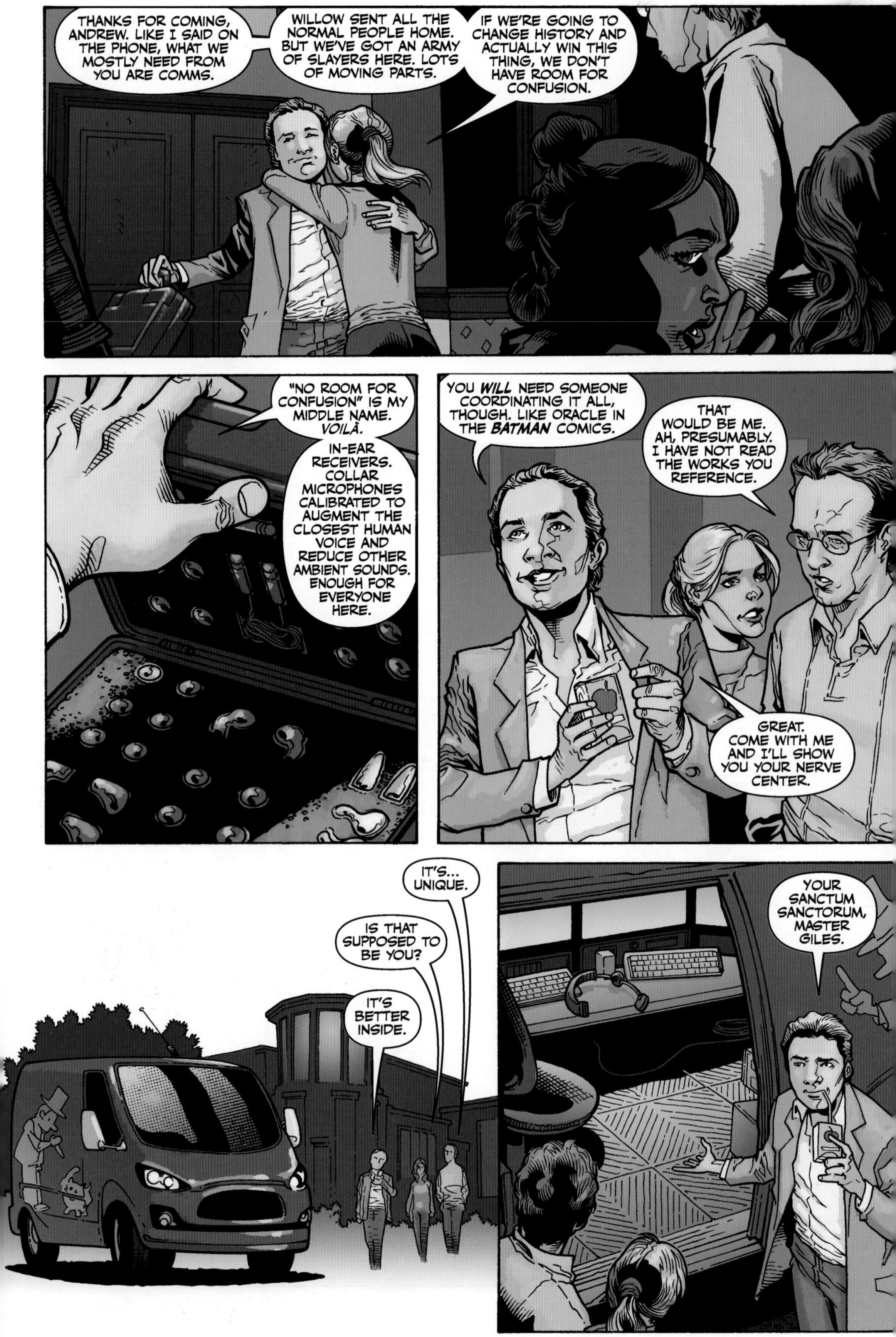

THANKS FOR COMING, ANDREW. LIKE I SAID ON THE PHONE, WHAT WE MOSTLY NEED FROM YOU ARE COMMS.
WILLOW SENT ALL THE NORMAL PEOPLE HOME. BUT WE'VE GOT AN ARMY OF SLAYERS HERE. LOTS OF MOVING PARTS.
IF WE'RE GOING TO CHANGE HISTORY AND ACTUALLY WIN THIS THING, WE DON'T HAVE ROOM FOR CONFUSION.
"NO ROOM FOR CONFUSION" IS MY MIDDLE NAME. *VOILÀ.*
IN-EAR RECEIVERS. COLLAR MICROPHONES CALIBRATED TO AUGMENT THE CLOSEST HUMAN VOICE AND REDUCE OTHER AMBIENT SOUNDS. ENOUGH FOR EVERYONE HERE.
YOU ***WILL*** NEED SOMEONE COORDINATING IT ALL, THOUGH. LIKE ORACLE IN THE ***BATMAN*** COMICS.
THAT WOULD BE ME. AH, PRESUMABLY. I HAVE NOT READ THE WORKS YOU REFERENCE.
GREAT. COME WITH ME AND I'LL SHOW YOU YOUR NERVE CENTER.
IT'S BETTER INSIDE.
IS THAT SUPPOSED TO BE YOU?
IT'S... UNIQUE.
YOUR SANCTUM SANCTORUM, MASTER GILES.

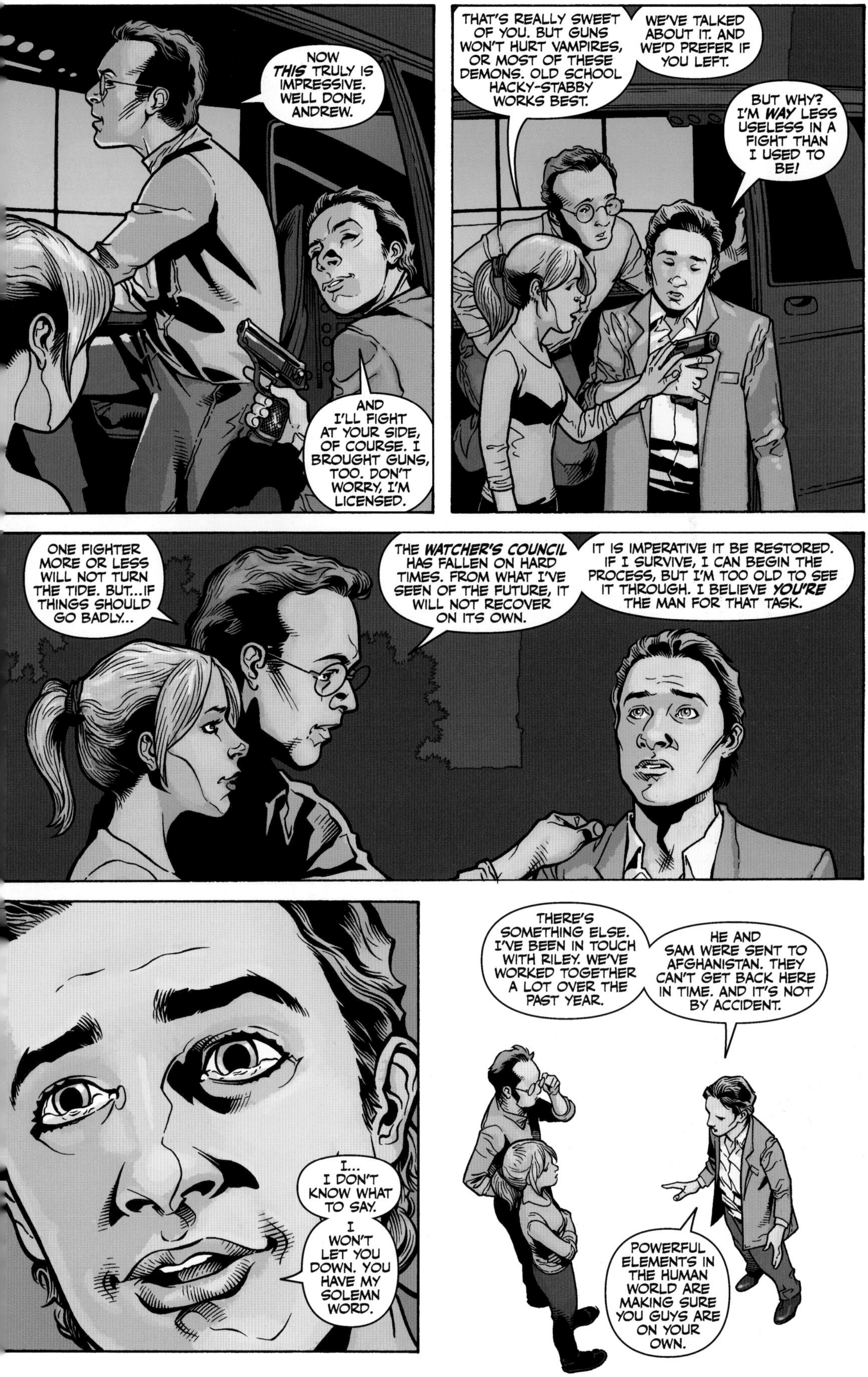
NOW THIS TRULY IS IMPRESSIVE. WELL DONE, ANDREW.
AND I'LL FIGHT AT YOUR SIDE, OF COURSE. I BROUGHT GUNS, TOO. DON'T WORRY, I'M LICENSED.
THAT'S REALLY SWEET OF YOU. BUT GUNS WON'T HURT VAMPIRES, OR MOST OF THESE DEMONS. OLD SCHOOL HACKY-STABBY WORKS BEST.
WE'VE TALKED ABOUT IT. AND WE'D PREFER IF YOU LEFT.
BUT WHY? I'M WAY LESS USELESS IN A FIGHT THAN I USED TO BE!
ONE FIGHTER MORE OR LESS WILL NOT TURN THE TIDE. BUT...IF THINGS SHOULD GO BADLY...
THE WATCHER'S COUNCIL HAS FALLEN ON HARD TIMES. FROM WHAT I'VE SEEN OF THE FUTURE, IT WILL NOT RECOVER ON ITS OWN.
IT IS IMPERATIVE IT BE RESTORED. IF I SURVIVE, I CAN BEGIN THE PROCESS, BUT I'M TOO OLD TO SEE IT THROUGH. I BELIEVE YOU'RE THE MAN FOR THAT TASK.
I... I DON'T KNOW WHAT TO SAY.
I WON'T LET YOU DOWN. YOU HAVE MY SOLEMN WORD.
THERE'S SOMETHING ELSE. I'VE BEEN IN TOUCH WITH RILEY. WE'VE WORKED TOGETHER A LOT OVER THE PAST YEAR.
HE AND SAM WERE SENT TO AFGHANISTAN. THEY CAN'T GET BACK HERE IN TIME. AND IT'S NOT BY ACCIDENT.
POWERFUL ELEMENTS IN THE HUMAN WORLD ARE MAKING SURE YOU GUYS ARE ON YOUR OWN.

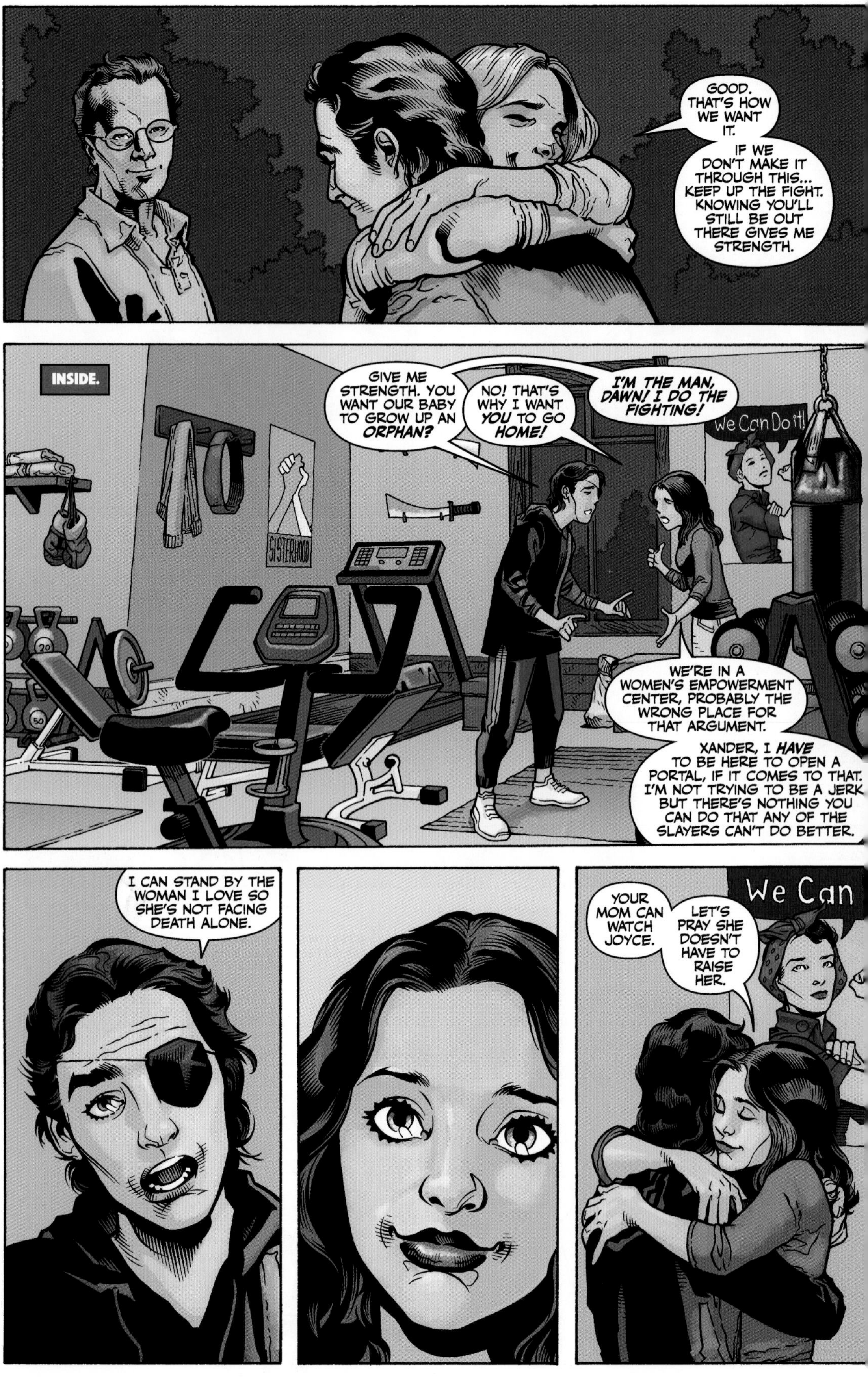
GOOD. THAT'S HOW WE WANT IT.
IF WE DON'T MAKE IT THROUGH THIS... KEEP UP THE FIGHT. KNOWING YOU'LL STILL BE OUT THERE GIVES ME STRENGTH.
INSIDE.
GIVE ME STRENGTH. YOU WANT OUR BABY TO GROW UP AN ORPHAN?
NO! THAT'S WHY I WANT YOU TO GO HOME!
I'M THE MAN, DAWN! I DO THE FIGHTING!
We Can Do it!
SISTERHOOD
WE'RE IN A WOMEN'S EMPOWERMENT CENTER, PROBABLY THE WRONG PLACE FOR THAT ARGUMENT.
XANDER, I HAVE TO BE HERE TO OPEN A PORTAL, IF IT COMES TO THAT. I'M NOT TRYING TO BE A JERK BUT THERE'S NOTHING YOU CAN DO THAT ANY OF THE SLAYERS CAN'T DO BETTER.
I CAN STAND BY THE WOMAN I LOVE SO SHE'S NOT FACING DEATH ALONE.
We Can
YOUR MOM CAN WATCH JOYCE.
LET'S PRAY SHE DOESN'T HAVE TO RAISE HER.

THE ROOF.

I UNDERSTAND, ANGEL. AND I'M IN.

ARE YOU *SURE* THIS IS YOUR DECISION, FRED? I STILL DON'T UNDERSTAND HOW YOUR BODY-SHARING ARRANGEMENT WITH ILLYRIA WORKS.

I'D HATE TO THINK YOU'RE BEING... I DON'T KNOW, *INFLUENCED.*

I DON'T REALLY UNDERSTAND IT EITHER. BUT I DO KNOW THIS.

I'M OKAY WITH HER FIGHTING THIS FIGHT. AND I'M OKAY WITH HER BEING WITH YOU. SO I KNOW IT'S HOW YOU GET YOUR KICKS, BUT STOP BEATING YOURSELF UP.

I'M NOT AFRAID OF DYING. I'VE ALREADY DONE IT, AND I HAD WAY MORE TO LOSE THEN.

TO BE HONEST, EVER SINCE I CAME BACK--RESURFACED, WHATEVER--I'VE FELT KIND OF... AT SEA.

THIS MIGHT BE THE FIRST TIME I KNOW FOR SURE WHAT I'M DOING AND WHY. IT FEELS GOOD.

I JUST WISH I COULD'VE SAID GOODBYE TO GUNN. BUT HE WOULD'VE RUSHED RIGHT OVER HERE.

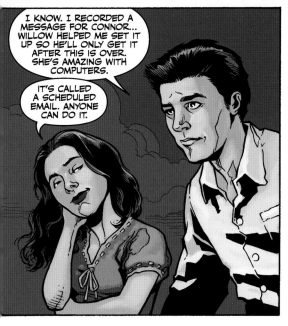

I KNOW. I RECORDED A MESSAGE FOR CONNOR... WILLOW HELPED ME SET IT UP SO HE'LL ONLY GET IT AFTER THIS IS OVER. SHE'S AMAZING WITH COMPUTERS.

IT'S CALLED A SCHEDULED EMAIL. ANYONE CAN DO IT.

REALLY?

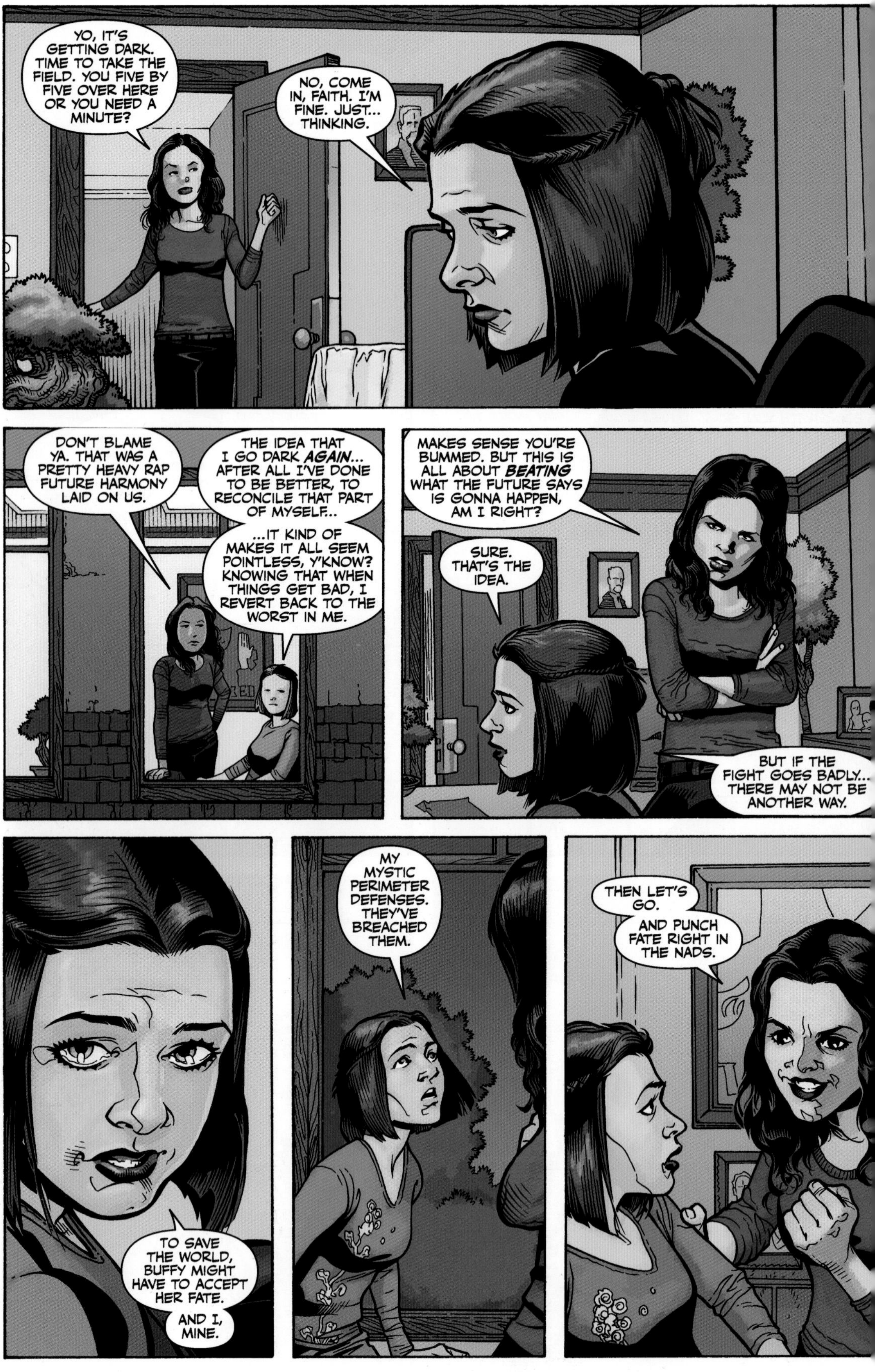

YO, IT'S GETTING DARK. TIME TO TAKE THE FIELD. YOU FIVE BY FIVE OVER HERE OR YOU NEED A MINUTE?
NO, COME IN, FAITH. I'M FINE. JUST... THINKING.
DON'T BLAME YA. THAT WAS A PRETTY HEAVY RAP FUTURE HARMONY LAID ON US.
THE IDEA THAT I GO DARK AGAIN... AFTER ALL I'VE DONE TO BE BETTER, TO RECONCILE THAT PART OF MYSELF...
...IT KIND OF MAKES IT ALL SEEM POINTLESS, Y'KNOW? KNOWING THAT WHEN THINGS GET BAD, I REVERT BACK TO THE WORST IN ME.
MAKES SENSE YOU'RE BUMMED. BUT THIS IS ALL ABOUT BEATING WHAT THE FUTURE SAYS IS GONNA HAPPEN, AM I RIGHT?
SURE. THAT'S THE IDEA.
BUT IF THE FIGHT GOES BADLY... THERE MAY NOT BE ANOTHER WAY.
TO SAVE THE WORLD, BUFFY MIGHT HAVE TO ACCEPT HER FATE.
AND I, MINE.
MY MYSTIC PERIMETER DEFENSES. THEY'VE BREACHED THEM.
THEN LET'S GO.
AND PUNCH FATE RIGHT IN THE NADS.

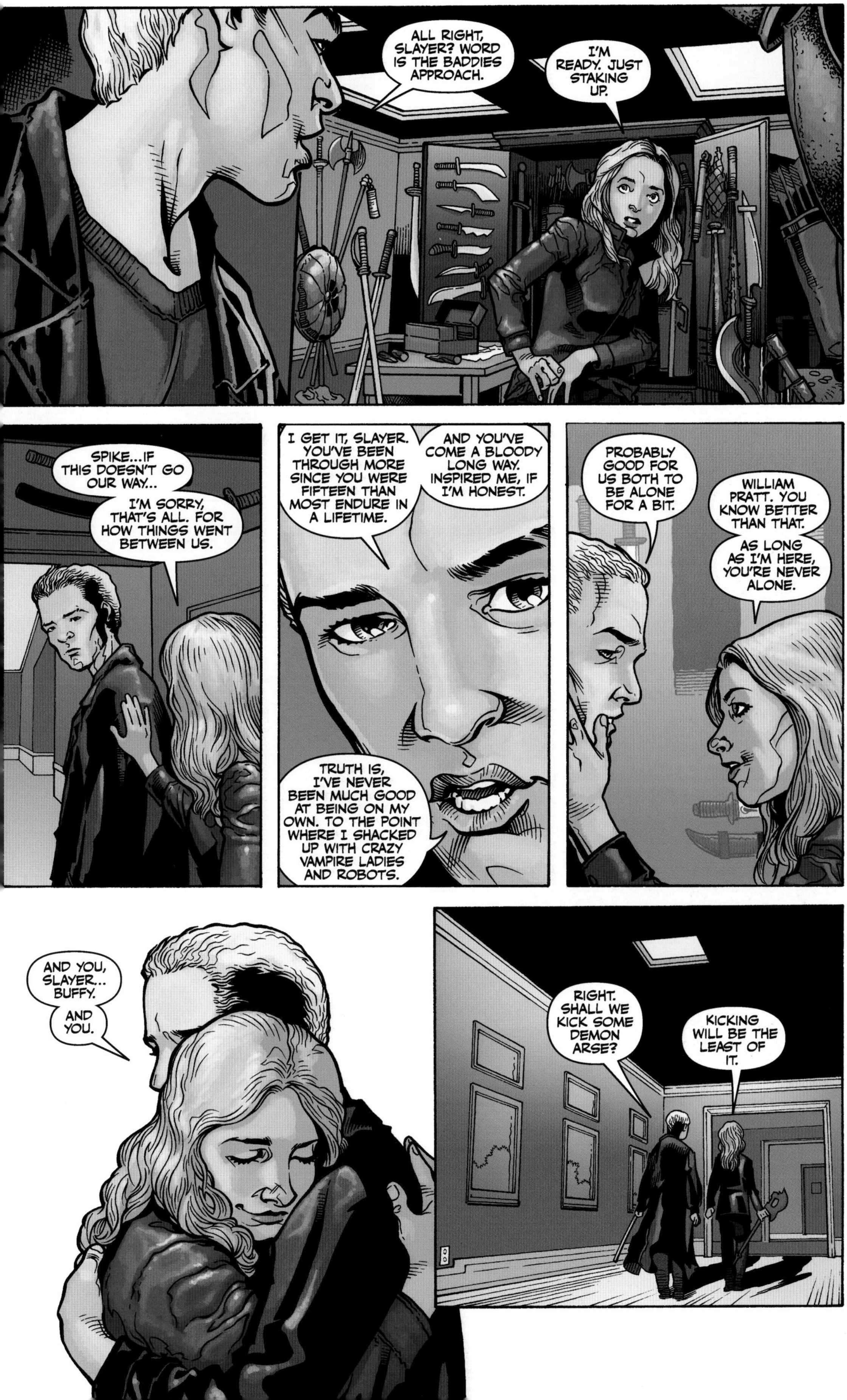
ALL RIGHT, SLAYER? WORD IS THE BADDIES APPROACH.
I'M READY. JUST STAKING UP.
SPIKE...IF THIS DOESN'T GO OUR WAY...
I'M SORRY, THAT'S ALL. FOR HOW THINGS WENT BETWEEN US.
I GET IT, SLAYER. YOU'VE BEEN THROUGH MORE SINCE YOU WERE FIFTEEN THAN MOST ENDURE IN A LIFETIME.
AND YOU'VE COME A BLOODY LONG WAY. INSPIRED ME, IF I'M HONEST.
TRUTH IS, I'VE NEVER BEEN MUCH GOOD AT BEING ON MY OWN. TO THE POINT WHERE I SHACKED UP WITH CRAZY VAMPIRE LADIES AND ROBOTS.
PROBABLY GOOD FOR US BOTH TO BE ALONE FOR A BIT.
WILLIAM PRATT. YOU KNOW BETTER THAN THAT.
AS LONG AS I'M HERE, YOU'RE NEVER ALONE.
AND YOU, SLAYER... BUFFY.
AND YOU.
RIGHT. SHALL WE KICK SOME DEMON ARSE?
KICKING WILL BE THE LEAST OF IT.

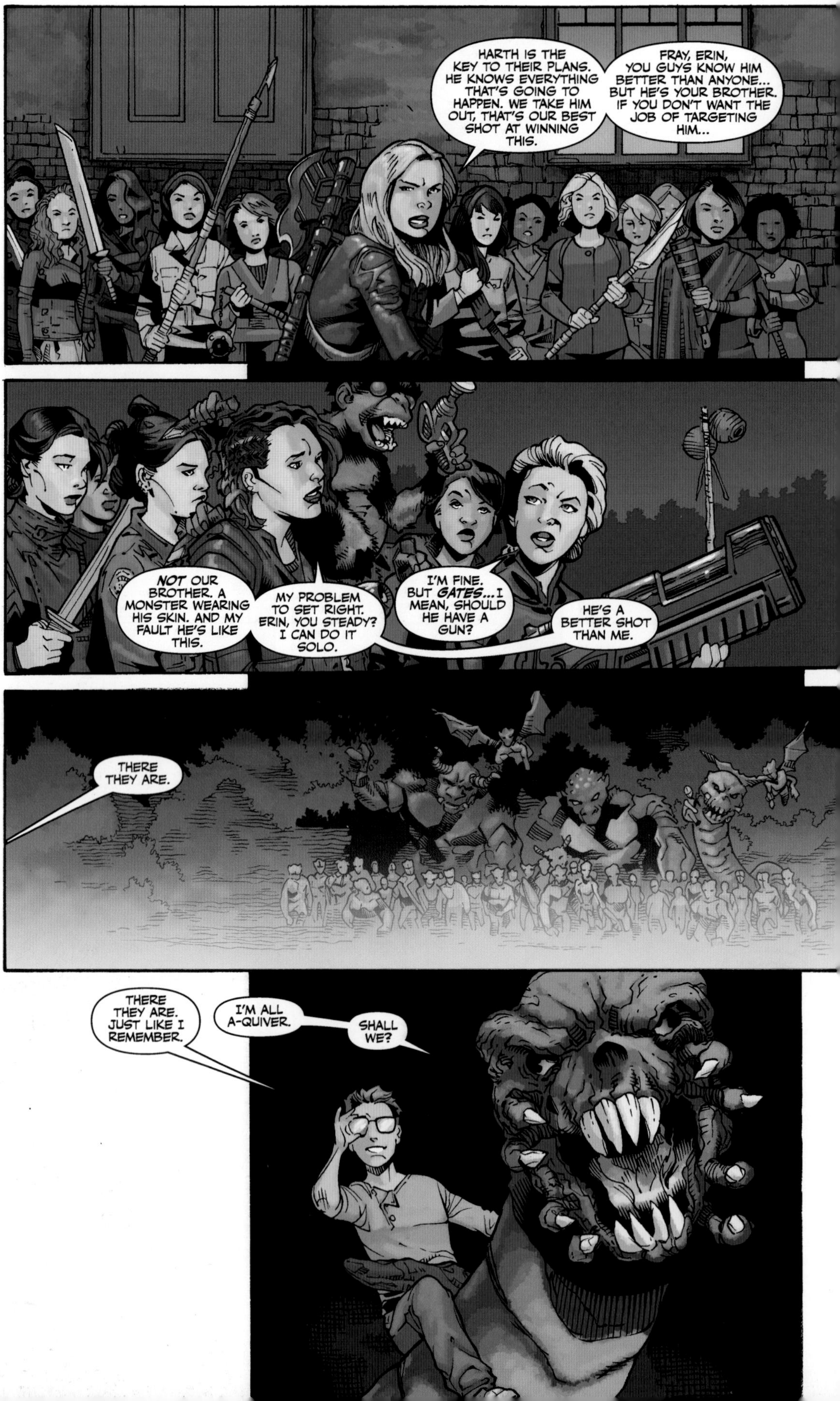
HARTH IS THE KEY TO THEIR PLANS. HE KNOWS EVERYTHING THAT'S GOING TO HAPPEN. WE TAKE HIM OUT, THAT'S OUR BEST SHOT AT WINNING THIS.
FRAY, ERIN, YOU GUYS KNOW HIM BETTER THAN ANYONE... BUT HE'S YOUR BROTHER. IF YOU DON'T WANT THE JOB OF TARGETING HIM...
NOT OUR BROTHER. A MONSTER WEARING HIS SKIN. AND MY FAULT HE'S LIKE THIS.
MY PROBLEM TO SET RIGHT. ERIN, YOU STEADY? I CAN DO IT SOLO.
I'M FINE. BUT GATES... I MEAN, SHOULD HE HAVE A GUN?
HE'S A BETTER SHOT THAN ME.
THERE THEY ARE.
THERE THEY ARE. JUST LIKE I REMEMBER.
I'M ALL A-QUIVER.
SHALL WE?

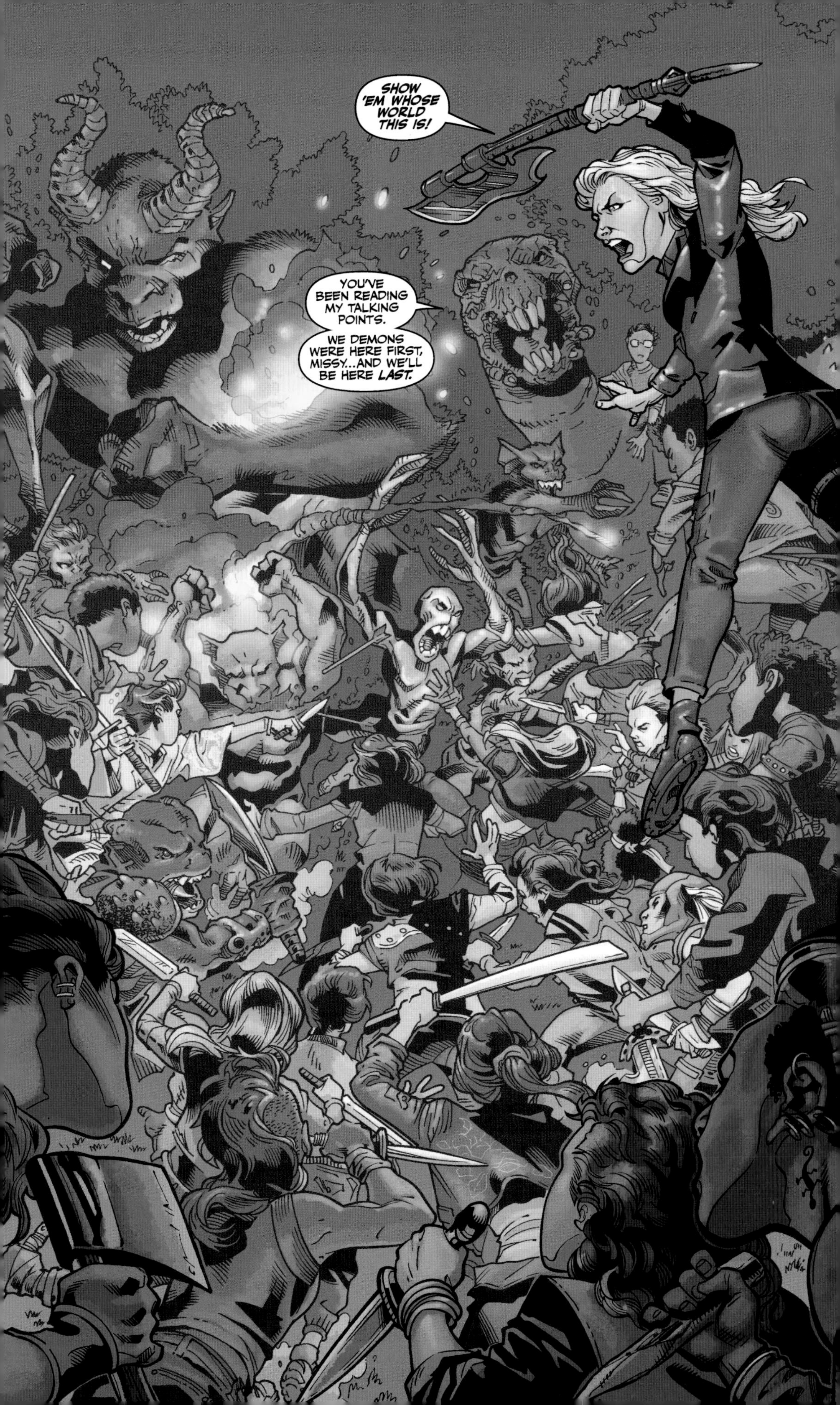
SHOW 'EM WHOSE WORLD THIS IS!
YOU'VE BEEN READING MY TALKING POINTS.
WE DEMONS WERE HERE FIRST, MISSY...AND WE'LL BE HERE LAST.

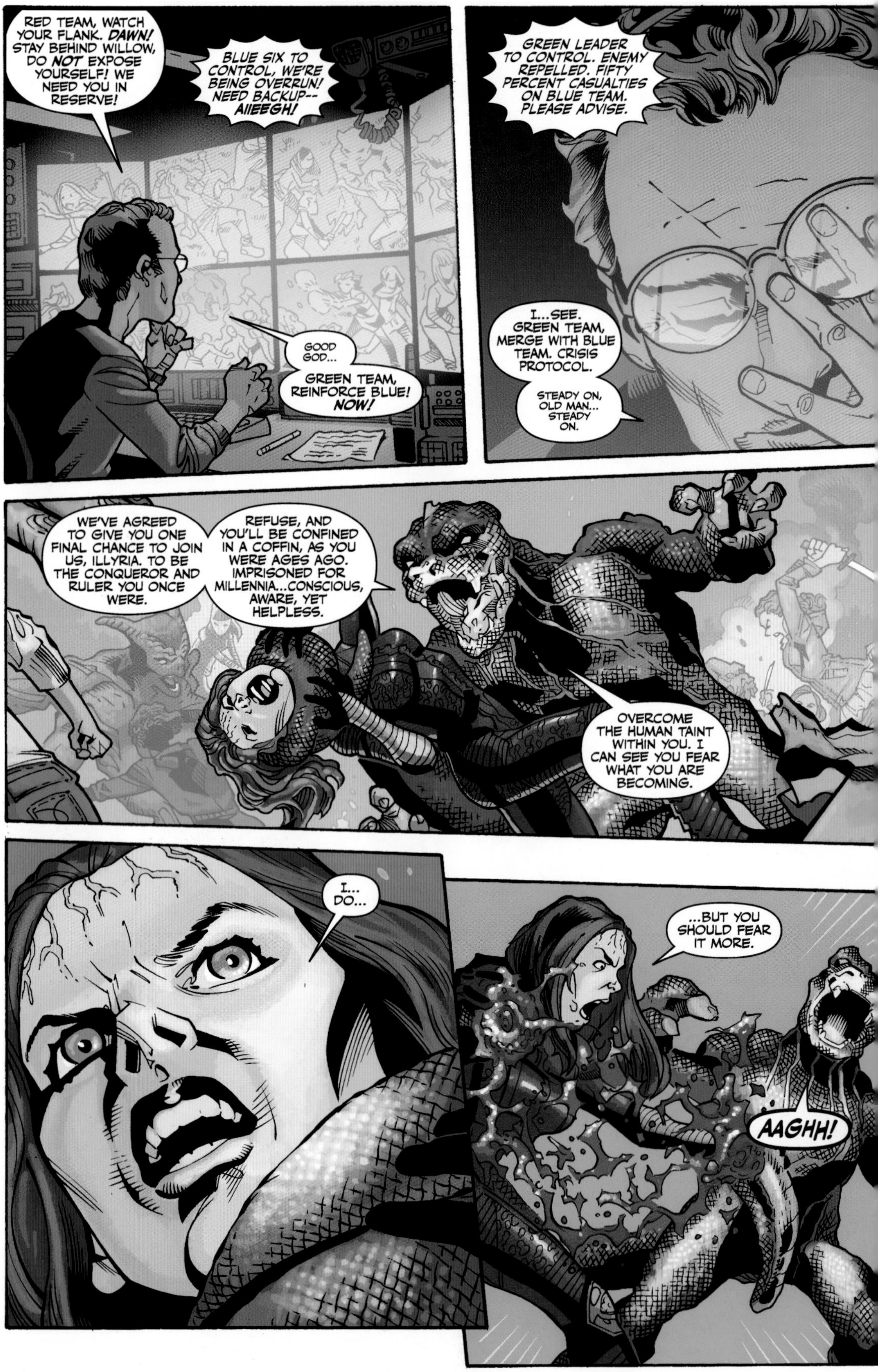

RED TEAM, WATCH YOUR FLANK. DAWN! STAY BEHIND WILLOW, DO NOT EXPOSE YOURSELF! WE NEED YOU IN RESERVE!
BLUE SIX TO CONTROL, WE'RE BEING OVERRUN! NEED BACKUP-- AIIEEGH!
GOOD GOD...
GREEN TEAM, REINFORCE BLUE! NOW!
GREEN LEADER TO CONTROL. ENEMY REPELLED. FIFTY PERCENT CASUALTIES ON BLUE TEAM. PLEASE ADVISE.
I...SEE. GREEN TEAM, MERGE WITH BLUE TEAM. CRISIS PROTOCOL.
STEADY ON, OLD MAN... STEADY ON.
WE'VE AGREED TO GIVE YOU ONE FINAL CHANCE TO JOIN US, ILLYRIA. TO BE THE CONQUEROR AND RULER YOU ONCE WERE.
REFUSE, AND YOU'LL BE CONFINED IN A COFFIN, AS YOU WERE AGES AGO. IMPRISONED FOR MILLENNIA...CONSCIOUS, AWARE, YET HELPLESS.
OVERCOME THE HUMAN TAINT WITHIN YOU. I CAN SEE YOU FEAR WHAT YOU ARE BECOMING.
I... DO...
...BUT YOU SHOULD FEAR IT MORE.
AAGHH!

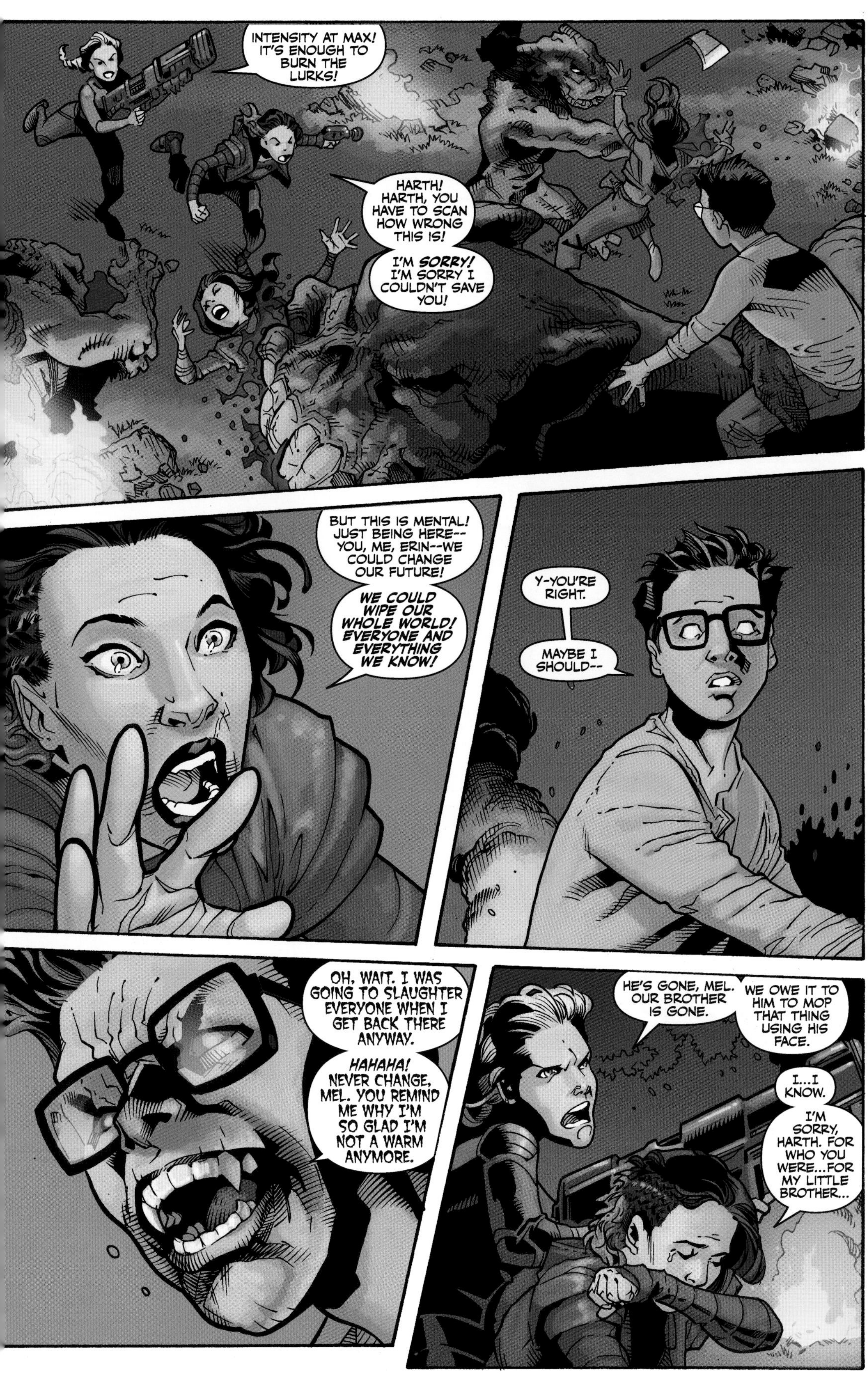

INTENSITY AT MAX! IT'S ENOUGH TO BURN THE LURKS!
HARTH! HARTH, YOU HAVE TO SCAN HOW WRONG THIS IS!
I'M SORRY! I'M SORRY I COULDN'T SAVE YOU!
BUT THIS IS MENTAL! JUST BEING HERE-- YOU, ME, ERIN--WE COULD CHANGE OUR FUTURE!
WE COULD WIPE OUR WHOLE WORLD! EVERYONE AND EVERYTHING WE KNOW!
Y-YOU'RE RIGHT.
MAYBE I SHOULD--
OH, WAIT. I WAS GOING TO SLAUGHTER EVERYONE WHEN I GET BACK THERE ANYWAY.
HAHAHA! NEVER CHANGE, MEL. YOU REMIND ME WHY I'M SO GLAD I'M NOT A WARM ANYMORE.
HE'S GONE, MEL. OUR BROTHER IS GONE.
WE OWE IT TO HIM TO MOP THAT THING USING HIS FACE.
I...I KNOW.
I'M SORRY, HARTH. FOR WHO YOU WERE...FOR MY LITTLE BROTHER...

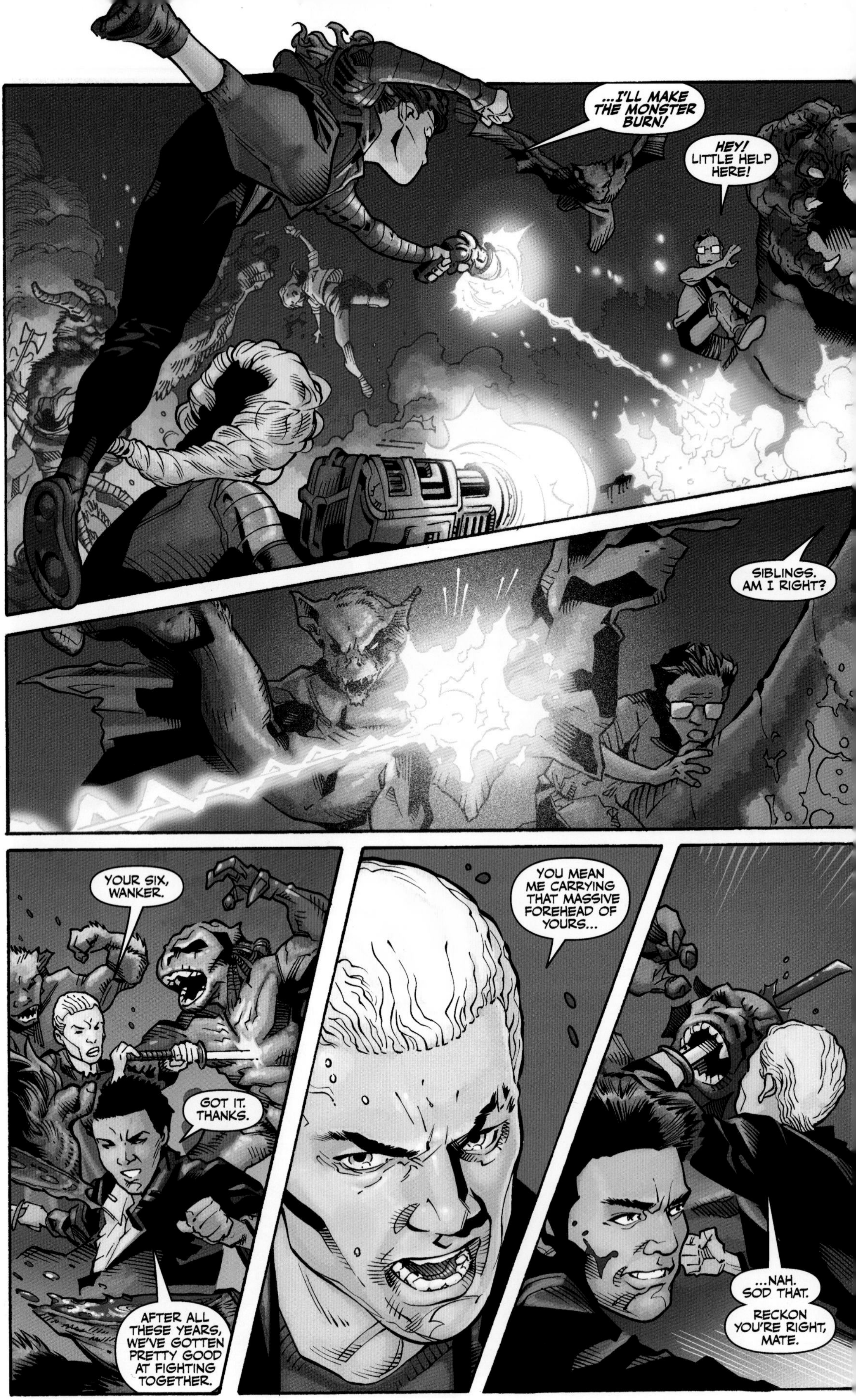
...I'LL MAKE THE MONSTER BURN!
HEY! LITTLE HELP HERE!
SIBLINGS. AM I RIGHT?
YOUR SIX, WANKER.
GOT IT. THANKS.
AFTER ALL THESE YEARS, WE'VE GOTTEN PRETTY GOOD AT FIGHTING TOGETHER.
YOU MEAN ME CARRYING THAT MASSIVE FOREHEAD OF YOURS...
...NAH. SOD THAT.
RECKON YOU'RE RIGHT, MATE.

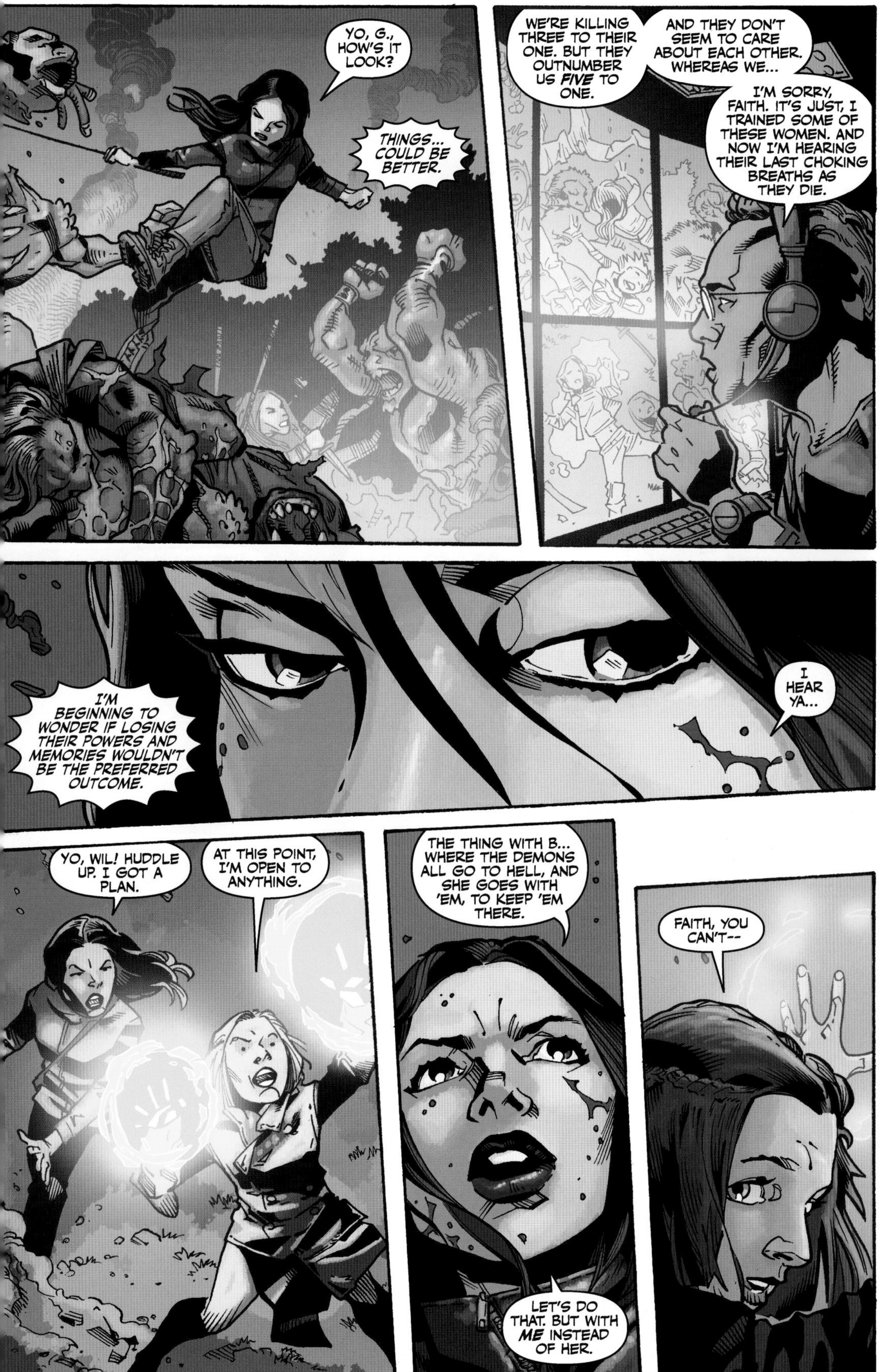
YO, G., HOW'S IT LOOK?
THINGS... COULD BE BETTER.
WE'RE KILLING THREE TO THEIR ONE. BUT THEY OUTNUMBER US FIVE TO ONE.
AND THEY DON'T SEEM TO CARE ABOUT EACH OTHER. WHEREAS WE...
I'M SORRY, FAITH. IT'S JUST, I TRAINED SOME OF THESE WOMEN. AND NOW I'M HEARING THEIR LAST CHOKING BREATHS AS THEY DIE.
I'M BEGINNING TO WONDER IF LOSING THEIR POWERS AND MEMORIES WOULDN'T BE THE PREFERRED OUTCOME.
I HEAR YA...
YO, WIL! HUDDLE UP. I GOT A PLAN.
AT THIS POINT, I'M OPEN TO ANYTHING.
THE THING WITH B... WHERE THE DEMONS ALL GO TO HELL, AND SHE GOES WITH 'EM, TO KEEP 'EM THERE.
LET'S DO THAT. BUT WITH ME INSTEAD OF HER.
FAITH, YOU CAN'T--

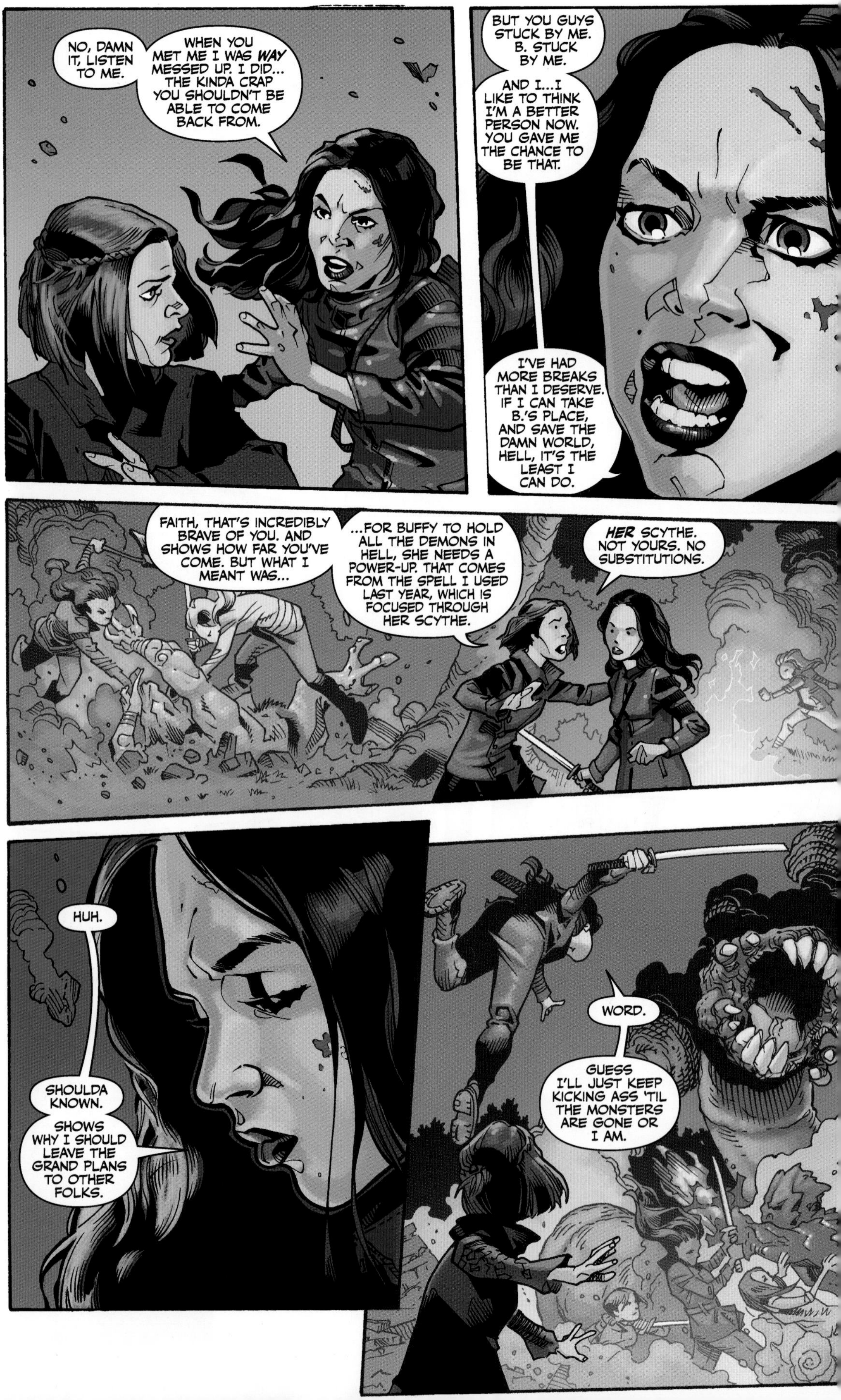
NO, DAMN IT, LISTEN TO ME.
WHEN YOU MET ME I WAS *WAY* MESSED UP. I DID... THE KINDA CRAP YOU SHOULDN'T BE ABLE TO COME BACK FROM.
BUT YOU GUYS STUCK BY ME. B. STUCK BY ME.
AND I...I LIKE TO THINK I'M A BETTER PERSON NOW. YOU GAVE ME THE CHANCE TO BE THAT.
I'VE HAD MORE BREAKS THAN I DESERVE. IF I CAN TAKE B.'S PLACE, AND SAVE THE DAMN WORLD, HELL, IT'S THE LEAST I CAN DO.
FAITH, THAT'S INCREDIBLY BRAVE OF YOU. AND SHOWS HOW FAR YOU'VE COME. BUT WHAT I MEANT WAS...
...FOR BUFFY TO HOLD ALL THE DEMONS IN HELL, SHE NEEDS A POWER-UP. THAT COMES FROM THE SPELL I USED LAST YEAR, WHICH IS FOCUSED THROUGH HER SCYTHE.
HER SCYTHE. NOT YOURS. NO SUBSTITUTIONS.
HUH.
SHOULDA KNOWN.
SHOWS WHY I SHOULD LEAVE THE GRAND PLANS TO OTHER FOLKS.
WORD.
GUESS I'LL JUST KEEP KICKING ASS 'TIL THE MONSTERS ARE GONE OR I AM.

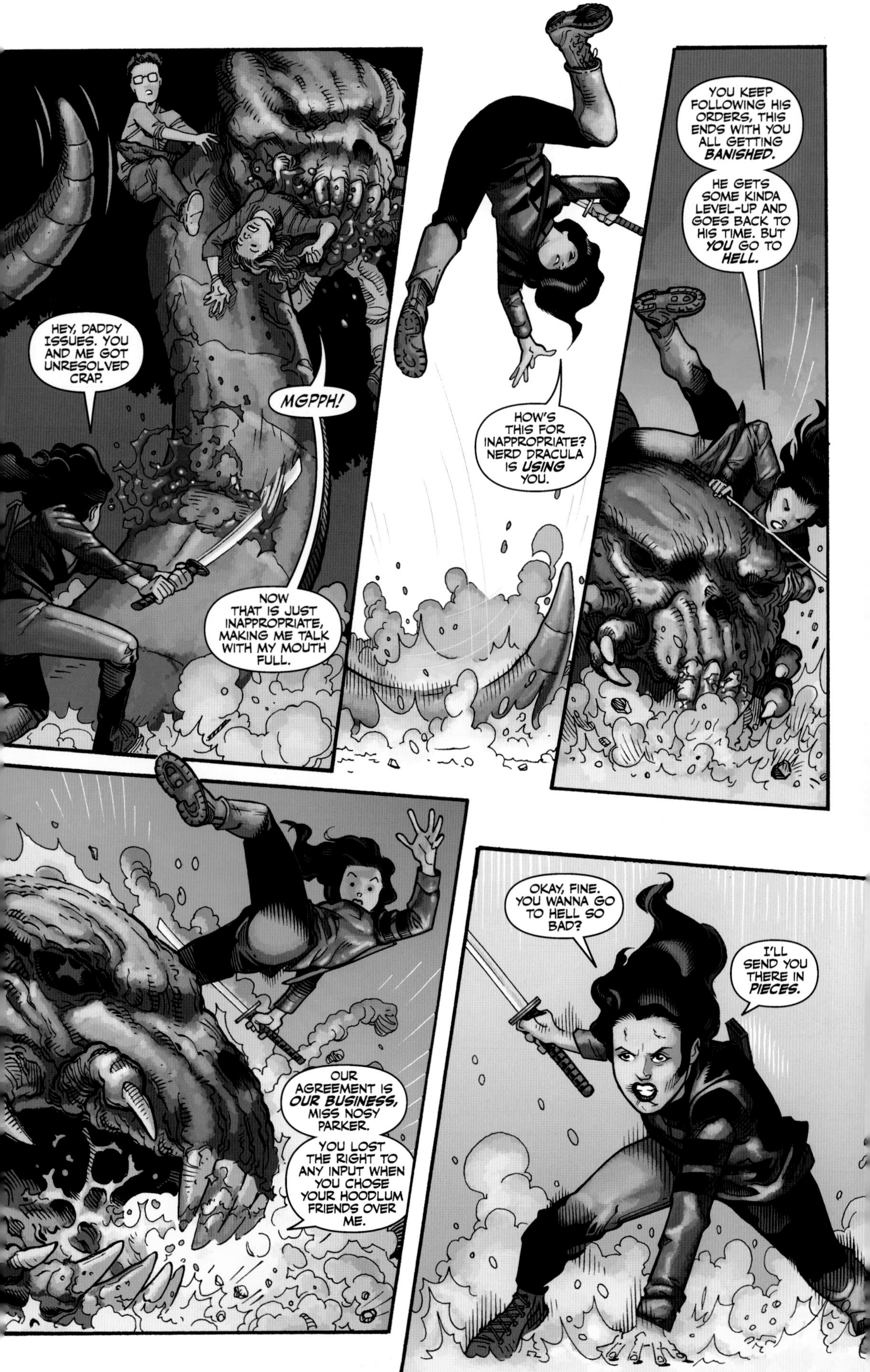
HEY, DADDY ISSUES. YOU AND ME GOT UNRESOLVED CRAP.
MGPPH!
NOW THAT IS JUST INAPPROPRIATE, MAKING ME TALK WITH MY MOUTH FULL.
HOW'S THIS FOR INAPPROPRIATE? NERD DRACULA IS USING YOU.
YOU KEEP FOLLOWING HIS ORDERS, THIS ENDS WITH YOU ALL GETTING BANISHED.
HE GETS SOME KINDA LEVEL-UP AND GOES BACK TO HIS TIME. BUT YOU GO TO HELL.
OUR AGREEMENT IS OUR BUSINESS, MISS NOSY PARKER.
YOU LOST THE RIGHT TO ANY INPUT WHEN YOU CHOSE YOUR HOODLUM FRIENDS OVER ME.
OKAY, FINE. YOU WANNA GO TO HELL SO BAD?
I'LL SEND YOU THERE IN PIECES.

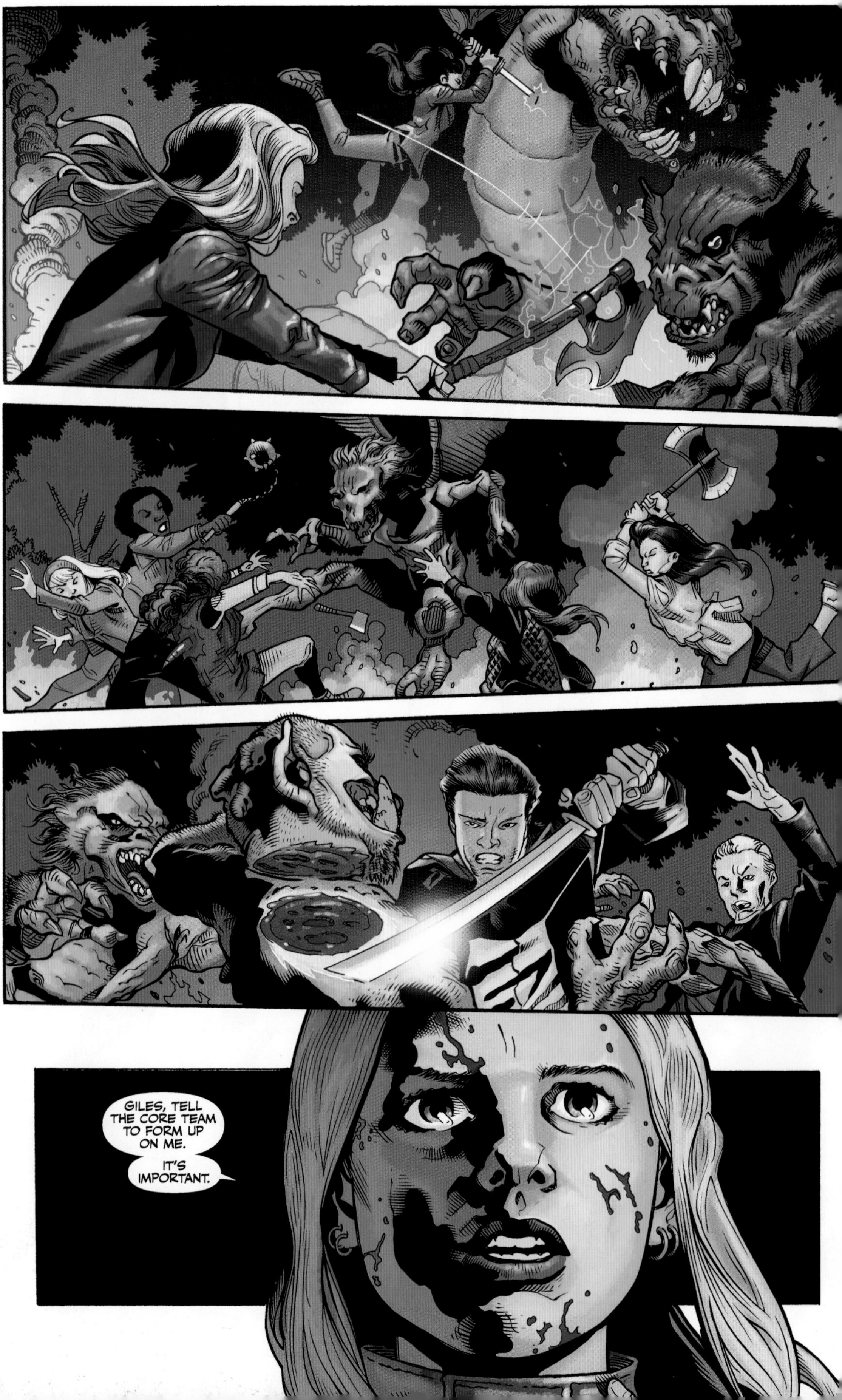
GILES, TELL THE CORE TEAM TO FORM UP ON ME.
IT'S IMPORTANT.

WHAT'S UP? THE OTHERS CAN'T HOLD THE LINE FOR LONG.

WE CAN'T WIN THIS. NOT THE WAY IT'S GOING.

THEY KNOW EVERYTHING WE'LL DO. AND THEY KNOW HOW TO COUNTER IT.

I COULD OPEN A PORTAL FOR US. IF WILLOW CAN PUSH THEM BACK WITH A SPELL, WE COULD ALL ESCAPE TO...I DON'T KNOW, WYOMING.

THAT CHANGES HISTORY. THEN IT'S A *FAIR FIGHT*, AT LEAST.

BUT THEN WE DON'T KNOW WHAT MIGHT HAPPEN. MAYBE THEY COME AFTER US WITH REINFORCEMENTS. CONFIDENT, BECAUSE THEY WON THE LAST BATTLE.

BUT THERE'S ONE WAY THIS ENDS THAT WE *KNOW* SAVES THE WORLD.

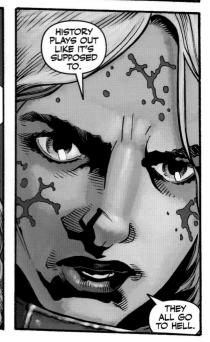

HISTORY PLAYS OUT LIKE IT'S SUPPOSED TO.

THEY ALL GO TO HELL.

AND I GO WITH THEM.

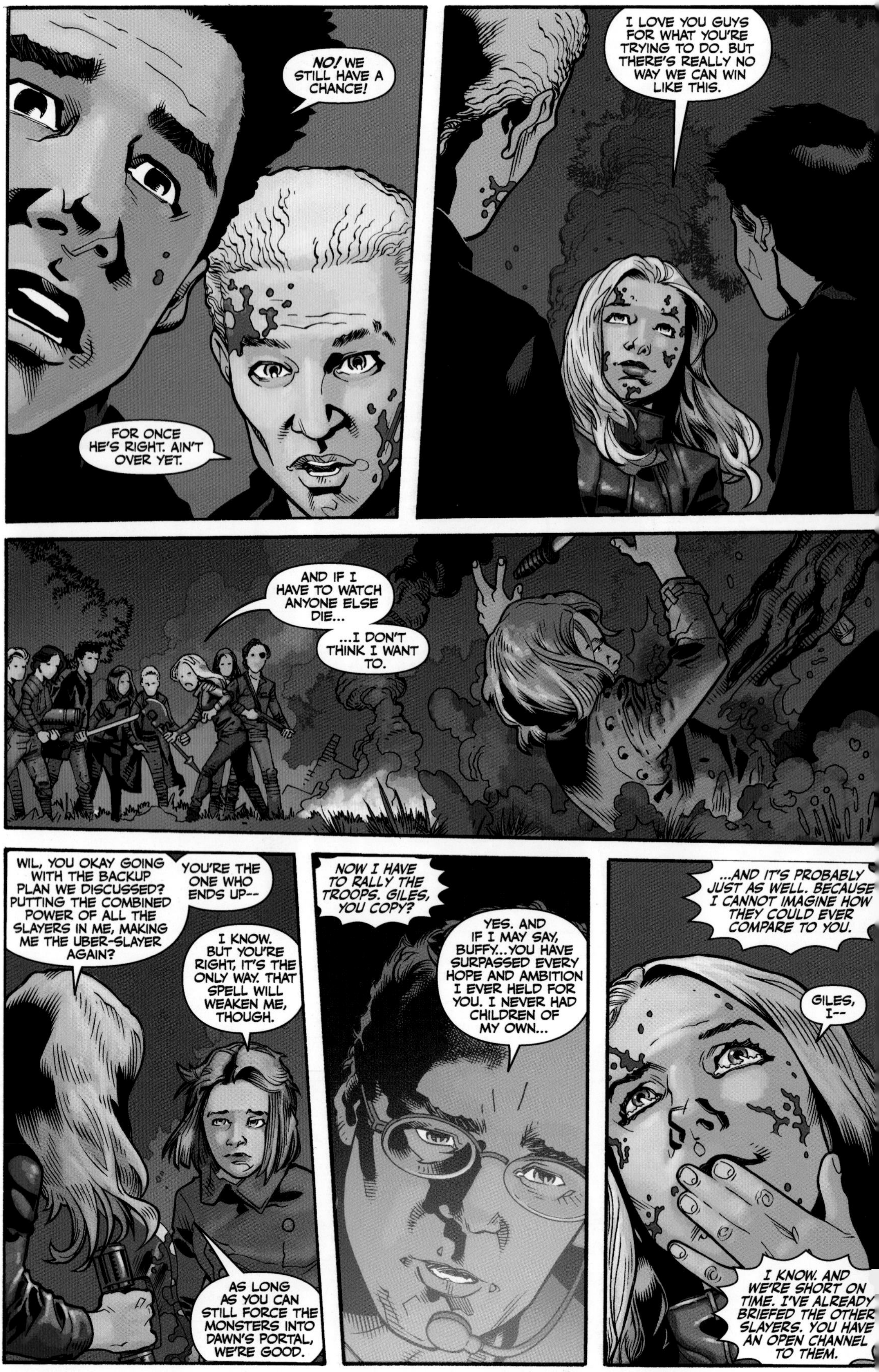
NO! WE STILL HAVE A CHANCE!
FOR ONCE HE'S RIGHT. AIN'T OVER YET.
I LOVE YOU GUYS FOR WHAT YOU'RE TRYING TO DO. BUT THERE'S REALLY NO WAY WE CAN WIN LIKE THIS.
AND IF I HAVE TO WATCH ANYONE ELSE DIE...
...I DON'T THINK I WANT TO.
WIL, YOU OKAY GOING WITH THE BACKUP PLAN WE DISCUSSED? PUTTING THE COMBINED POWER OF ALL THE SLAYERS IN ME, MAKING ME THE UBER-SLAYER AGAIN?
YOU'RE THE ONE WHO ENDS UP--
I KNOW. BUT YOU'RE RIGHT, IT'S THE ONLY WAY. THAT SPELL WILL WEAKEN ME, THOUGH.
AS LONG AS YOU CAN STILL FORCE THE MONSTERS INTO DAWN'S PORTAL, WE'RE GOOD.
NOW I HAVE TO RALLY THE TROOPS. GILES, YOU COPY?
YES. AND IF I MAY SAY, BUFFY...YOU HAVE SURPASSED EVERY HOPE AND AMBITION I EVER HELD FOR YOU. I NEVER HAD CHILDREN OF MY OWN...
...AND IT'S PROBABLY JUST AS WELL. BECAUSE I CANNOT IMAGINE HOW THEY COULD EVER COMPARE TO YOU.
GILES, I--
I KNOW. AND WE'RE SHORT ON TIME. I'VE ALREADY BRIEFED THE OTHER SLAYERS. YOU HAVE AN OPEN CHANNEL TO THEM.

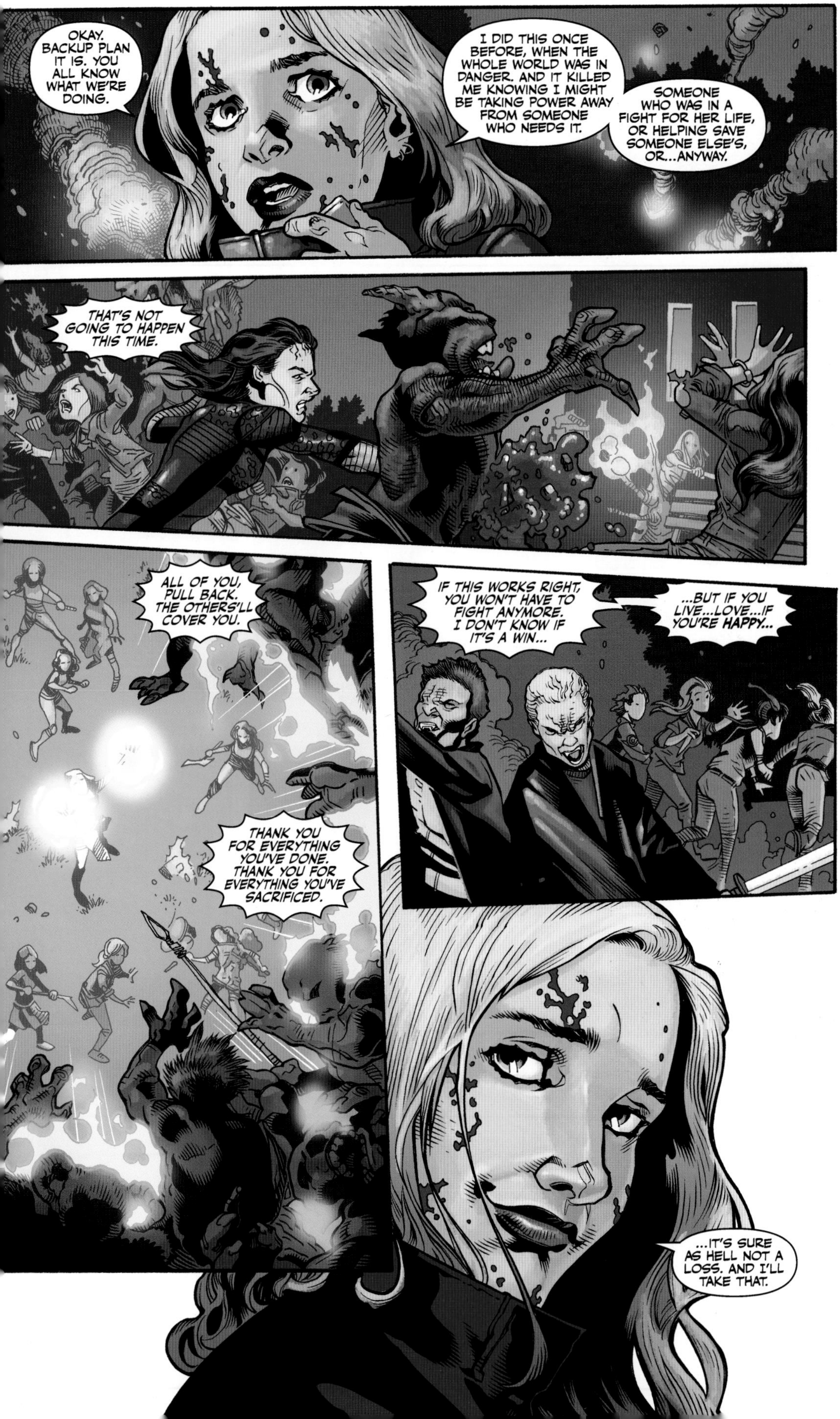
OKAY. BACKUP PLAN IT IS. YOU ALL KNOW WHAT WE'RE DOING.
I DID THIS ONCE BEFORE, WHEN THE WHOLE WORLD WAS IN DANGER. AND IT KILLED ME KNOWING I MIGHT BE TAKING POWER AWAY FROM SOMEONE WHO NEEDS IT.
SOMEONE WHO WAS IN A FIGHT FOR HER LIFE, OR HELPING SAVE SOMEONE ELSE'S, OR...ANYWAY.
THAT'S NOT GOING TO HAPPEN THIS TIME.
ALL OF YOU, PULL BACK. THE OTHERS'LL COVER YOU.
THANK YOU FOR EVERYTHING YOU'VE DONE. THANK YOU FOR EVERYTHING YOU'VE SACRIFICED.
IF THIS WORKS RIGHT, YOU WON'T HAVE TO FIGHT ANYMORE. I DON'T KNOW IF IT'S A WIN...
...BUT IF YOU LIVE...LOVE...IF YOU'RE HAPPY...
...IT'S SURE AS HELL NOT A LOSS. AND I'LL TAKE THAT.

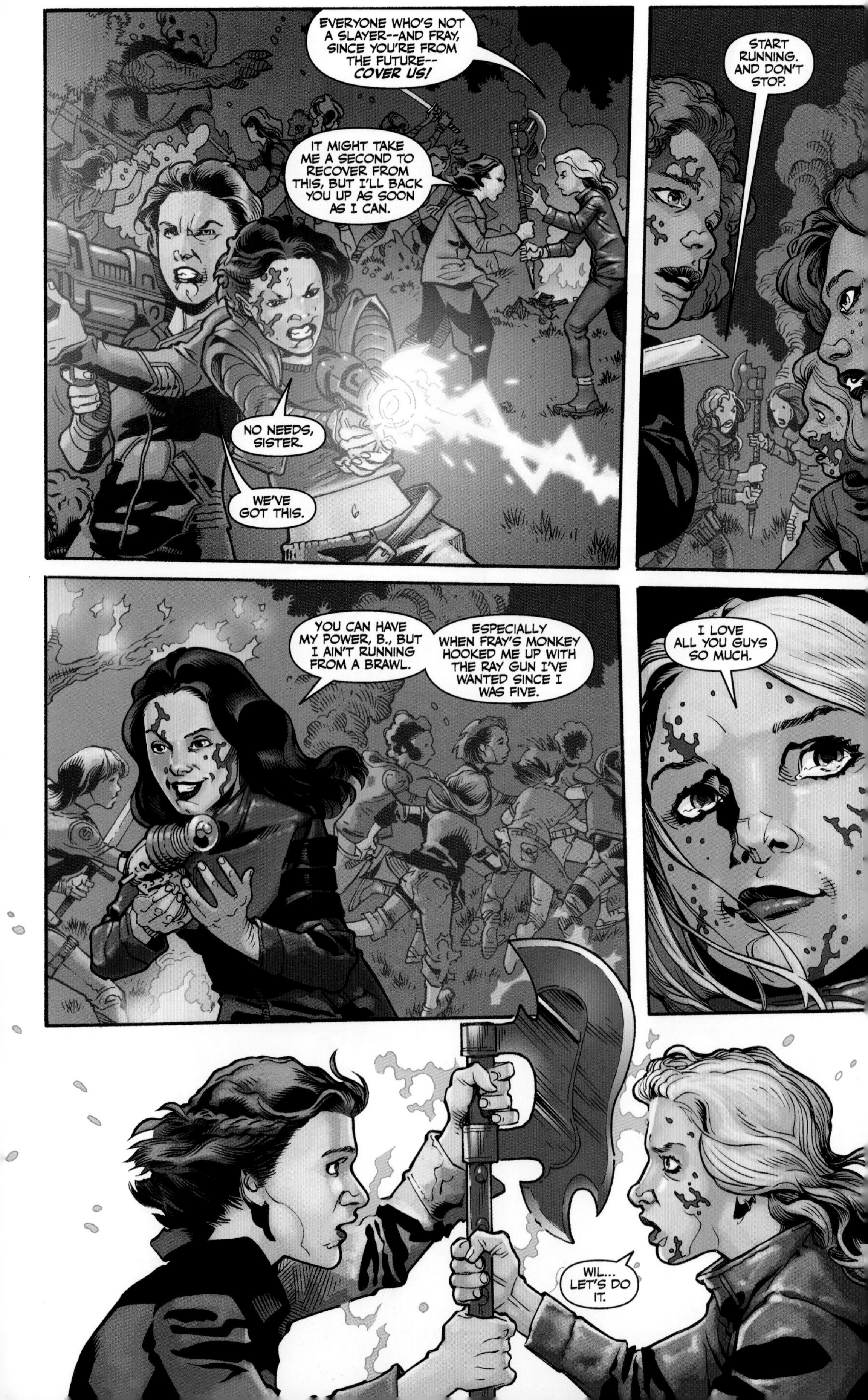
EVERYONE WHO'S NOT A SLAYER--AND FRAY, SINCE YOU'RE FROM THE FUTURE-- COVER US!
IT MIGHT TAKE ME A SECOND TO RECOVER FROM THIS, BUT I'LL BACK YOU UP AS SOON AS I CAN.
NO NEEDS, SISTER.
WE'VE GOT THIS.
START RUNNING. AND DON'T STOP.
YOU CAN HAVE MY POWER, B., BUT I AIN'T RUNNING FROM A BRAWL.
ESPECIALLY WHEN FRAY'S MONKEY HOOKED ME UP WITH THE RAY GUN I'VE WANTED SINCE I WAS FIVE.
I LOVE ALL YOU GUYS SO MUCH.
WIL... LET'S DO IT.

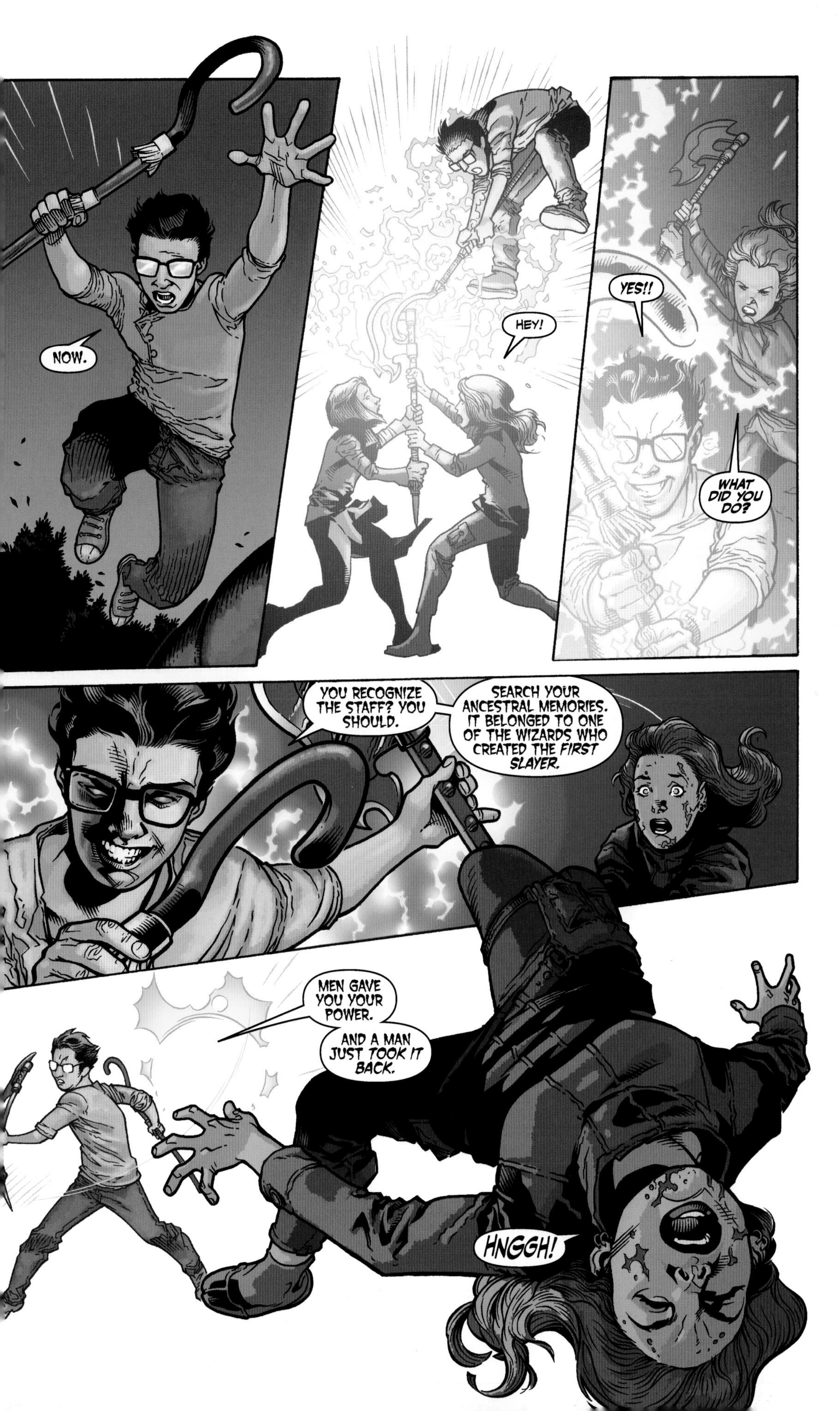
NOW.
HEY!
YES!!
WHAT DID YOU DO?
YOU RECOGNIZE THE STAFF? YOU SHOULD.
SEARCH YOUR ANCESTRAL MEMORIES. IT BELONGED TO ONE OF THE WIZARDS WHO CREATED THE *FIRST* SLAYER.
MEN GAVE YOU YOUR POWER.
AND A MAN JUST *TOOK IT* BACK.
HNGGH!

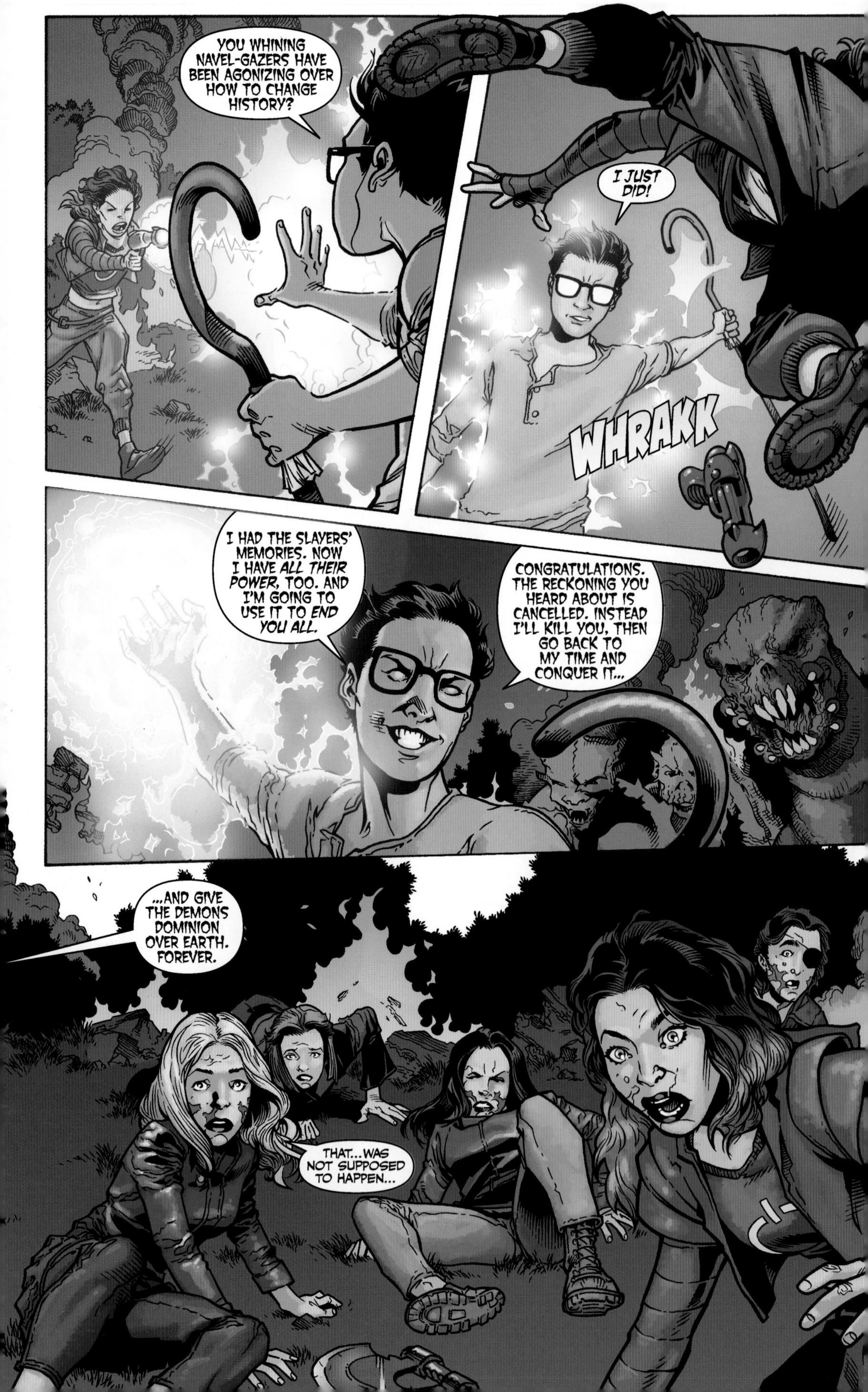
YOU WHINING NAVEL-GAZERS HAVE BEEN AGONIZING OVER HOW TO CHANGE HISTORY?
I JUST DID!
WHRAKK
I HAD THE SLAYERS' MEMORIES. NOW I HAVE *ALL THEIR POWER*, TOO. AND I'M GOING TO USE IT TO *END YOU ALL.*
CONGRATULATIONS. THE RECKONING YOU HEARD ABOUT IS CANCELLED. INSTEAD I'LL KILL YOU, THEN GO BACK TO MY TIME AND CONQUER IT...
...AND GIVE THE DEMONS DOMINION OVER EARTH. FOREVER.
THAT...WAS NOT SUPPOSED TO HAPPEN...

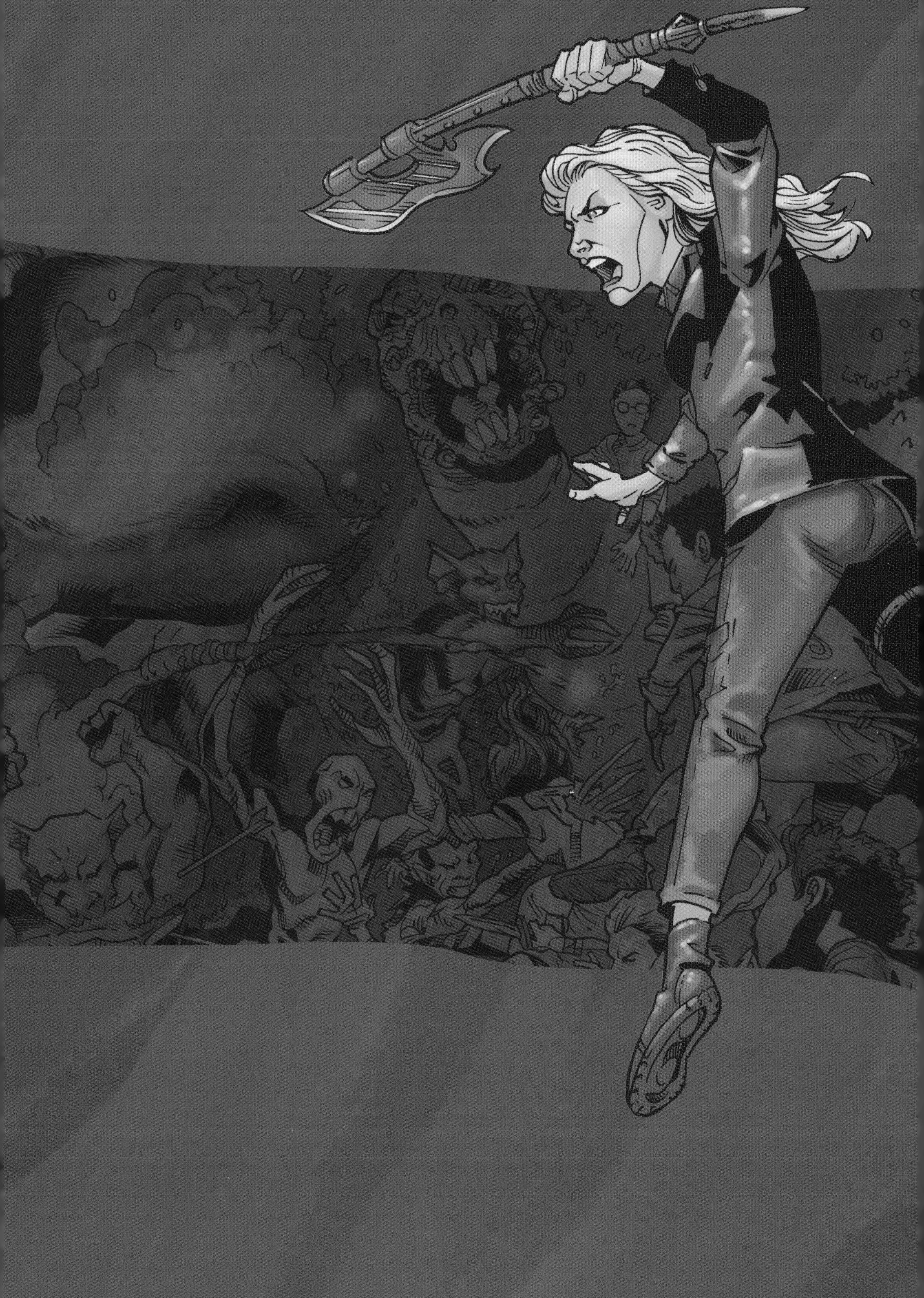

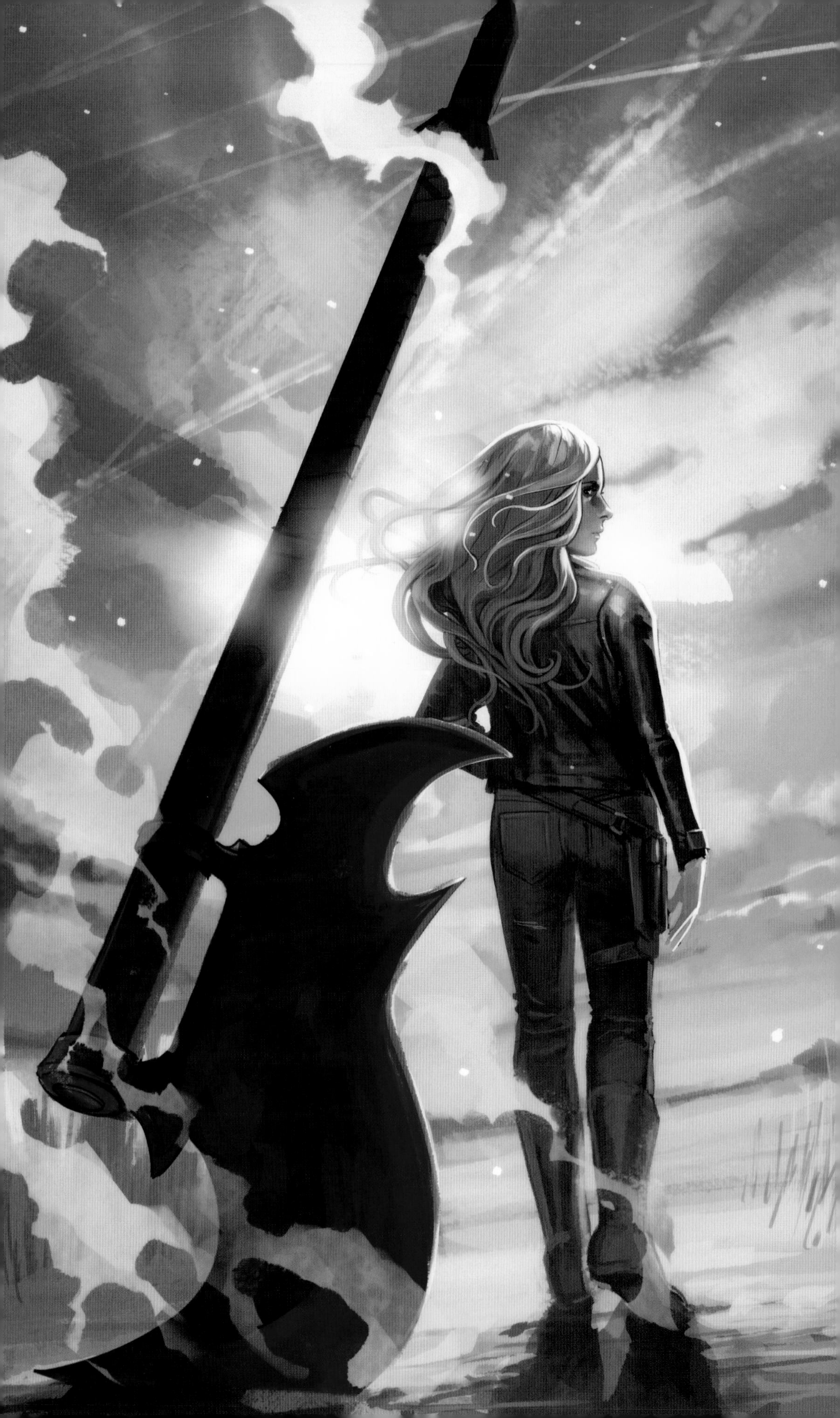

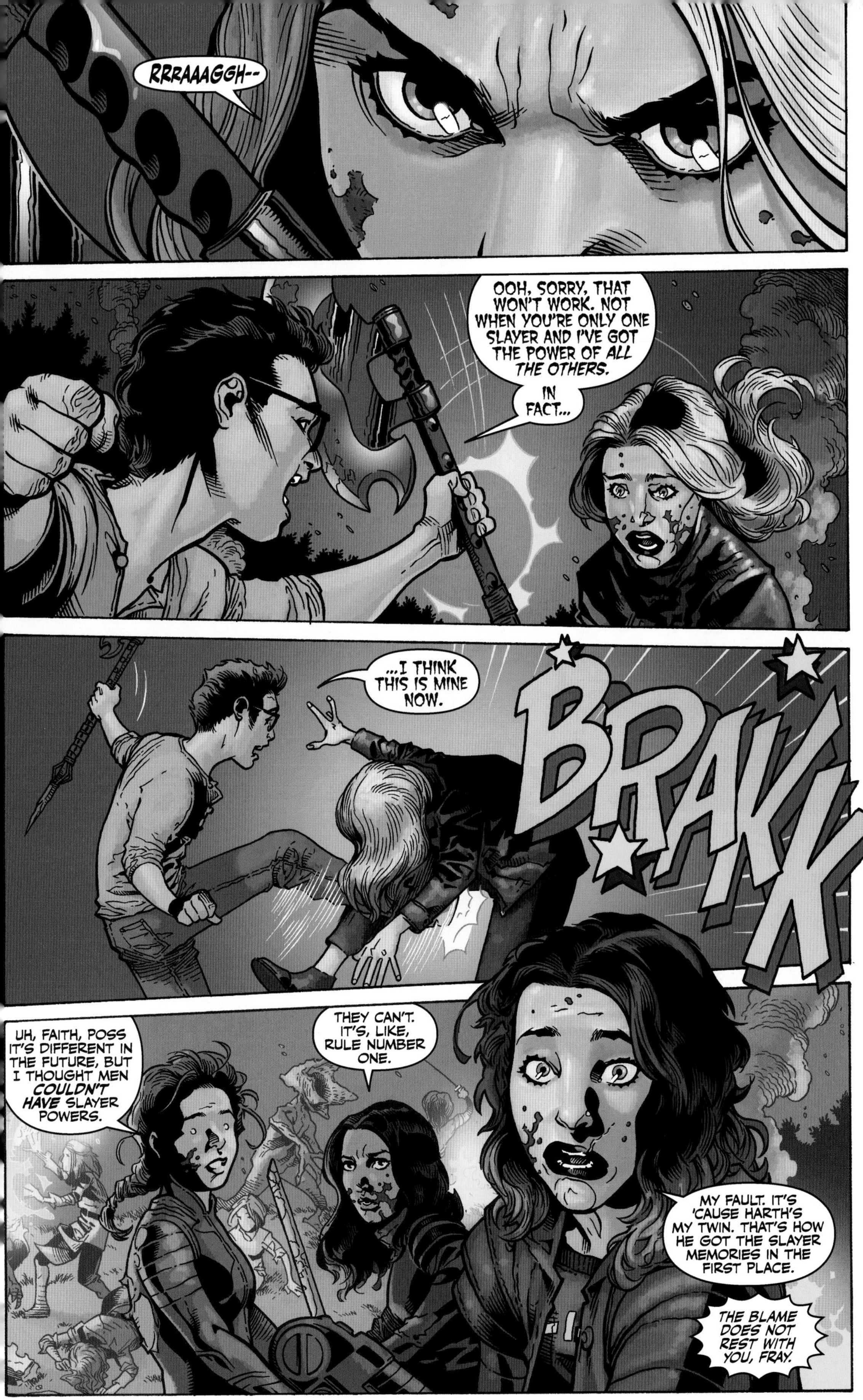

RRRAAAGGH--
OOH, SORRY, THAT WON'T WORK. NOT WHEN YOU'RE ONLY ONE SLAYER AND I'VE GOT THE POWER OF ALL THE OTHERS.
IN FACT...
...I THINK THIS IS MINE NOW.
BRAKK
UH, FAITH, POSS IT'S DIFFERENT IN THE FUTURE, BUT I THOUGHT MEN COULDN'T HAVE SLAYER POWERS.
THEY CAN'T. IT'S, LIKE, RULE NUMBER ONE.
MY FAULT. IT'S 'CAUSE HARTH'S MY TWIN. THAT'S HOW HE GOT THE SLAYER MEMORIES IN THE FIRST PLACE.
THE BLAME DOES NOT REST WITH YOU, FRAY.

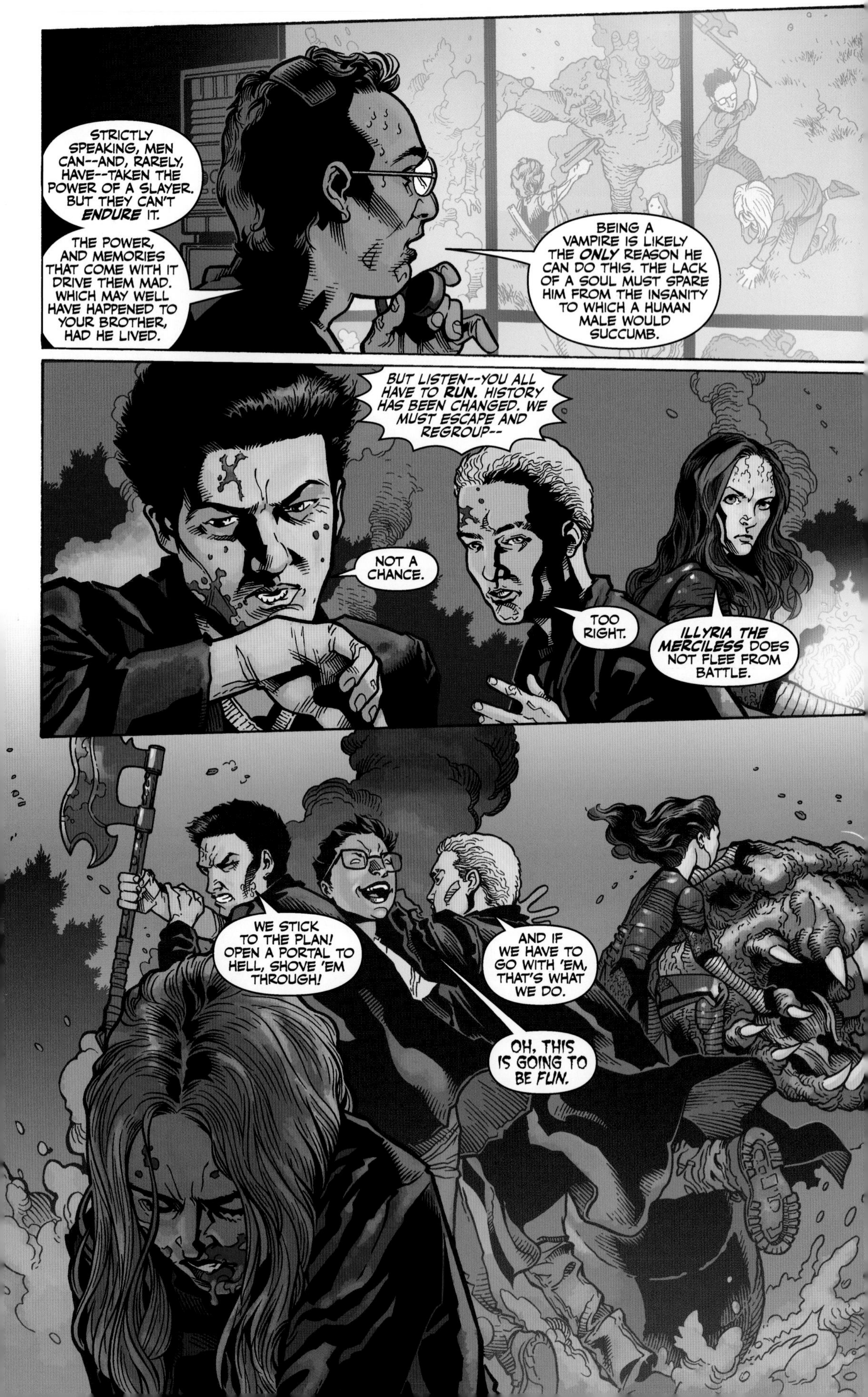
STRICTLY SPEAKING, MEN CAN--AND, RARELY, HAVE--TAKEN THE POWER OF A SLAYER. BUT THEY CAN'T *ENDURE* IT.
THE POWER, AND MEMORIES THAT COME WITH IT DRIVE THEM MAD. WHICH MAY WELL HAVE HAPPENED TO YOUR BROTHER, HAD HE LIVED.
BEING A VAMPIRE IS LIKELY THE *ONLY* REASON HE CAN DO THIS. THE LACK OF A SOUL MUST SPARE HIM FROM THE INSANITY TO WHICH A HUMAN MALE WOULD SUCCUMB.
*BUT LISTEN--YOU ALL HAVE TO **RUN**. HISTORY HAS BEEN CHANGED. WE MUST ESCAPE AND REGROUP--*
NOT A CHANCE.
TOO RIGHT.
ILLYRIA THE MERCILESS DOES NOT FLEE FROM BATTLE.
WE STICK TO THE PLAN! OPEN A PORTAL TO HELL, SHOVE 'EM THROUGH!
AND IF WE HAVE TO GO WITH 'EM, THAT'S WHAT WE DO.
OH, THIS IS GOING TO BE *FUN*.

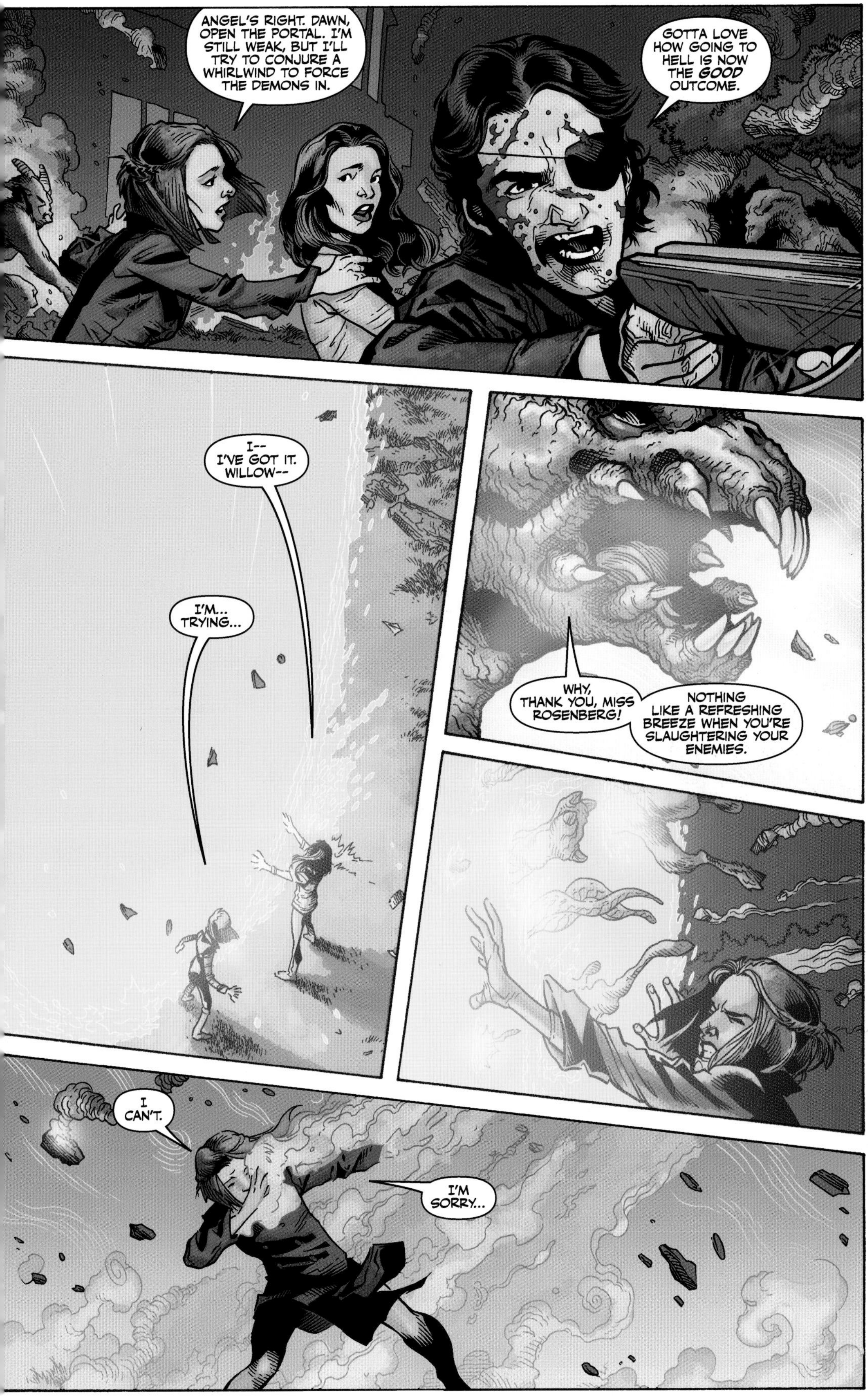
ANGEL'S RIGHT. DAWN, OPEN THE PORTAL. I'M STILL WEAK, BUT I'LL TRY TO CONJURE A WHIRLWIND TO FORCE THE DEMONS IN.
GOTTA LOVE HOW GOING TO HELL IS NOW THE GOOD OUTCOME.
I-- I'VE GOT IT. WILLOW--
I'M... TRYING...
WHY, THANK YOU, MISS ROSENBERG!
NOTHING LIKE A REFRESHING BREEZE WHEN YOU'RE SLAUGHTERING YOUR ENEMIES.
I CAN'T.
I'M SORRY...

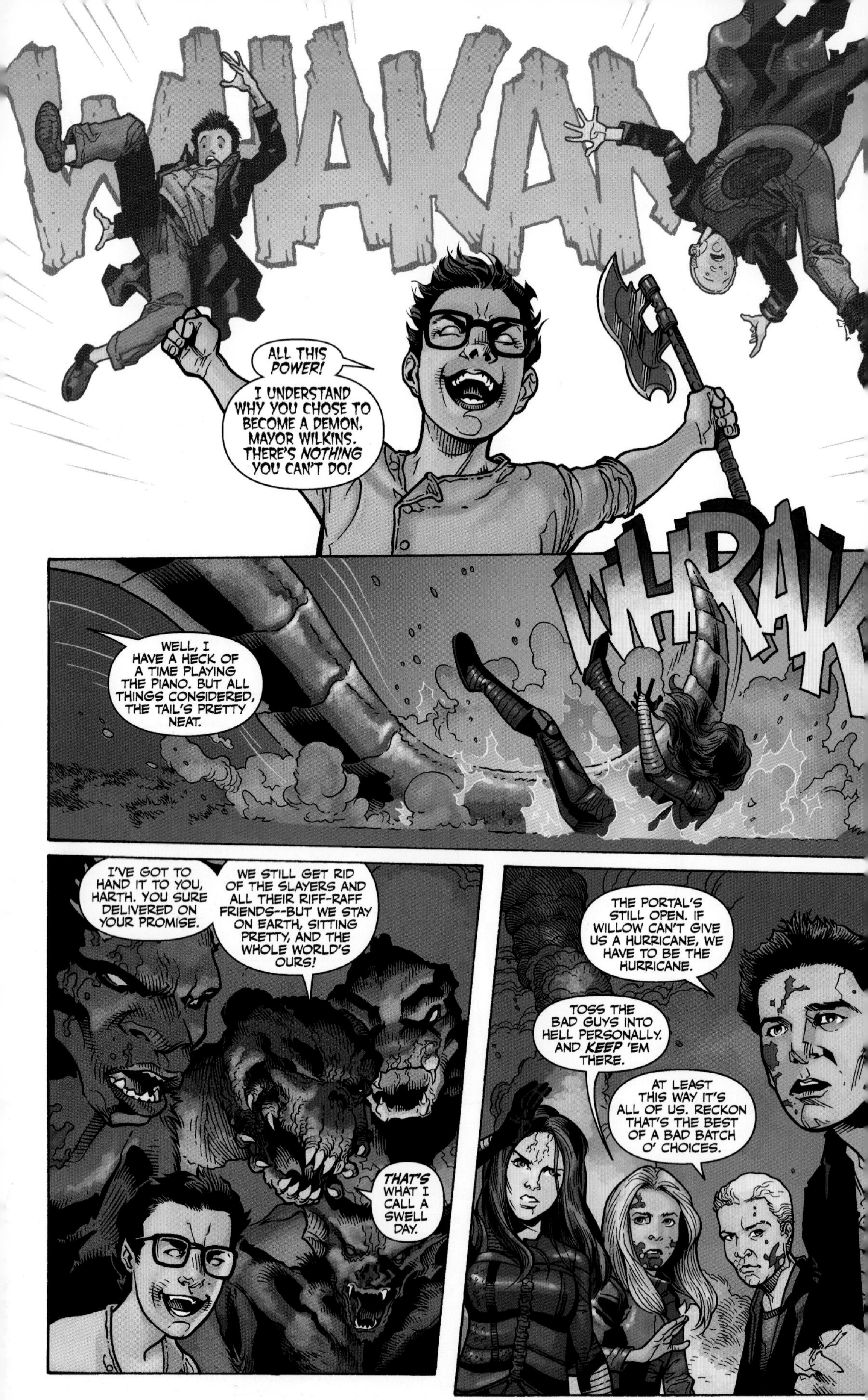
WHAKAM
ALL THIS POWER!
I UNDERSTAND WHY YOU CHOSE TO BECOME A DEMON, MAYOR WILKINS. THERE'S NOTHING YOU CAN'T DO!
WHRAK
WELL, I HAVE A HECK OF A TIME PLAYING THE PIANO. BUT ALL THINGS CONSIDERED, THE TAIL'S PRETTY NEAT.
I'VE GOT TO HAND IT TO YOU, HARTH. YOU SURE DELIVERED ON YOUR PROMISE.
WE STILL GET RID OF THE SLAYERS AND ALL THEIR RIFF-RAFF FRIENDS--BUT WE STAY ON EARTH, SITTING PRETTY, AND THE WHOLE WORLD'S OURS!
THAT'S WHAT I CALL A SWELL DAY.
THE PORTAL'S STILL OPEN. IF WILLOW CAN'T GIVE US A HURRICANE, WE HAVE TO BE THE HURRICANE.
TOSS THE BAD GUYS INTO HELL PERSONALLY. AND KEEP 'EM THERE.
AT LEAST THIS WAY IT'S ALL OF US. RECKON THAT'S THE BEST OF A BAD BATCH O' CHOICES.

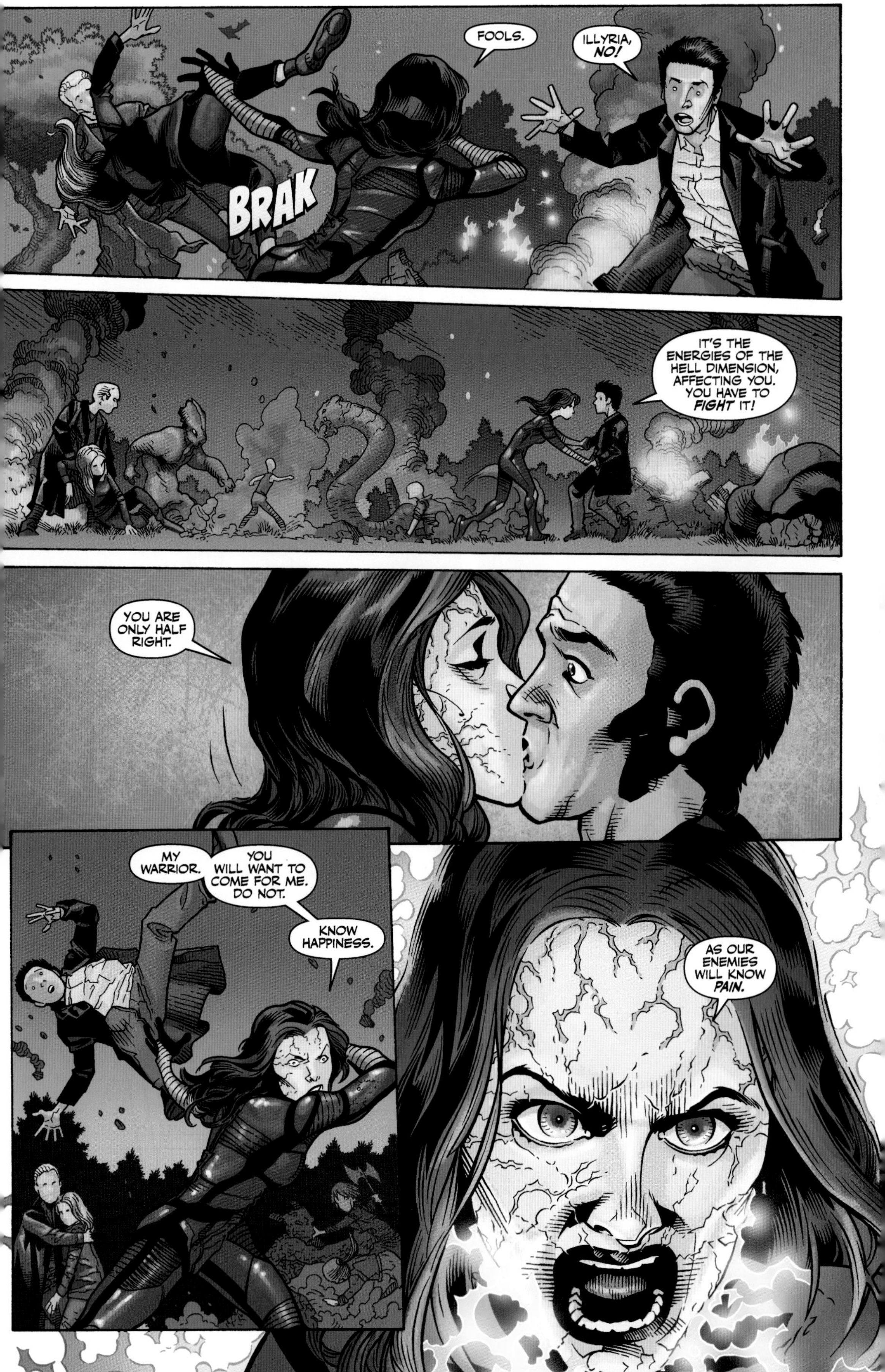
FOOLS.
ILLYRIA, NO!
BRAK
IT'S THE ENERGIES OF THE HELL DIMENSION, AFFECTING YOU. YOU HAVE TO FIGHT IT!
YOU ARE ONLY HALF RIGHT.
MY WARRIOR.
YOU WILL WANT TO COME FOR ME. DO NOT.
KNOW HAPPINESS.
AS OUR ENEMIES WILL KNOW PAIN.

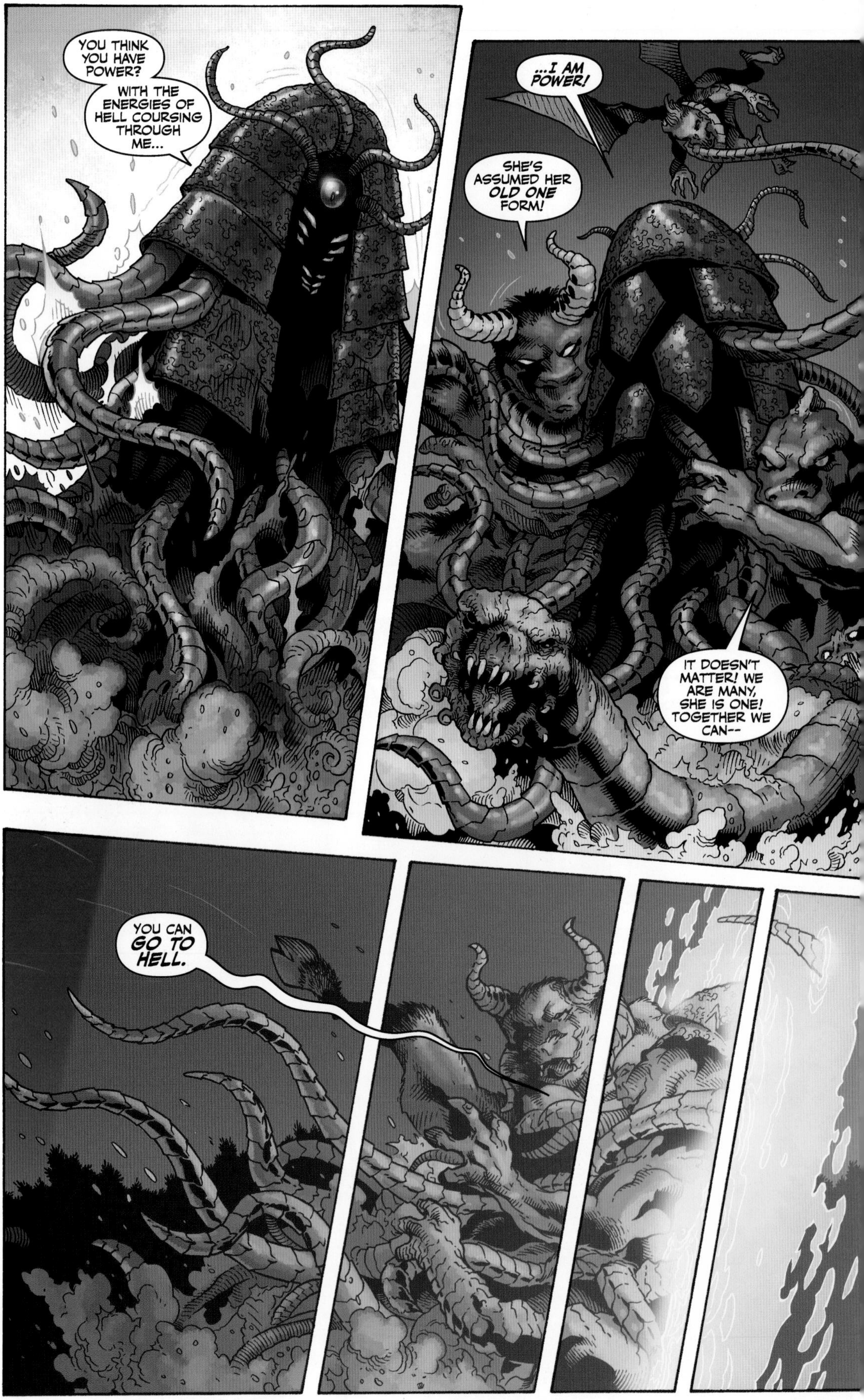
YOU THINK YOU HAVE POWER?
WITH THE ENERGIES OF HELL COURSING THROUGH ME...
...I AM POWER!
SHE'S ASSUMED HER OLD ONE FORM!
IT DOESN'T MATTER! WE ARE MANY, SHE IS ONE! TOGETHER WE CAN--
YOU CAN GO TO HELL.

CLOSE THE GATE, CHILD.

AND FAREWELL...

ILLYRIA! NO!

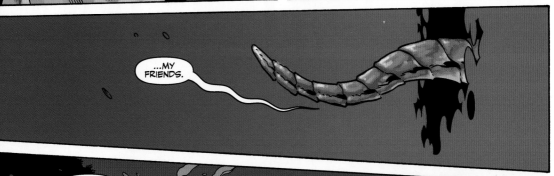

...MY FRIENDS.

OPEN IT! OPEN IT!

I... NEED TO REST FIRST.

SO BACK OFF. BESIDES...

...WE'VE STILL GOT PROBLEMS.

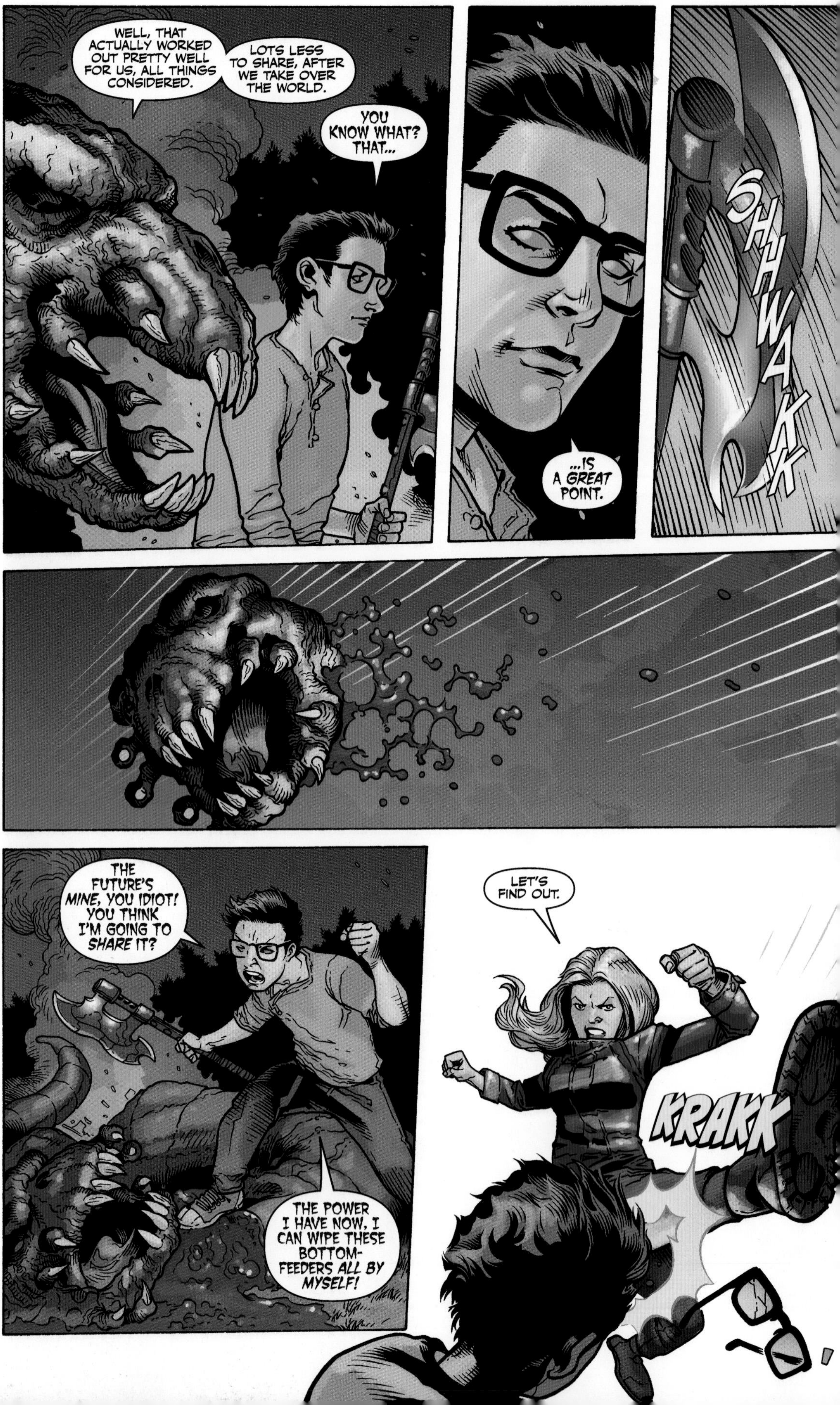
WELL, THAT ACTUALLY WORKED OUT PRETTY WELL FOR US, ALL THINGS CONSIDERED.
LOTS LESS TO SHARE, AFTER WE TAKE OVER THE WORLD.
YOU KNOW WHAT? THAT...
...IS A GREAT POINT.
SHHWAKK
THE FUTURE'S MINE, YOU IDIOT! YOU THINK I'M GOING TO SHARE IT?
THE POWER I HAVE NOW, I CAN WIPE THESE BOTTOM-FEEDERS ALL BY MYSELF!
LET'S FIND OUT.
KRAKK

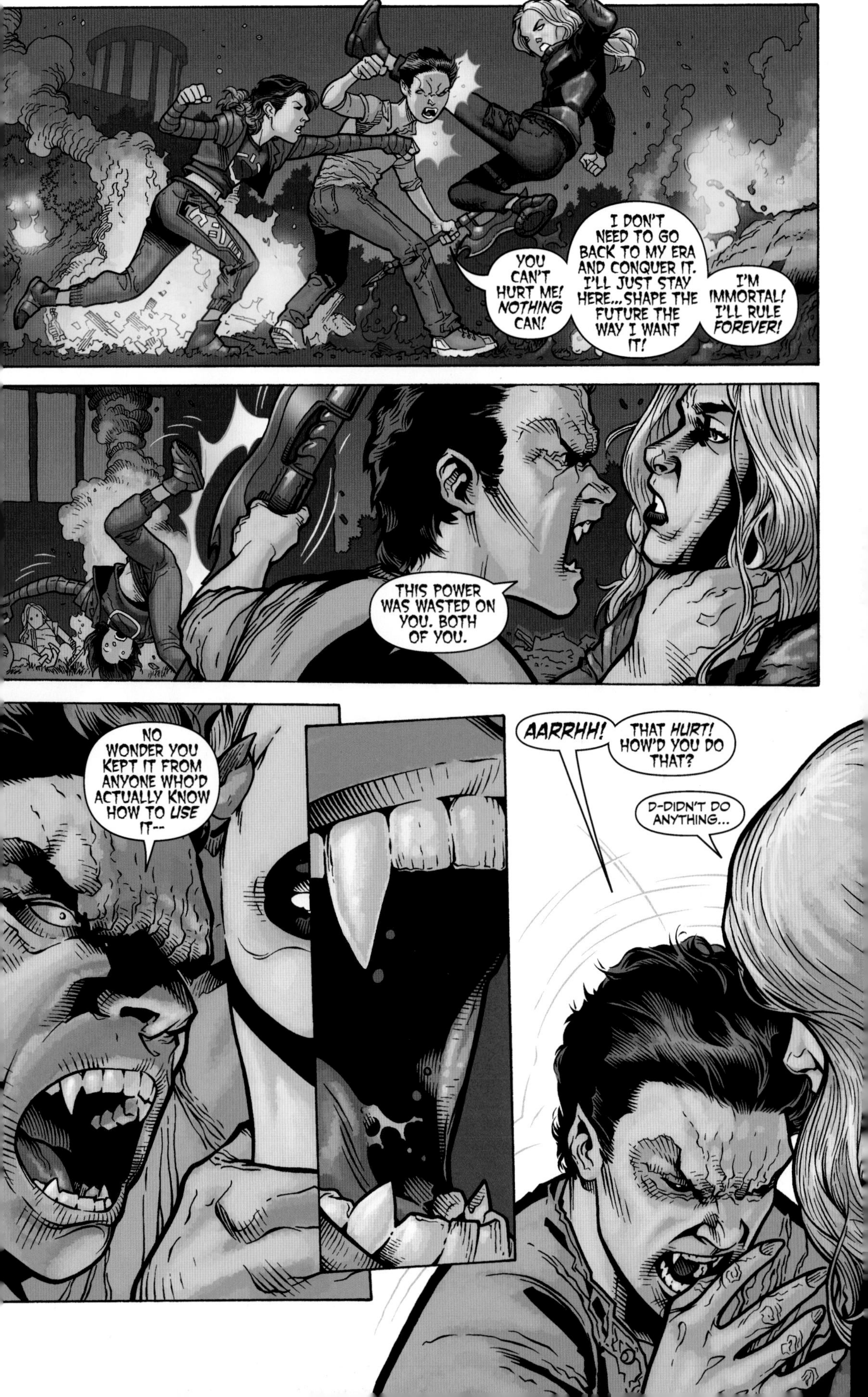
YOU CAN'T HURT ME! NOTHING CAN!
I DON'T NEED TO GO BACK TO MY ERA AND CONQUER IT. I'LL JUST STAY HERE...SHAPE THE FUTURE THE WAY I WANT IT!
I'M IMMORTAL! I'LL RULE FOREVER!
THIS POWER WAS WASTED ON YOU. BOTH OF YOU.
NO WONDER YOU KEPT IT FROM ANYONE WHO'D ACTUALLY KNOW HOW TO USE IT--
AARRHH!
THAT HURT! HOW'D YOU DO THAT?
D-DIDN'T DO ANYTHING...

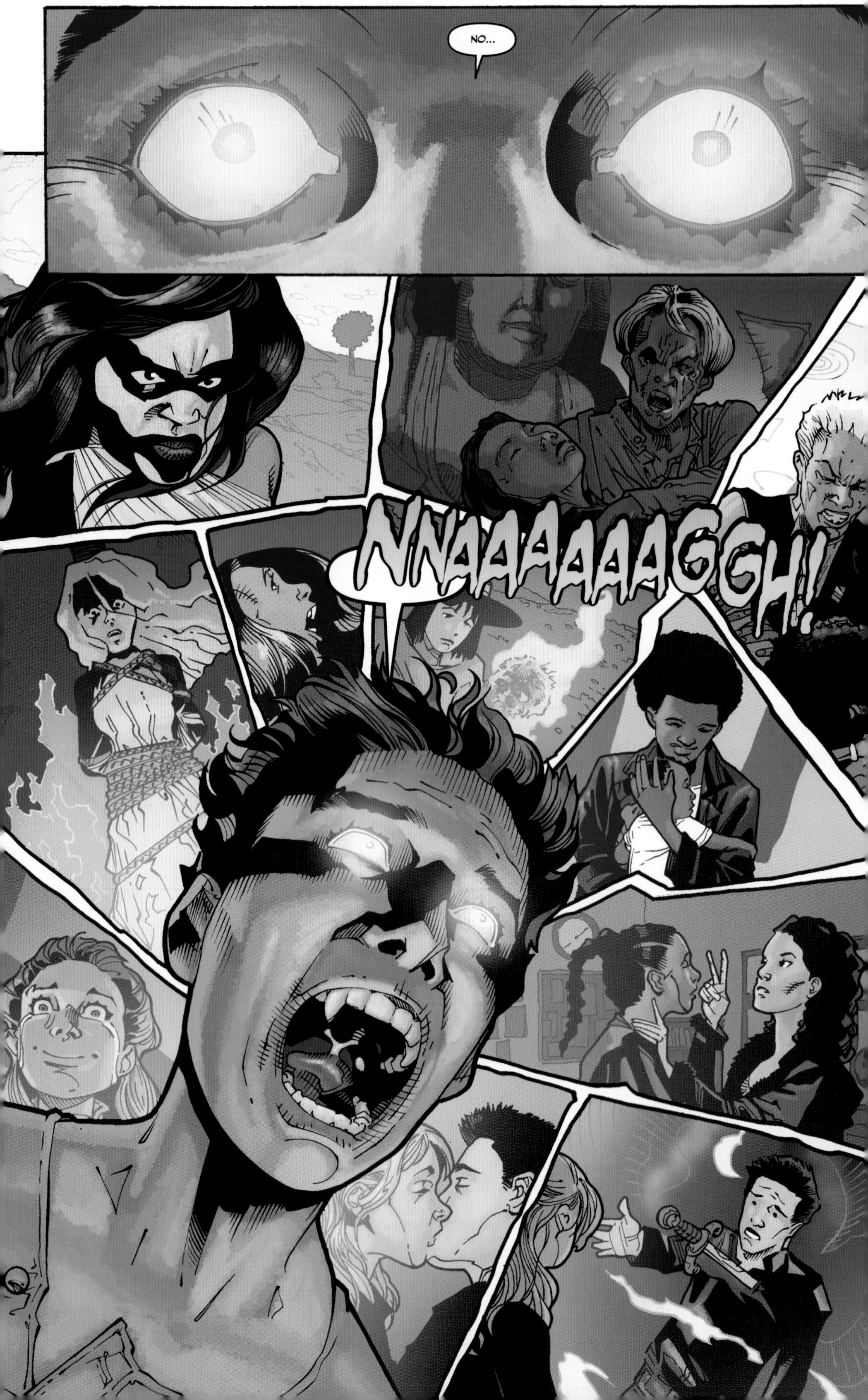
NO...
NNAAAAAAAGGH!

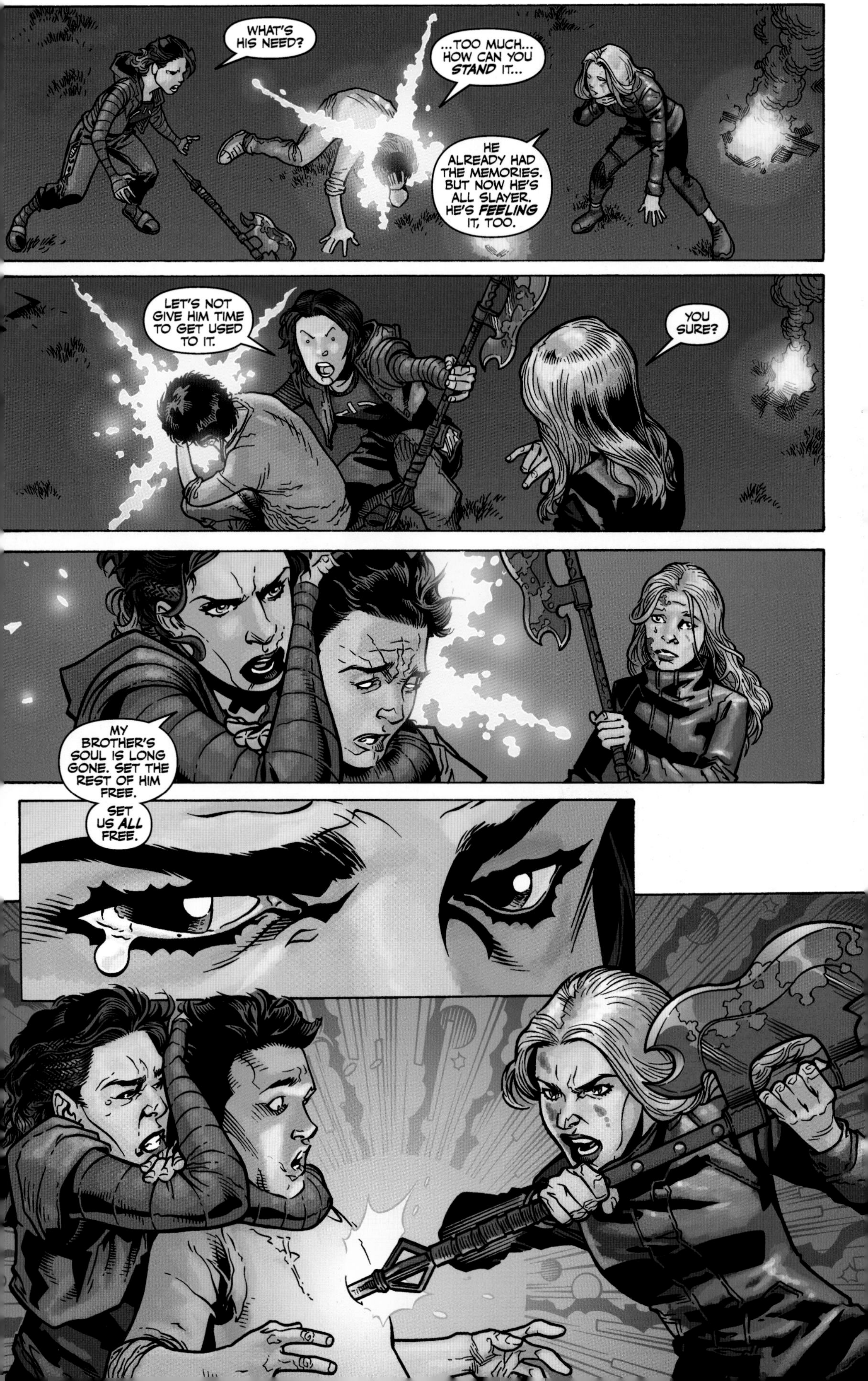
WHAT'S HIS NEED?
...TOO MUCH... HOW CAN YOU *STAND* IT...
HE ALREADY HAD THE MEMORIES. BUT NOW HE'S ALL SLAYER. HE'S *FEELING* IT, TOO.
LET'S NOT GIVE HIM TIME TO GET USED TO IT.
YOU SURE?
MY BROTHER'S SOUL IS LONG GONE. SET THE REST OF HIM FREE.
SET US *ALL* FREE.

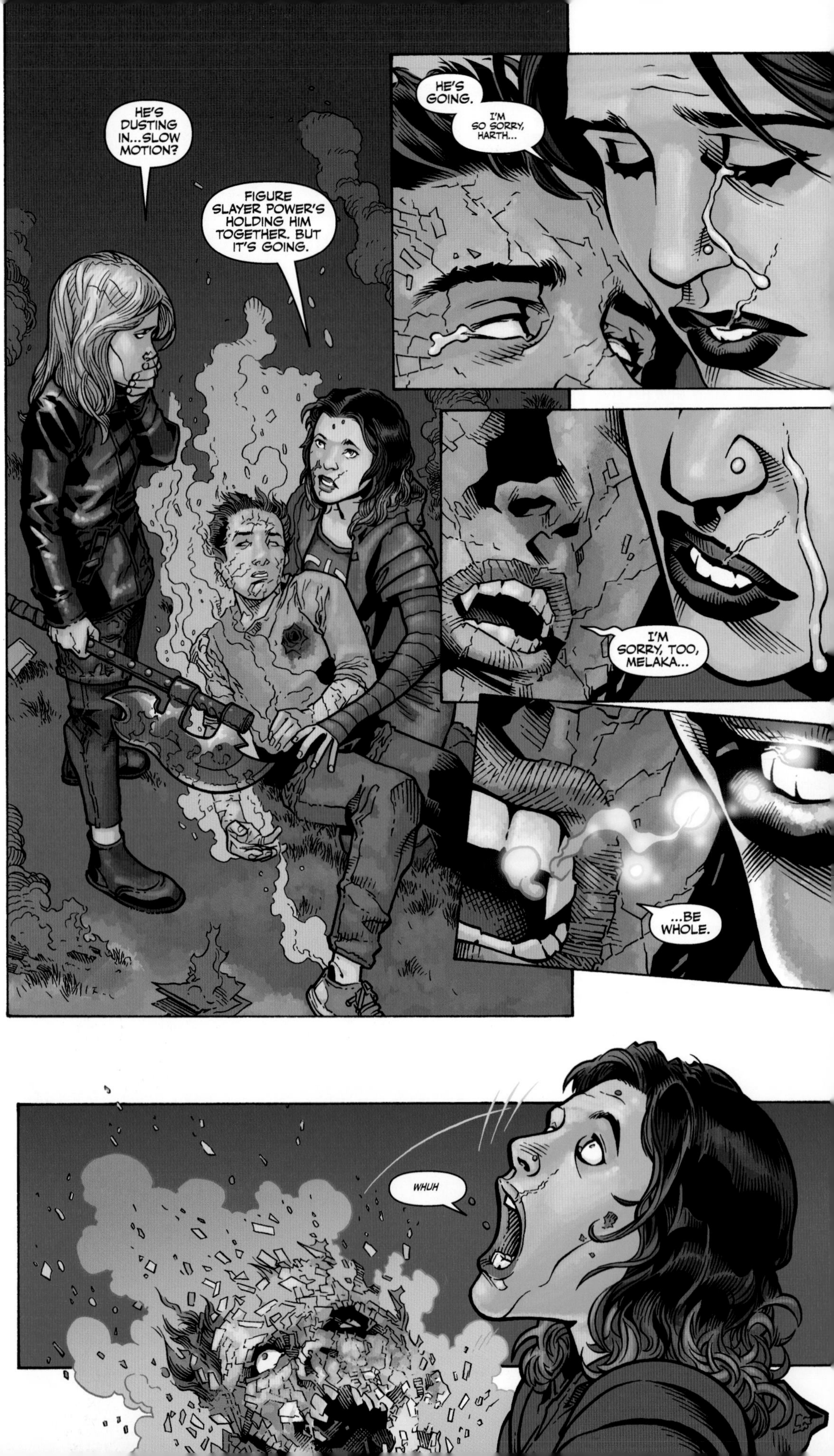
HE'S DUSTING IN...SLOW MOTION?
FIGURE SLAYER POWER'S HOLDING HIM TOGETHER. BUT IT'S GOING.
HE'S GOING.
I'M SO SORRY, HARTH...
I'M SORRY, TOO, MELAKA...
...BE WHOLE.
WHUH

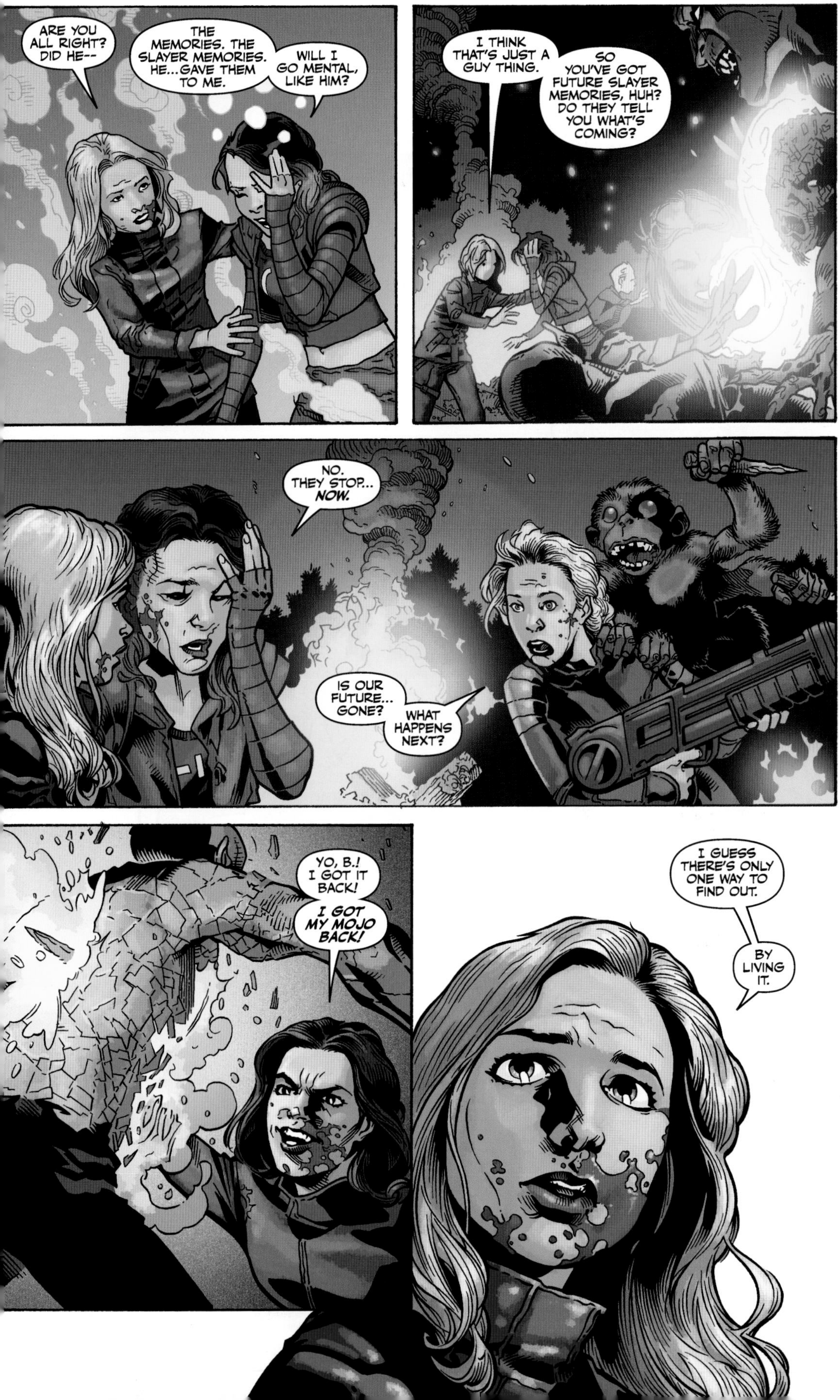
ARE YOU ALL RIGHT? DID HE--
THE MEMORIES. THE SLAYER MEMORIES. HE...GAVE THEM TO ME.
WILL I GO MENTAL, LIKE HIM?
I THINK THAT'S JUST A GUY THING.
SO YOU'VE GOT FUTURE SLAYER MEMORIES, HUH? DO THEY TELL YOU WHAT'S COMING?
NO. THEY STOP... *NOW.*
IS OUR FUTURE... GONE?
WHAT HAPPENS NEXT?
YO, B.! I GOT IT BACK!
I GOT MY MOJO BACK!
I GUESS THERE'S ONLY ONE WAY TO FIND OUT.
BY LIVING IT.

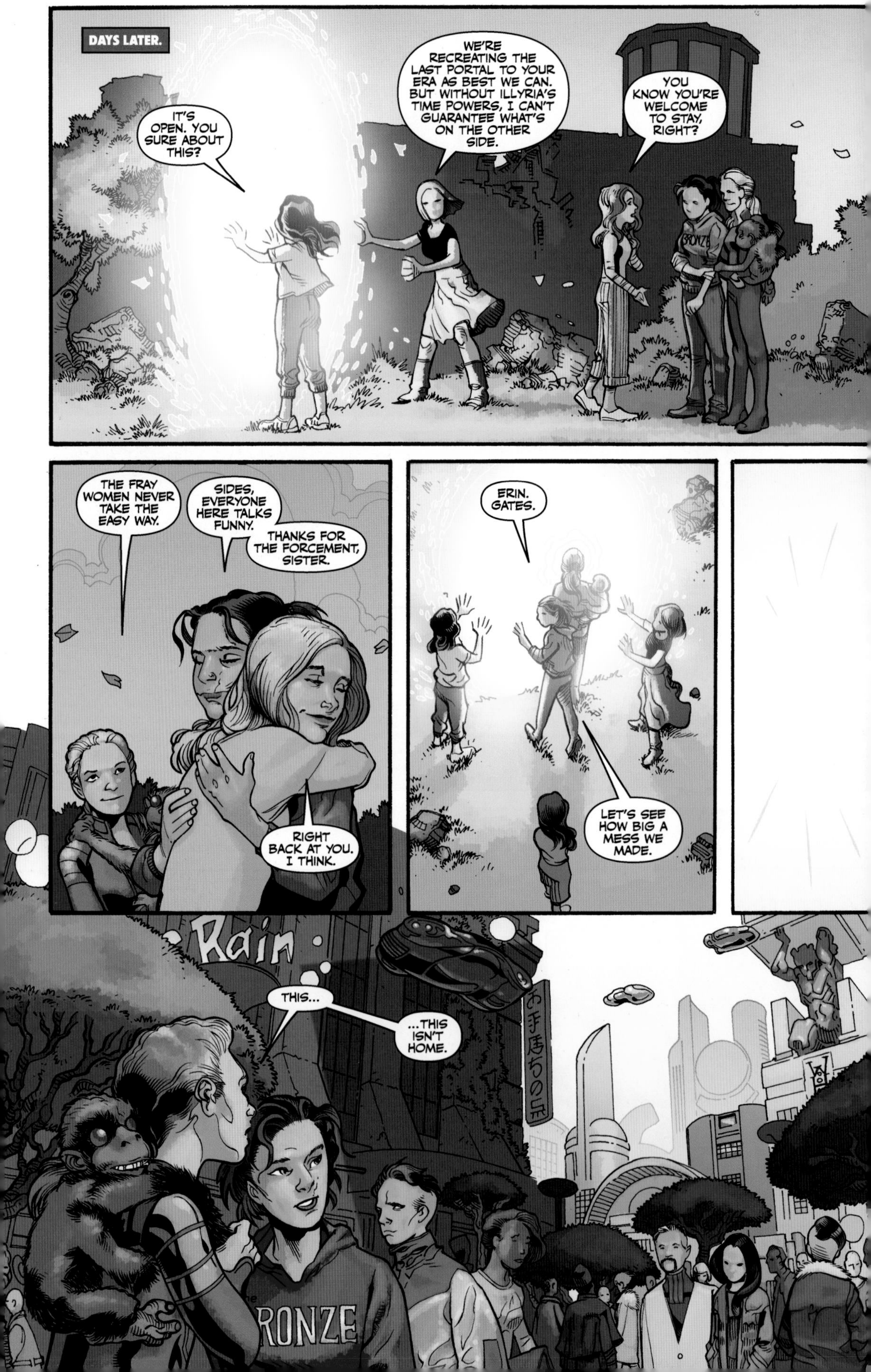
DAYS LATER.
IT'S OPEN. YOU SURE ABOUT THIS?
WE'RE RECREATING THE LAST PORTAL TO YOUR ERA AS BEST WE CAN. BUT WITHOUT ILLYRIA'S TIME POWERS, I CAN'T GUARANTEE WHAT'S ON THE OTHER SIDE.
YOU KNOW YOU'RE WELCOME TO STAY, RIGHT?
BRONZE
THE FRAY WOMEN NEVER TAKE THE EASY WAY.
SIDES, EVERYONE HERE TALKS FUNNY.
THANKS FOR THE FORCEMENT, SISTER.
RIGHT BACK AT YOU. I THINK.
ERIN. GATES.
LET'S SEE HOW BIG A MESS WE MADE.
Rain
THIS...
...THIS ISN'T HOME.
お手盾ちの品
the
RONZE

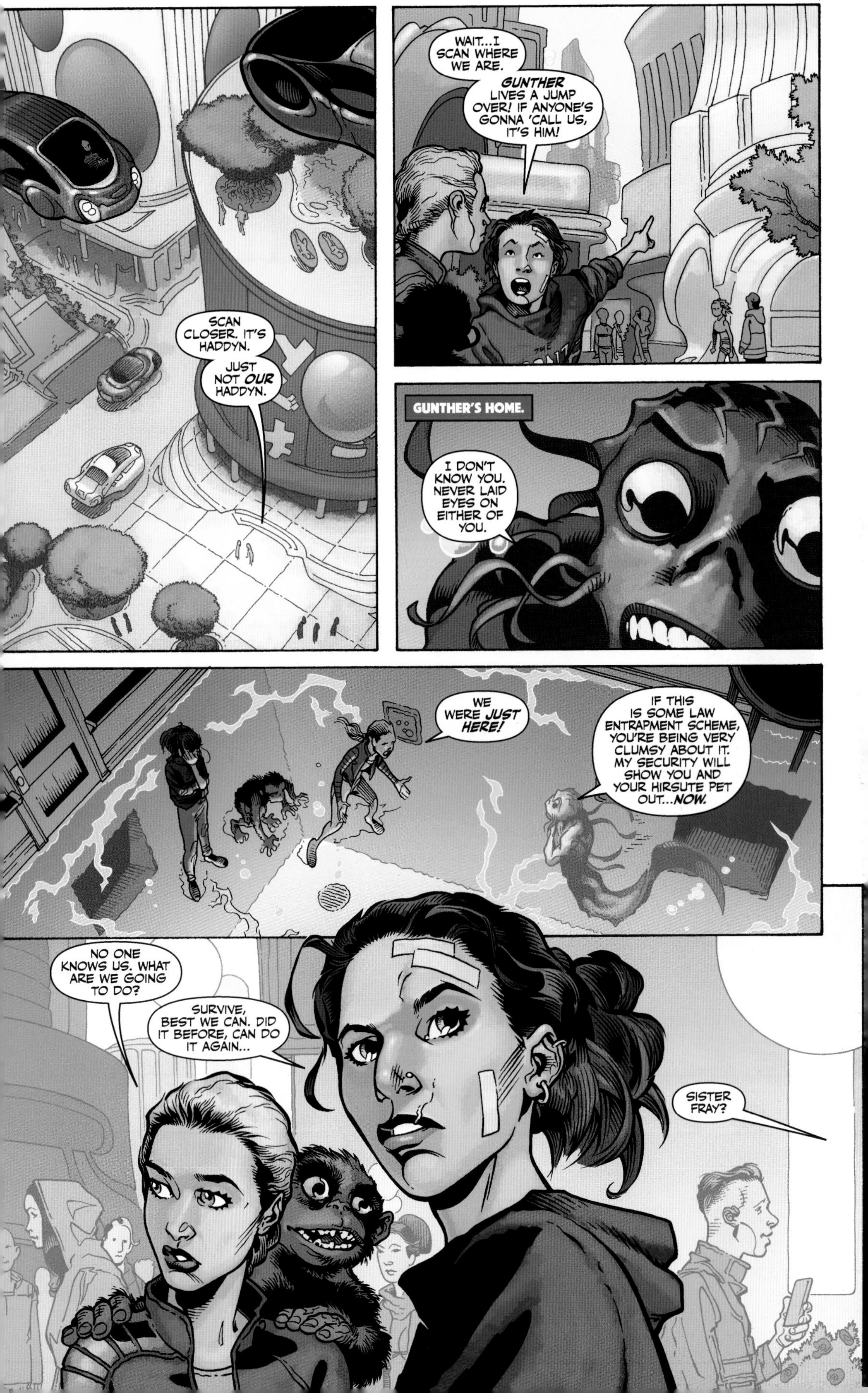
SCAN CLOSER. IT'S HADDYN.
JUST NOT *OUR* HADDYN.
WAIT...I SCAN WHERE WE ARE.
GUNTHER LIVES A JUMP OVER! IF ANYONE'S GONNA 'CALL US, IT'S HIM!
GUNTHER'S HOME.
I DON'T KNOW YOU. NEVER LAID EYES ON EITHER OF YOU.
WE WERE *JUST HERE!*
IF THIS IS SOME LAW ENTRAPMENT SCHEME, YOU'RE BEING VERY CLUMSY ABOUT IT. MY SECURITY WILL SHOW YOU AND YOUR HIRSUTE PET OUT...*NOW.*
NO ONE KNOWS US. WHAT ARE WE GOING TO DO?
SURVIVE, BEST WE CAN. DID IT BEFORE, CAN DO IT AGAIN...
SISTER FRAY?

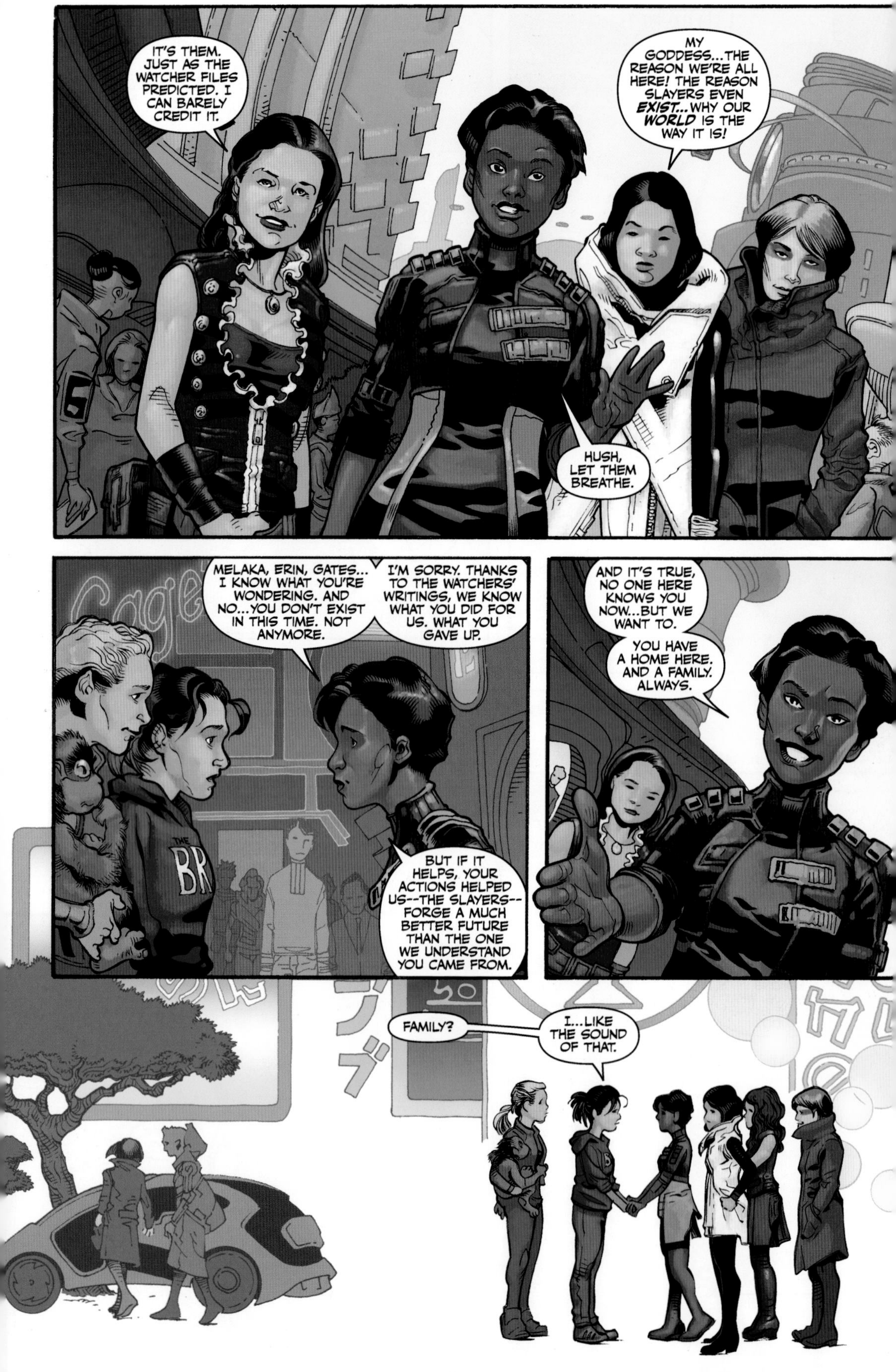
IT'S THEM. JUST AS THE WATCHER FILES PREDICTED. I CAN BARELY CREDIT IT.
MY GODDESS...THE REASON WE'RE ALL HERE! THE REASON SLAYERS EVEN *EXIST...* WHY OUR *WORLD* IS THE WAY IT IS!
HUSH, LET THEM BREATHE.
MELAKA, ERIN, GATES... I KNOW WHAT YOU'RE WONDERING. AND NO...YOU DON'T EXIST IN THIS TIME. NOT ANYMORE.
I'M SORRY. THANKS TO THE WATCHERS' WRITINGS, WE KNOW WHAT YOU DID FOR US. WHAT YOU GAVE UP.
BUT IF IT HELPS, YOUR ACTIONS HELPED US--THE SLAYERS--FORGE A MUCH BETTER FUTURE THAN THE ONE WE UNDERSTAND YOU CAME FROM.
AND IT'S TRUE, NO ONE HERE KNOWS YOU NOW...BUT WE WANT TO.
YOU HAVE A HOME HERE. AND A FAMILY. ALWAYS.
FAMILY?
I...LIKE THE SOUND OF THAT.

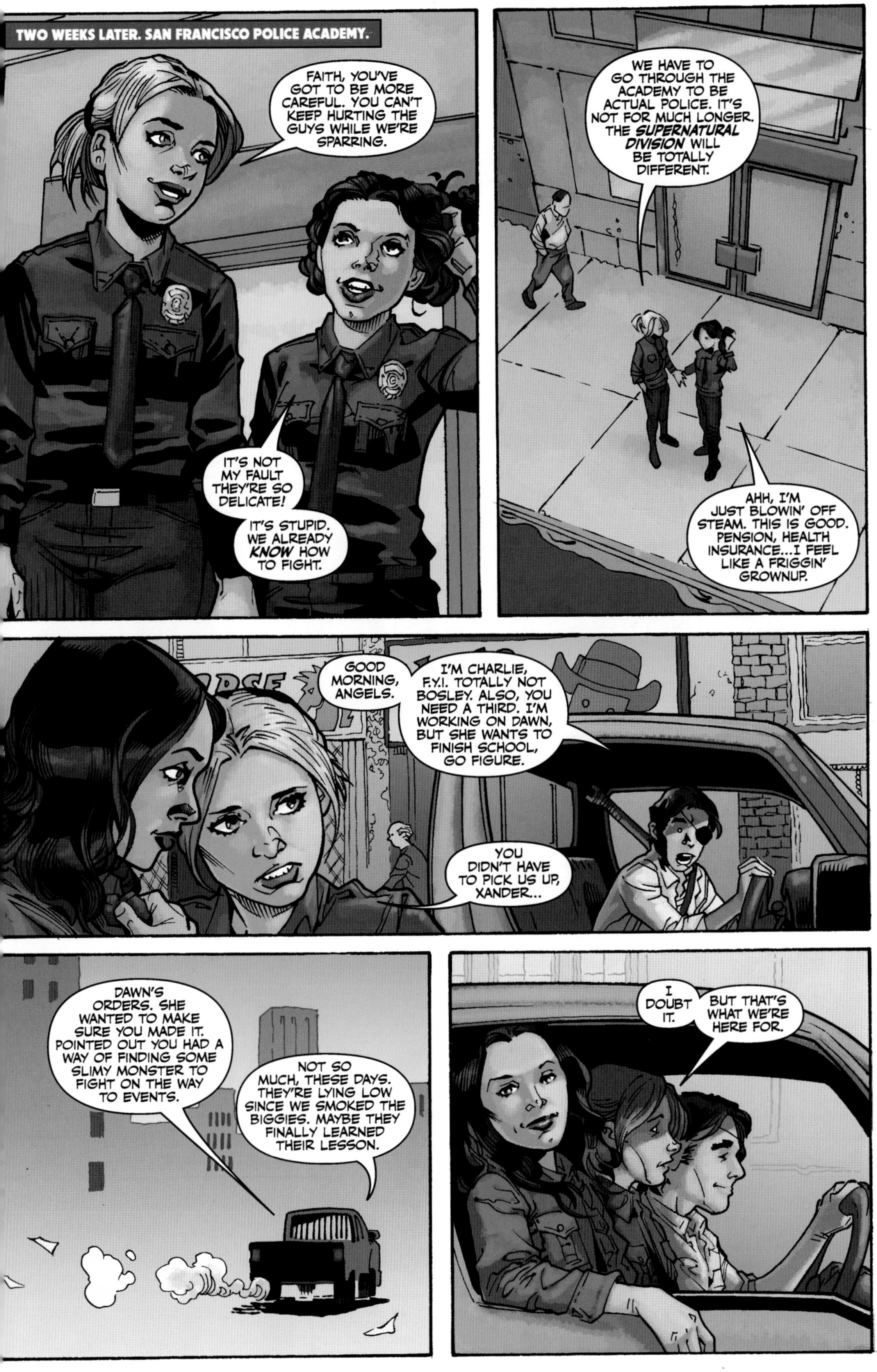
TWO WEEKS LATER. SAN FRANCISCO POLICE ACADEMY.
FAITH, YOU'VE GOT TO BE MORE CAREFUL. YOU CAN'T KEEP HURTING THE GUYS WHILE WE'RE SPARRING.
IT'S NOT MY FAULT THEY'RE SO DELICATE!
IT'S STUPID. WE ALREADY KNOW HOW TO FIGHT.
WE HAVE TO GO THROUGH THE ACADEMY TO BE ACTUAL POLICE. IT'S NOT FOR MUCH LONGER. THE SUPERNATURAL DIVISION WILL BE TOTALLY DIFFERENT.
AHH, I'M JUST BLOWIN' OFF STEAM. THIS IS GOOD. PENSION, HEALTH INSURANCE...I FEEL LIKE A FRIGGIN' GROWNUP.
GOOD MORNING, ANGELS.
I'M CHARLIE, F.Y.I. TOTALLY NOT BOSLEY. ALSO, YOU NEED A THIRD. I'M WORKING ON DAWN, BUT SHE WANTS TO FINISH SCHOOL, GO FIGURE.
YOU DIDN'T HAVE TO PICK US UP, XANDER...
DAWN'S ORDERS. SHE WANTED TO MAKE SURE YOU MADE IT. POINTED OUT YOU HAD A WAY OF FINDING SOME SLIMY MONSTER TO FIGHT ON THE WAY TO EVENTS.
NOT SO MUCH, THESE DAYS. THEY'RE LYING LOW SINCE WE SMOKED THE BIGGIES. MAYBE THEY FINALLY LEARNED THEIR LESSON.
I DOUBT IT.
BUT THAT'S WHAT WE'RE HERE FOR.

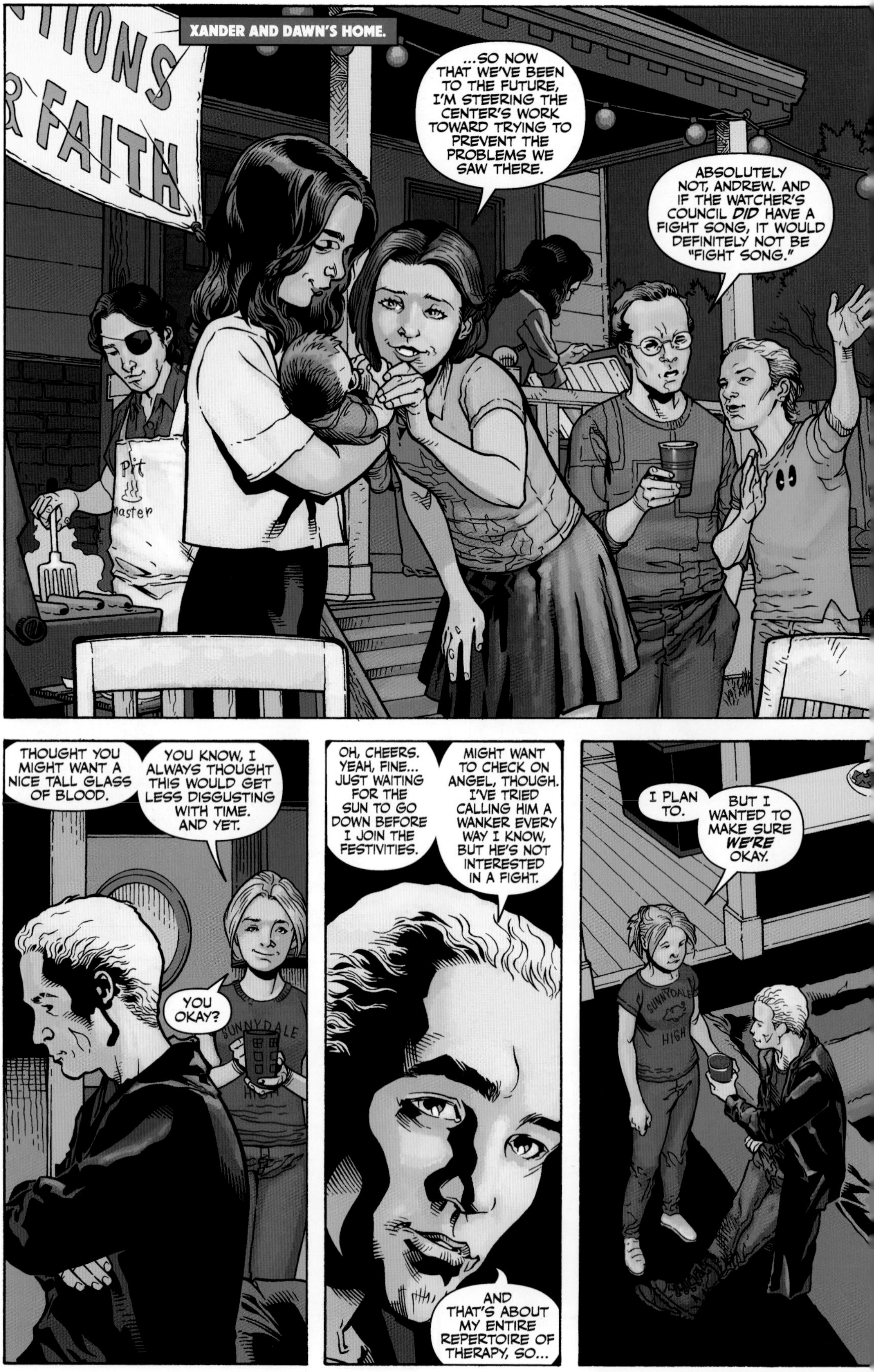

XANDER AND DAWN'S HOME.
TIONS
R FAITH
...SO NOW THAT WE'VE BEEN TO THE FUTURE, I'M STEERING THE CENTER'S WORK TOWARD TRYING TO PREVENT THE PROBLEMS WE SAW THERE.
ABSOLUTELY NOT, ANDREW. AND IF THE WATCHER'S COUNCIL DID HAVE A FIGHT SONG, IT WOULD DEFINITELY NOT BE "FIGHT SONG."
Pit master
THOUGHT YOU MIGHT WANT A NICE TALL GLASS OF BLOOD.
YOU KNOW, I ALWAYS THOUGHT THIS WOULD GET LESS DISGUSTING WITH TIME. AND YET.
YOU OKAY?
SUNNYDALE HIGH
OH, CHEERS. YEAH, FINE... JUST WAITING FOR THE SUN TO GO DOWN BEFORE I JOIN THE FESTIVITIES.
MIGHT WANT TO CHECK ON ANGEL, THOUGH. I'VE TRIED CALLING HIM A WANKER EVERY WAY I KNOW, BUT HE'S NOT INTERESTED IN A FIGHT.
AND THAT'S ABOUT MY ENTIRE REPERTOIRE OF THERAPY, SO...
I PLAN TO.
BUT I WANTED TO MAKE SURE WE'RE OKAY.
SUNNYDALE HIGH

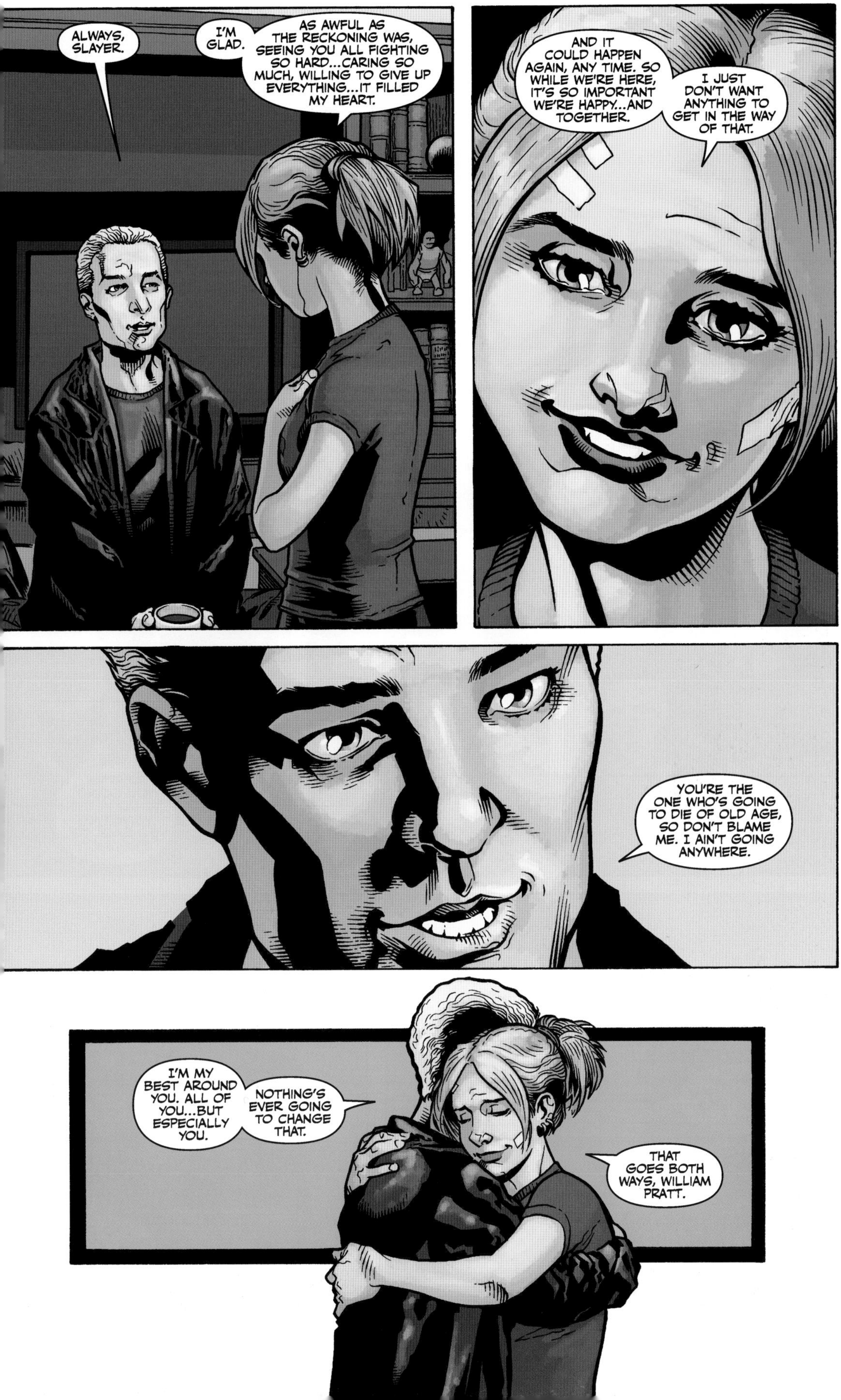
ALWAYS, SLAYER.
I'M GLAD.
AS AWFUL AS THE RECKONING WAS, SEEING YOU ALL FIGHTING SO HARD...CARING SO MUCH, WILLING TO GIVE UP EVERYTHING...IT FILLED MY HEART.
AND IT COULD HAPPEN AGAIN, ANY TIME. SO WHILE WE'RE HERE, IT'S SO IMPORTANT WE'RE HAPPY...AND TOGETHER.
I JUST DON'T WANT ANYTHING TO GET IN THE WAY OF THAT.
YOU'RE THE ONE WHO'S GOING TO DIE OF OLD AGE, SO DON'T BLAME ME. I AIN'T GOING ANYWHERE.
I'M MY BEST AROUND YOU. ALL OF YOU...BUT ESPECIALLY YOU.
NOTHING'S EVER GOING TO CHANGE THAT.
THAT GOES BOTH WAYS, WILLIAM PRATT.

HEY.

HEY.

YOU KNOW WE'RE ALL READY TO GO AFTER ILLYRIA ANY TIME.

SHE ASKED ME NOT TO BEFORE SHE WENT. SHE KNEW IT'S TOO DANGEROUS TO REOPEN THE PORTAL WHEN SO MANY DEMONS MIGHT COME THROUGH.

SHE WANTS US TO GIVE HER TIME TO KILL AS MANY AS SHE CAN. I'M JUST WORRIED...

THAT THEY'LL KILL HER FIRST?

THAT BY THE TIME WE GET THERE, SHE'LL WANT TO STAY.

BUT IT'S WHAT SHE WANTS. AND SHE'S RIGHT.

WE'RE BOTH IMMORTALS. I CAN WAIT.

WHAT'RE YOU GOING TO DO IN THE MEANTIME? GO BACK TO ENGLAND?

I THINK... I'D LIKE TO STAY AROUND HERE A WHILE.

I MEAN, IF YOU DON'T MIND.

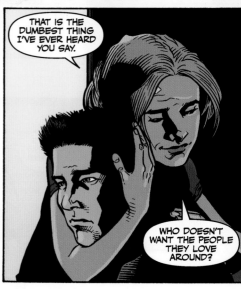

THAT IS THE DUMBEST THING I'VE EVER HEARD YOU SAY.

WHO DOESN'T WANT THE PEOPLE THEY LOVE AROUND?

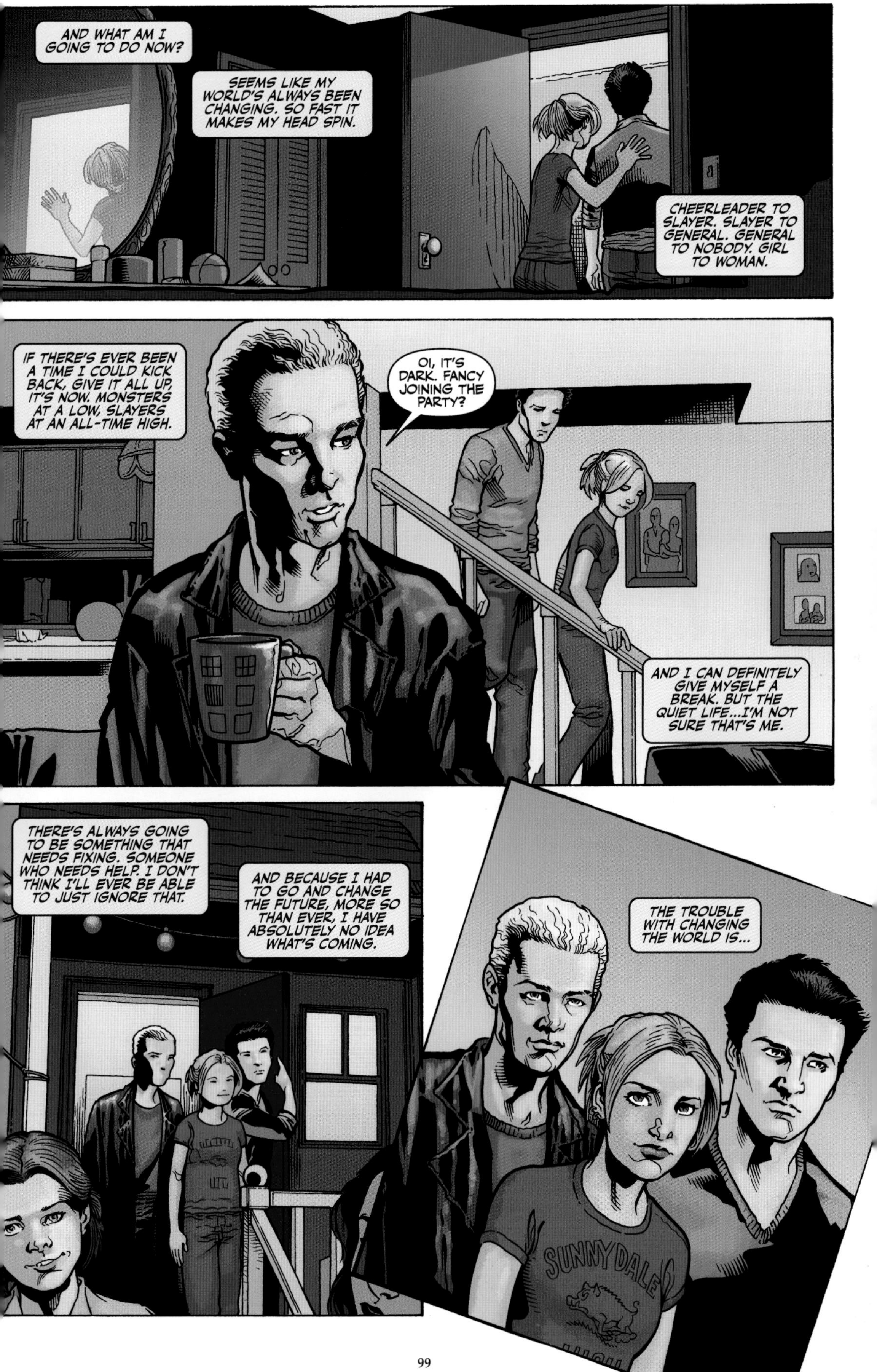
AND WHAT AM I GOING TO DO NOW?
SEEMS LIKE MY WORLD'S ALWAYS BEEN CHANGING. SO FAST IT MAKES MY HEAD SPIN.
CHEERLEADER TO SLAYER. SLAYER TO GENERAL. GENERAL TO NOBODY. GIRL TO WOMAN.
IF THERE'S EVER BEEN A TIME I COULD KICK BACK, GIVE IT ALL UP, IT'S NOW. MONSTERS AT A LOW, SLAYERS AT AN ALL-TIME HIGH.
OI, IT'S DARK. FANCY JOINING THE PARTY?
AND I CAN DEFINITELY GIVE MYSELF A BREAK. BUT THE QUIET LIFE...I'M NOT SURE THAT'S ME.
THERE'S ALWAYS GOING TO BE SOMETHING THAT NEEDS FIXING. SOMEONE WHO NEEDS HELP. I DON'T THINK I'LL EVER BE ABLE TO JUST IGNORE THAT.
AND BECAUSE I HAD TO GO AND CHANGE THE FUTURE, MORE SO THAN EVER, I HAVE ABSOLUTELY NO IDEA WHAT'S COMING.
THE TROUBLE WITH CHANGING THE WORLD IS...
SUNNYDALE

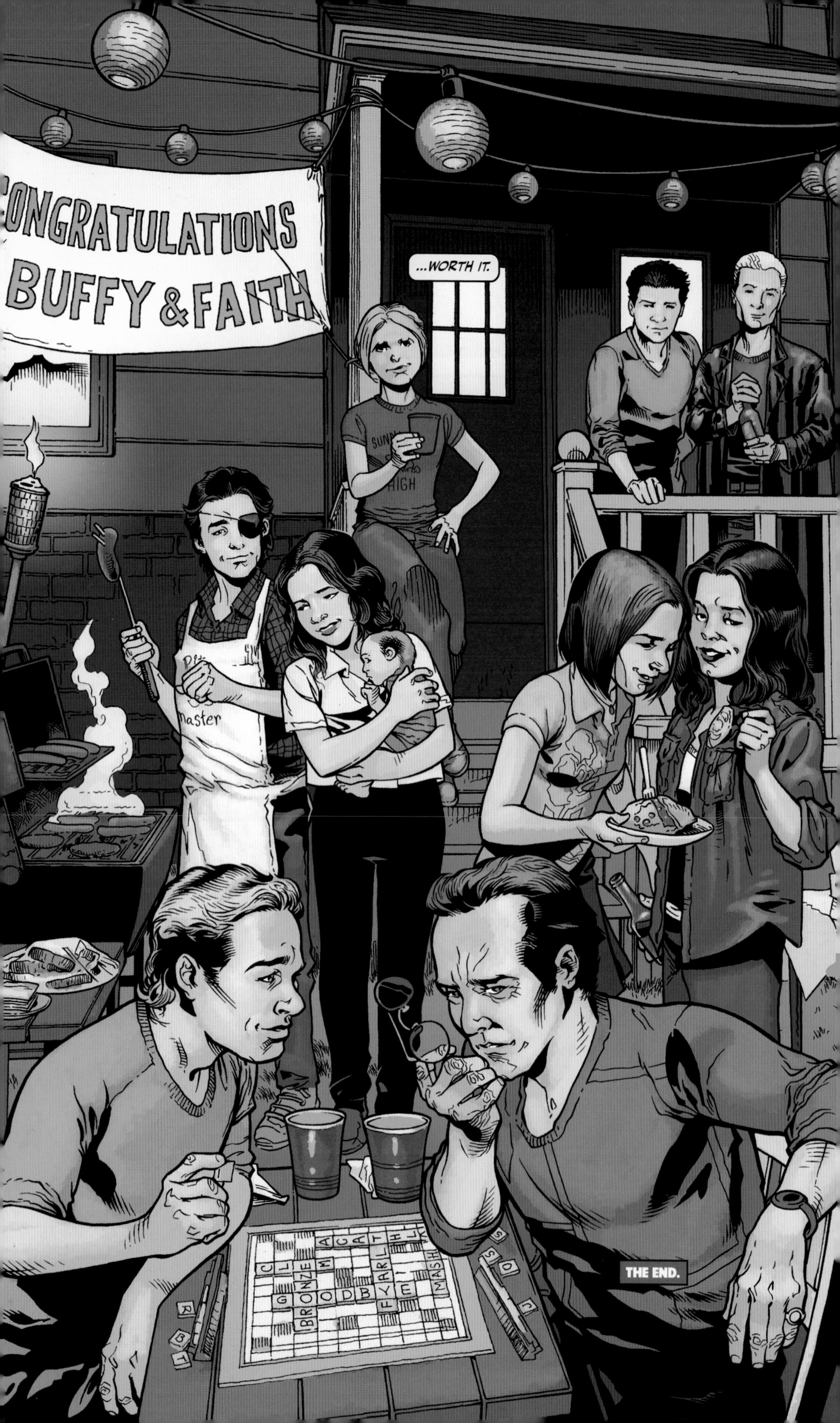
CONGRATULATIONS BUFFY & FAITH
...WORTH IT.
THE END.

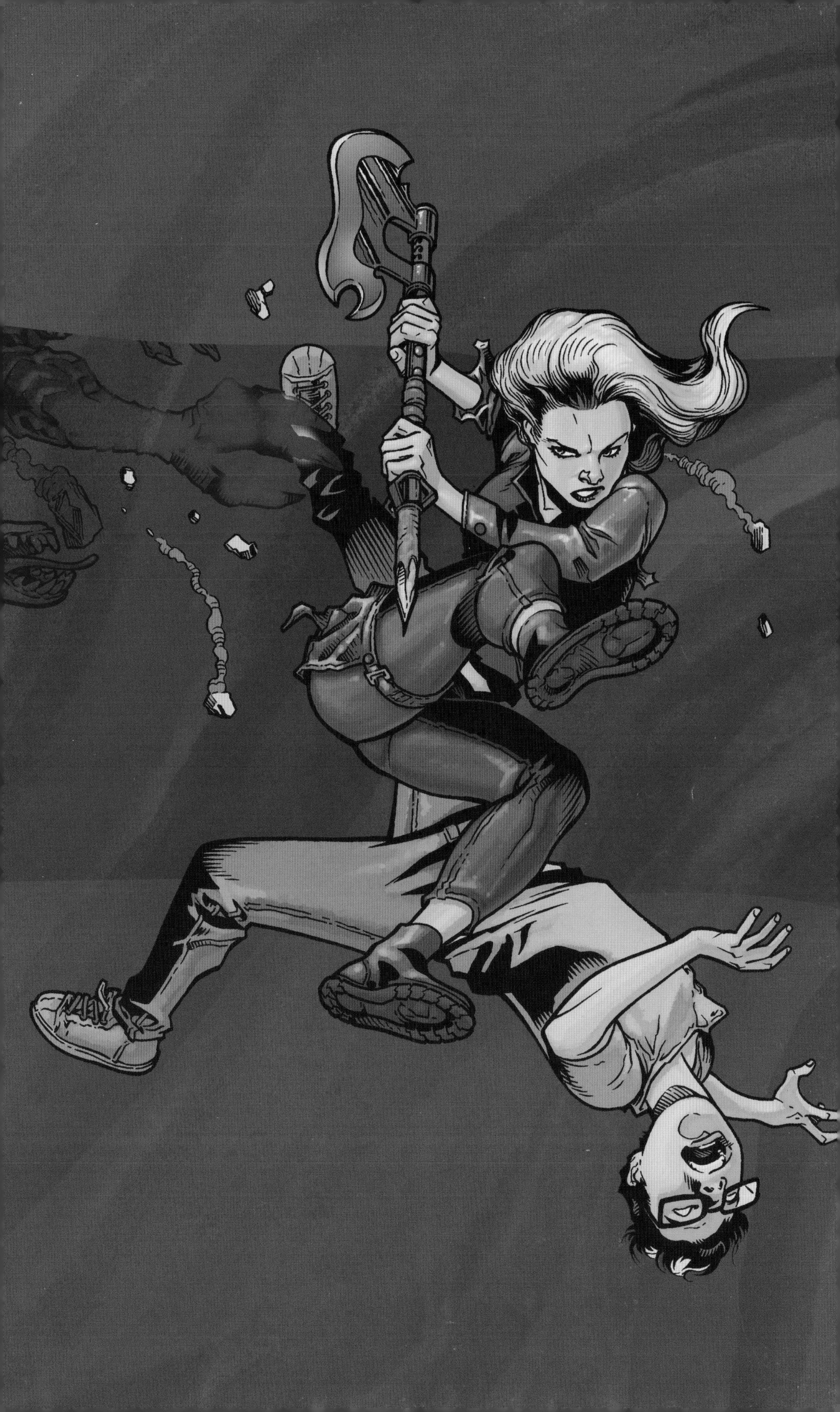

Buffy the Vampire Slayer™

COVER GALLERY & SKETCHBOOK

Season 12

Here is the sketch Georges created of Buffy in battle gear, preparing her to face Harth and his demon army.

For this culminating season of *Buffy*, artist Georges Jeanty moved us into the art for the series with sketches of Buffy and some of her crew, setting up their general appearance—and also, outfits and hairstyles! Here in this gallery, you'll see these sketches as well as all the variant covers that were created for Season 12.

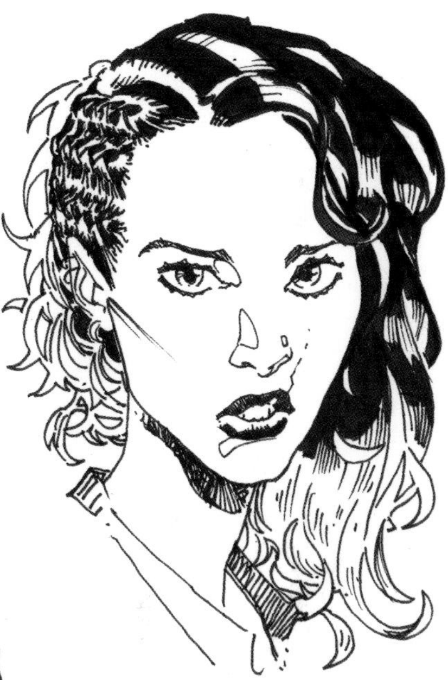

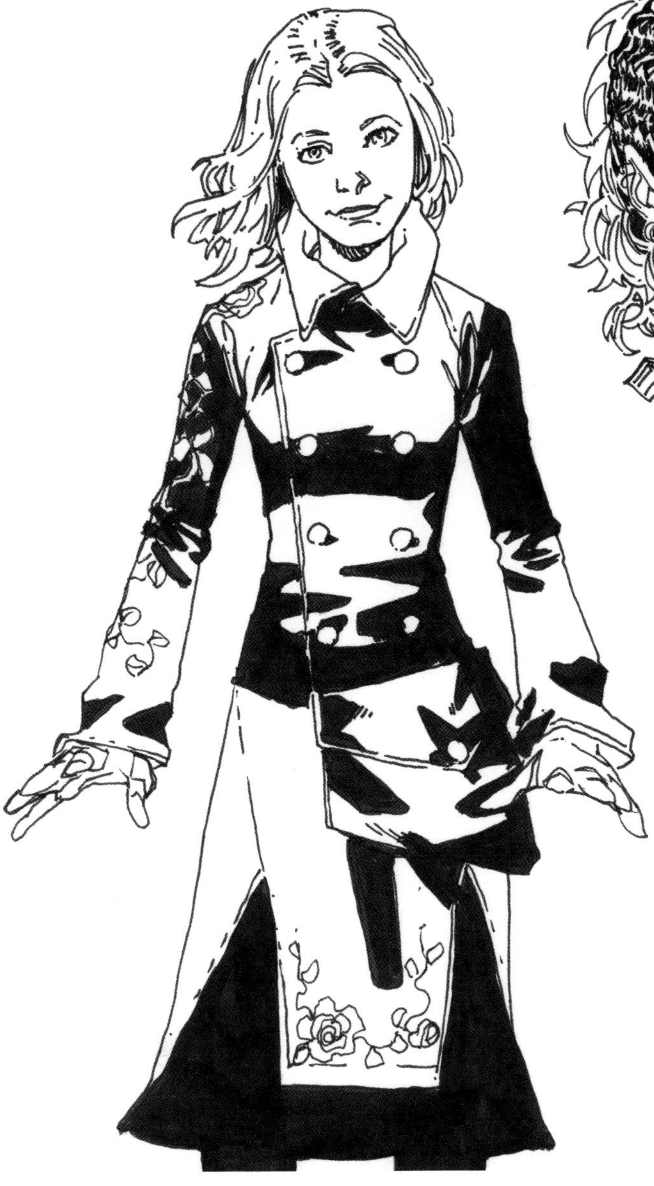

Above:
And, though not the first time Georges would draw future Slayer, Melaka Fray, he created a new hairstyle for her for the series. This headshot shows the final look.

Left:
Here is Willow in her gear, ready for battle.

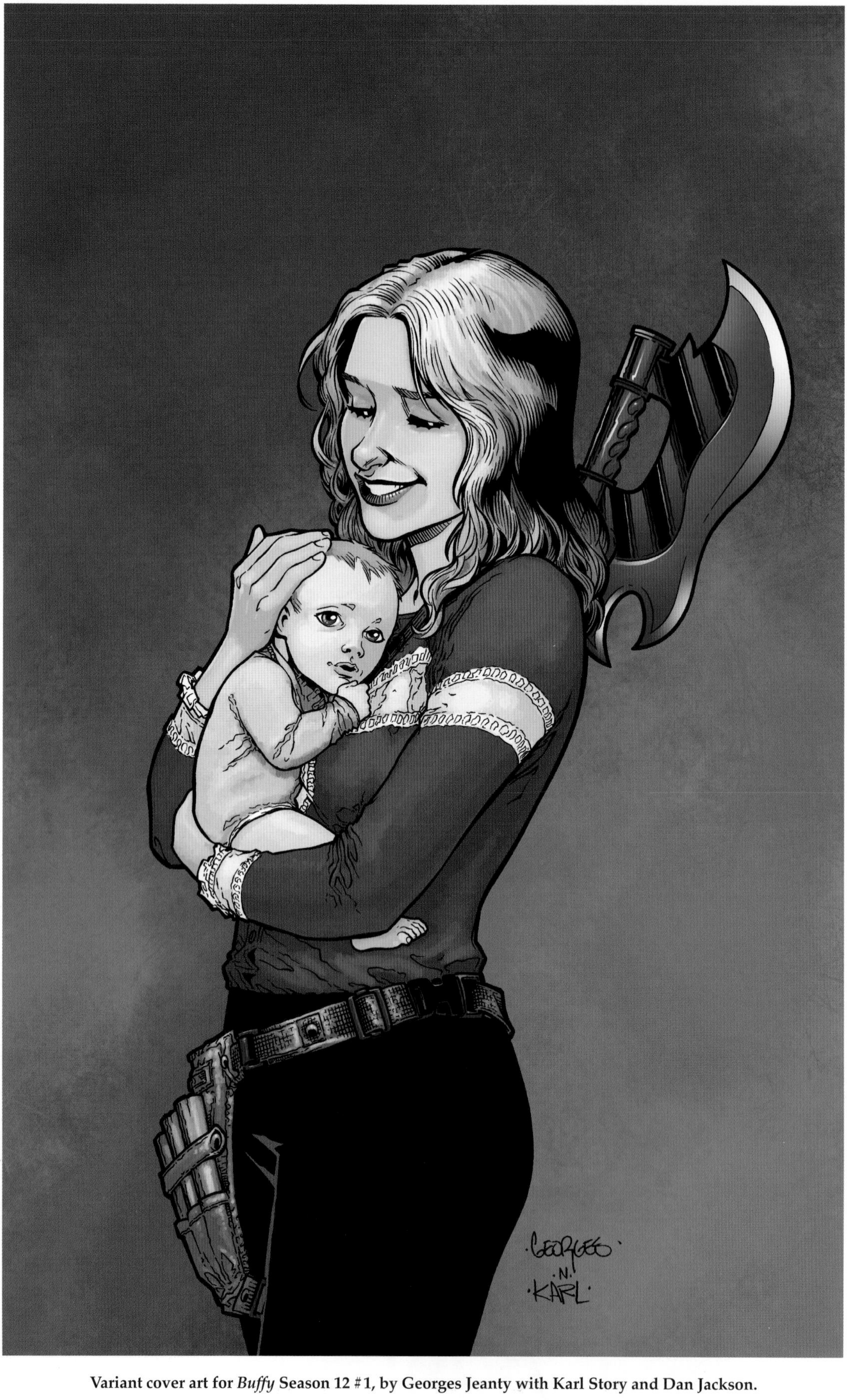
·GEORGES·
·N·
·KARL·

Variant cover art for *Buffy* Season 12 #1, by Georges Jeanty with Karl Story and Dan Jackson.

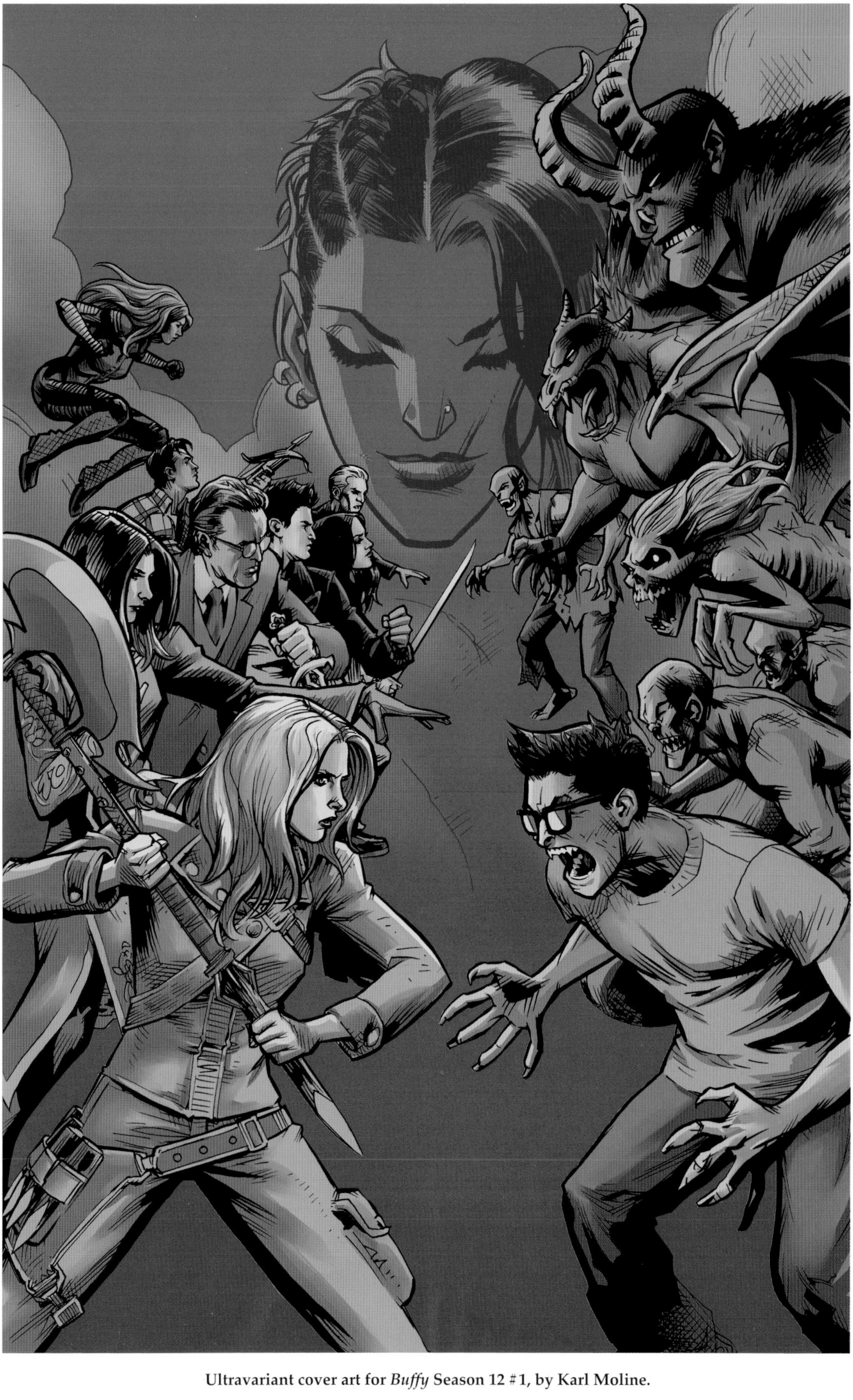

Ultravariant cover art for *Buffy* Season 12 #1, by Karl Moline.

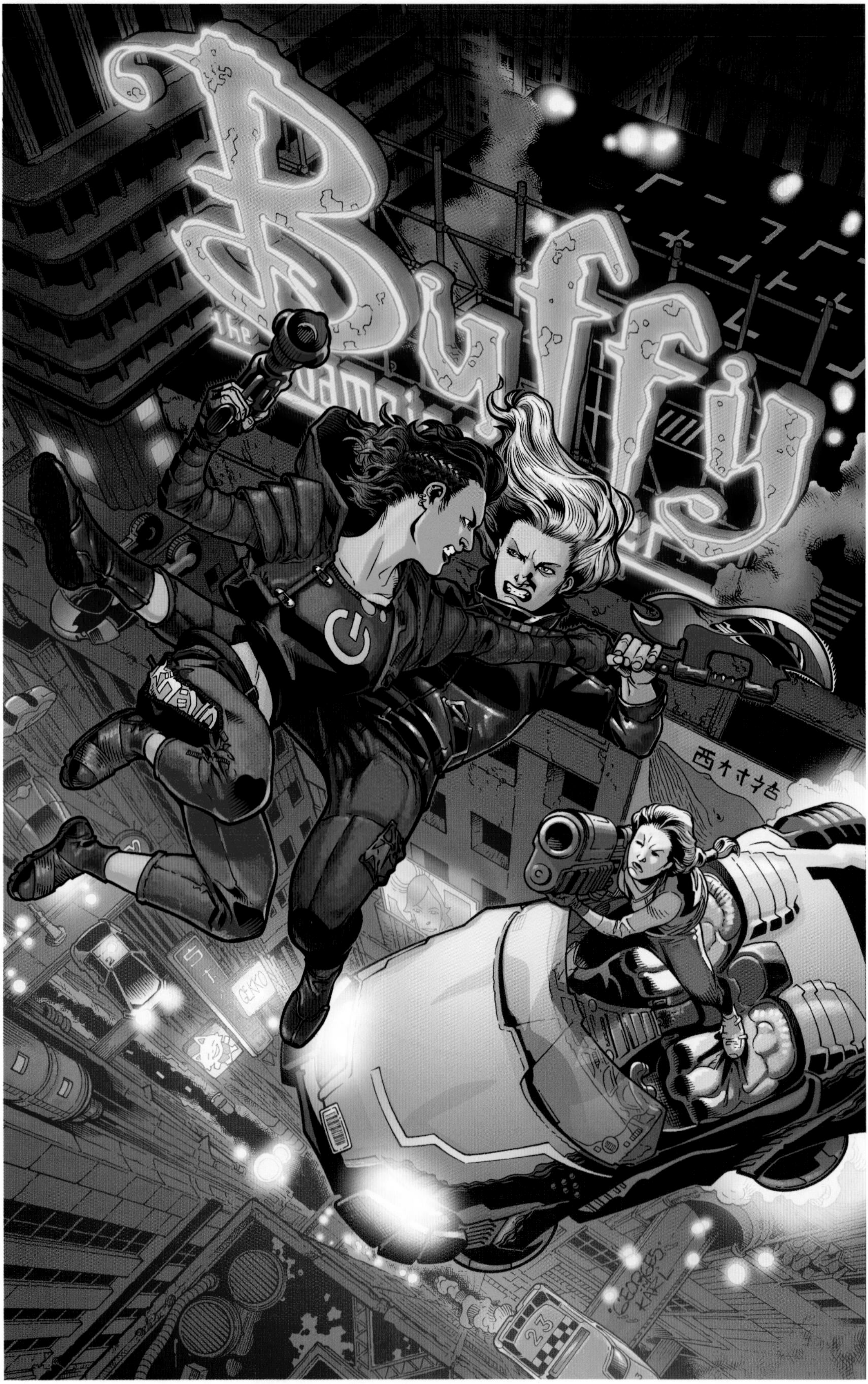
Buffy
The
GEKKO

Variant cover art for *Buffy* Season 12 #2, by Georges Jeanty with Karl Story and Dan Jackson.

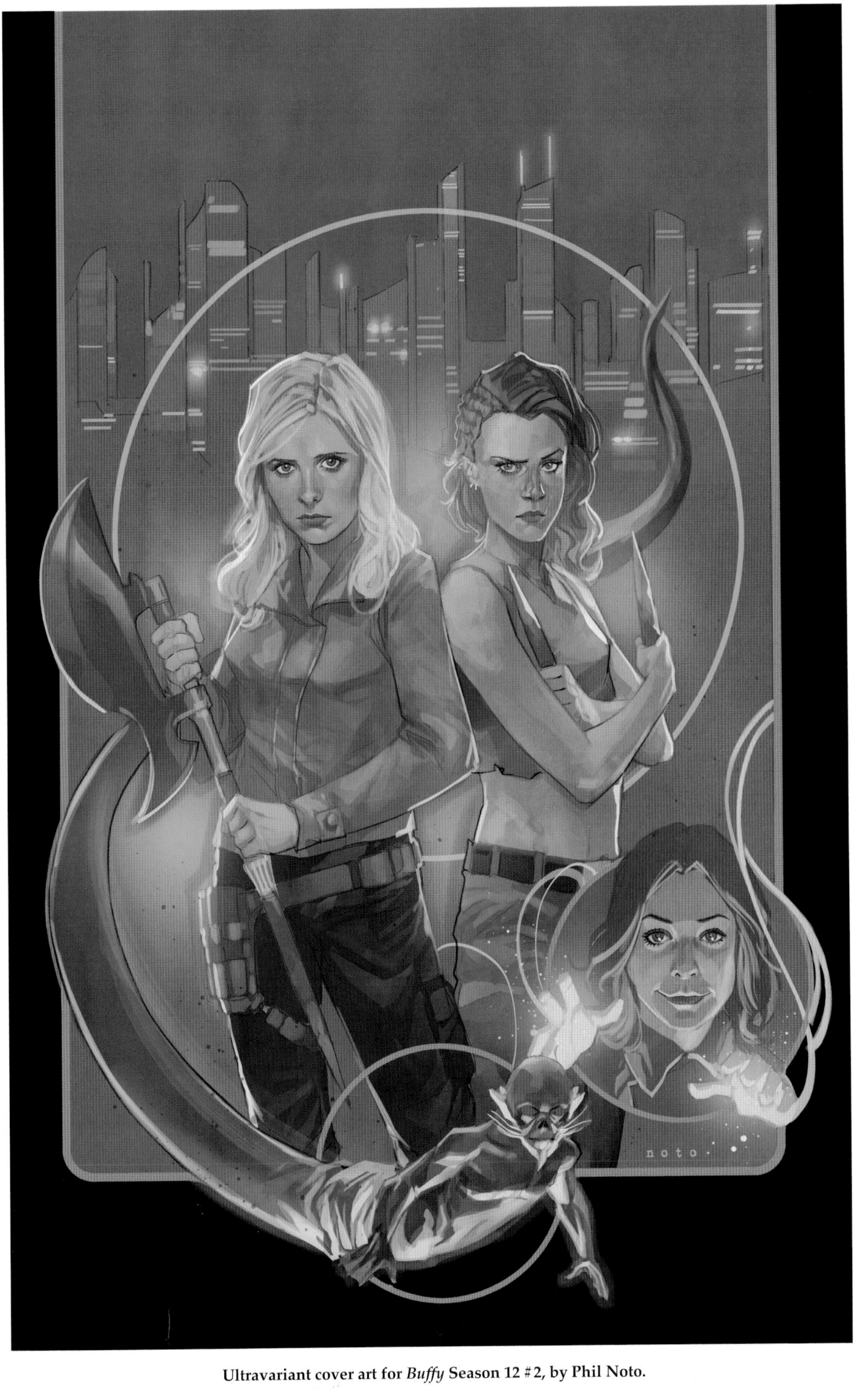
noto

Ultravariant cover art for *Buffy* Season 12 #2, by Phil Noto.

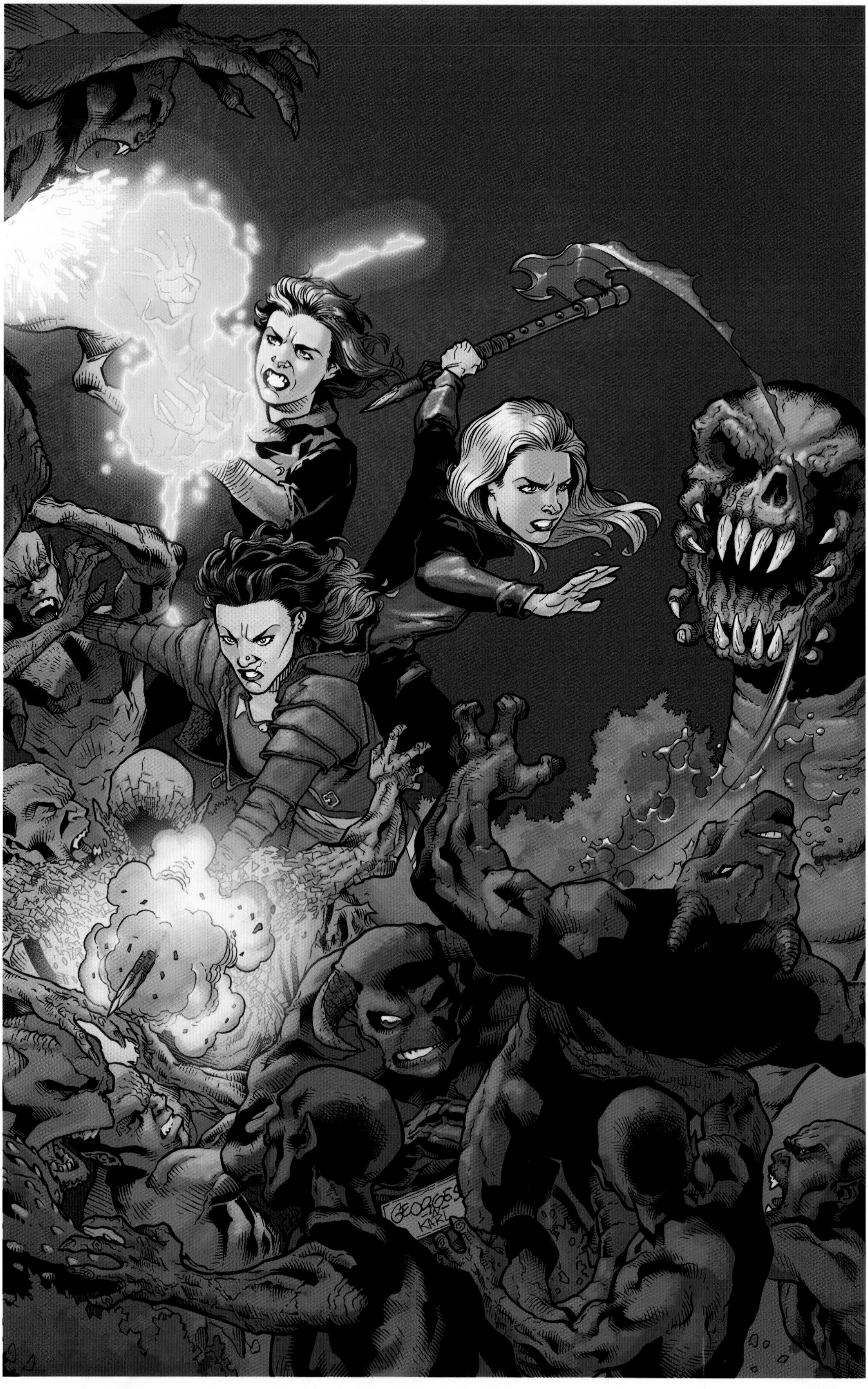
GEORGES
KARL

Variant cover art for *Buffy* Season 12 #3, by Georges Jeanty with Karl Story and Dan Jackson.

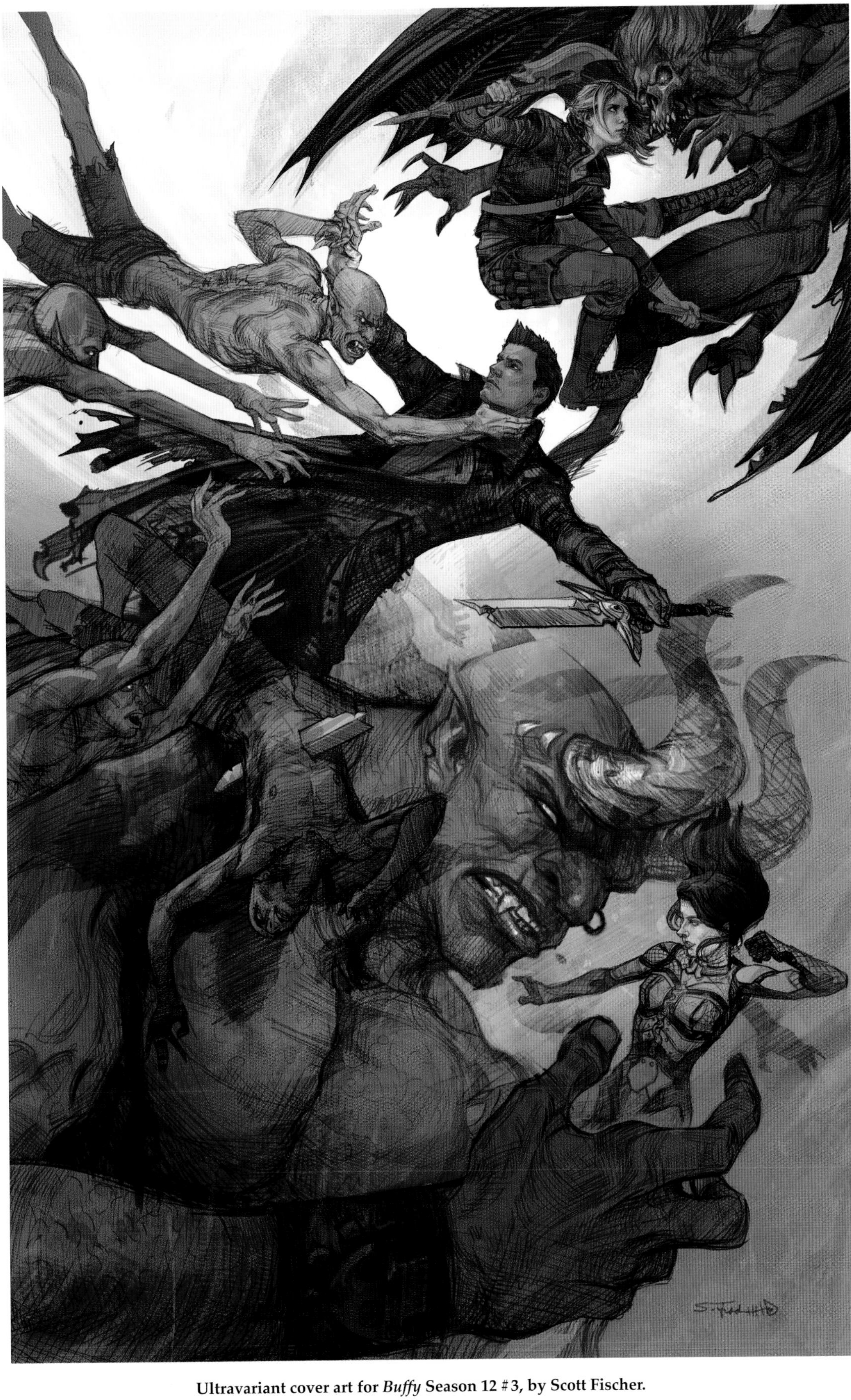

Ultravariant cover art for *Buffy* Season 12 #3, by Scott Fischer.

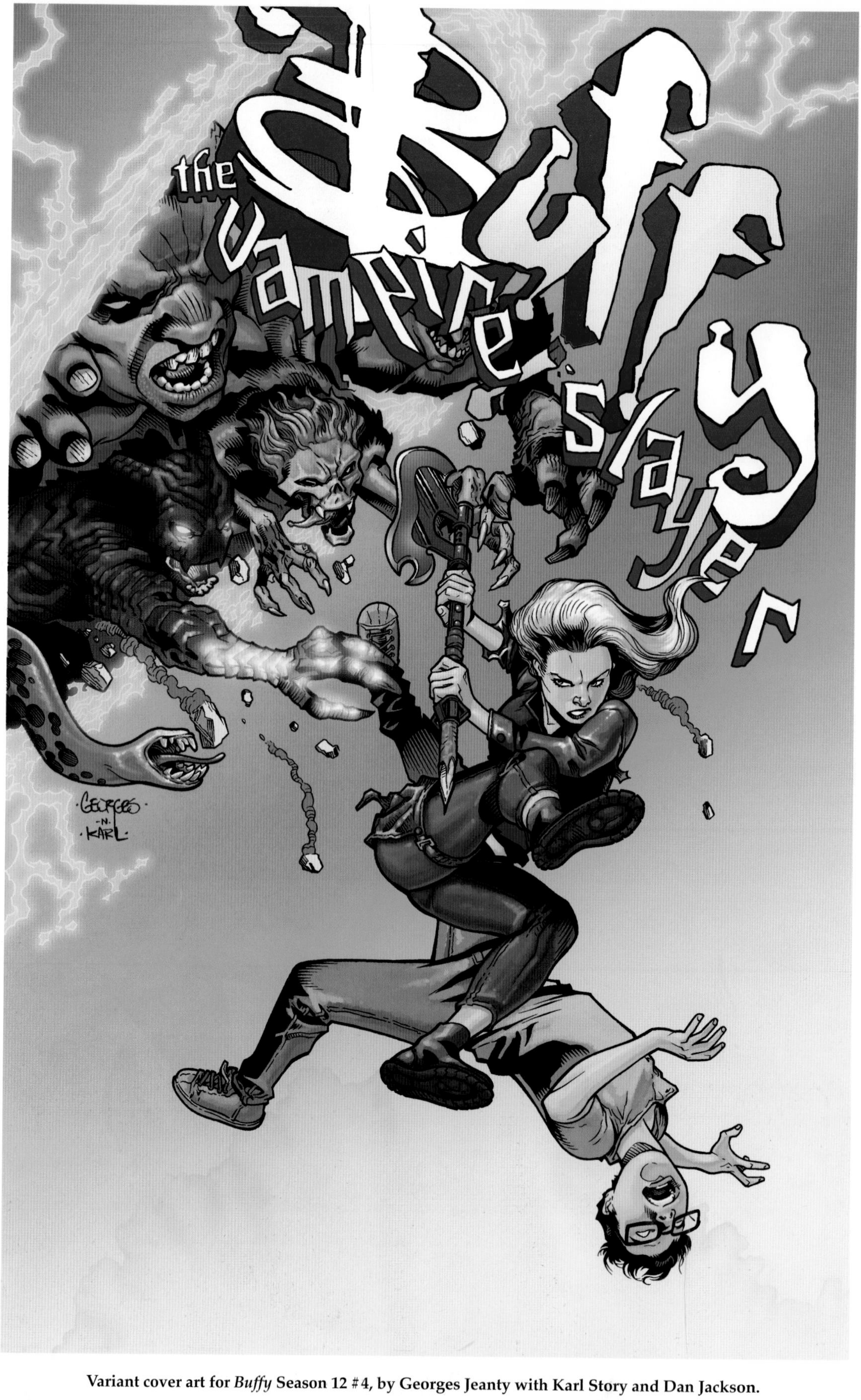

the
vampire
slayer
GEORGES -N- KARL

Variant cover art for *Buffy* Season 12 #4, by Georges Jeanty with Karl Story and Dan Jackson.

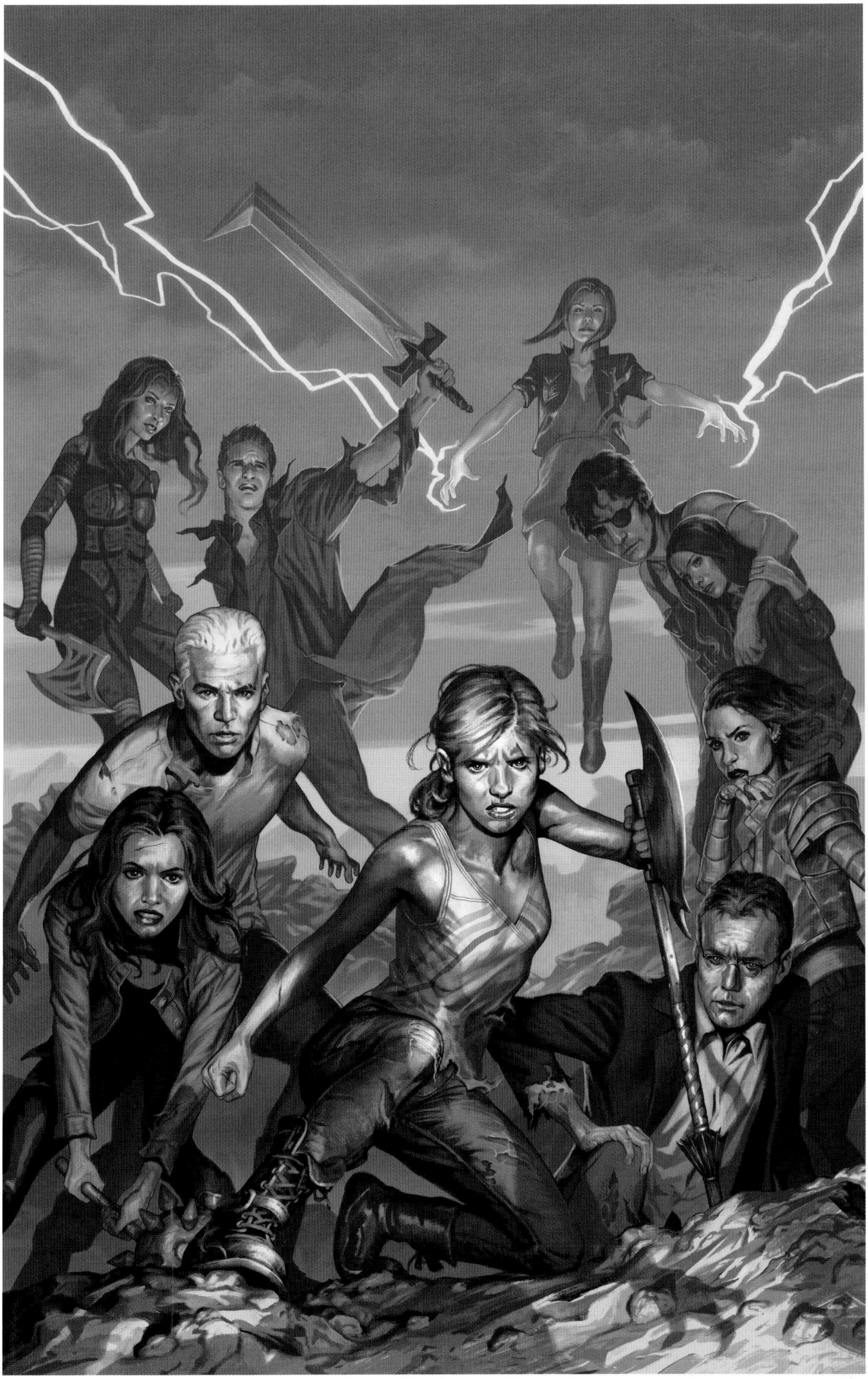

Ultravariant cover art for *Buffy* Season 12 #4, by Steve Morris.

Buffy the Vampire Slayer™

BUFFY THE VAMPIRE SLAYER SEASON 8

VOLUME 1: THE LONG WAY HOME
Joss Whedon and Georges Jeanty
ISBN 978-1-59307-822-5 | $15.99

VOLUME 2: NO FUTURE FOR YOU
Brian K. Vaughan, Georges Jeanty, and Joss Whedon
ISBN 978-1-59307-963-5 | $15.99

VOLUME 3: WOLVES AT THE GATE
Drew Goddard, Georges Jeanty, and Joss Whedon
ISBN 978-1-59582-165-2 | $15.99

VOLUME 4: TIME OF YOUR LIFE
Joss Whedon, Jeph Loeb, Georges Jeanty, and others
ISBN 978-1-59582-310-6 | $15.99

VOLUME 5: PREDATORS AND PREY
Joss Whedon, Jane Espenson, Georges Jeanty, Cliff Richards, and others
ISBN 978-1-59582-342-7 | $15.99

VOLUME 6: RETREAT
Joss Whedon, Jane Espenson, Georges Jeanty, Karl Moline, and others
ISBN 978-1-59582-415-8 | $15.99

VOLUME 7: TWILIGHT
Joss Whedon, Brad Meltzer, and Georges Jeanty
ISBN 978-1-59582-558-2 | $16.99

VOLUME 8: LAST GLEAMING
Joss Whedon, Scott Allie, and Georges Jeanty
ISBN 978-1-59582-610-7 | $16.99

BUFFY THE VAMPIRE SLAYER SEASON 8 LIBRARY EDITION

VOLUME 1
ISBN 978-1-59582-888-0 | $29.99

VOLUME 2
ISBN 978-1-59582-935-1 | $29.99

VOLUME 3
ISBN 978-1-59582-978-8 | $29.99

VOLUME 4
ISBN 978-1-61655-127-8 | $29.99

BUFFY THE VAMPIRE SLAYER OMNIBUS: SEASON 8

VOLUME 1
ISBN 978-1-63008-941-2 | $24.99

VOLUME 2
ISBN 978-1-63008-942-9 | $24.99

BUFFY THE VAMPIRE SLAYER SEASON 9

VOLUME 1: FREEFALL
Joss Whedon, Andrew Chambliss, Georges Jeanty, and others
ISBN 978-1-59582-922-1 | $17.99

VOLUME 2: ON YOUR OWN
Andrew Chambliss, Scott Allie, Georges Jeanty, and others
ISBN 978-1-59582-990-0 | $17.99

VOLUME 3: GUARDED
Joss Whedon, Jane Espenson, Drew Z. Greenberg, Georges Jeanty, and others
ISBN 978-1-61655-099-8 | $17.99

VOLUME 4: WELCOME TO THE TEAM
Andrew Chambliss, Georges Jeanty, Karl Moline, and others
ISBN 978-1-61655-166-7 | $17.99

VOLUME 5: THE CORE
Andrew Chambliss, Georges Jeanty, and others
ISBN 978-1-61655-254-1 | $17.99

BUFFY THE VAMPIRE SLAYER SEASON 9 LIBRARY EDITION

VOLUME 1
ISBN 978-1-61655-715-7 | $29.99

VOLUME 2
ISBN 978-1-61655-716-4 | $29.99

VOLUME 3
ISBN 978-1-61655-717-1 | $29.99

BUFFY THE VAMPIRE SLAYER SEASON 10

VOLUME 1: NEW RULES
Christos Gage, Rebekah Isaacs, Nicholas Brendon, and others
ISBN 978-1-61655-490-3 | $18.99

VOLUME 2: I WISH
Christos Gage, Rebekah Isaacs, Nicholas Brendon, and others
ISBN 978-1-61655-600-6 | $18.99

VOLUME 3: LOVE DARES YOU
Christos Gage, Rebekah Isaacs, Nicholas Brendon, and Megan Levens
ISBN 978-1-61655-758-4 | $18.99

VOLUME 4: OLD DEMONS
Christos Gage and Rebekah Isaacs
ISBN 978-1-61655-802-4 | $18.99

VOLUME 5: IN PIECES ON THE GROUND
Christos Gage, Megan Levens, and Rebekah Isaacs
ISBN 978-1-61655-944-1 | $18.99

VOLUME 6: OWN IT
Christos Gage and Rebekah Isaacs
ISBN 978-1-50670-034-2 | $18.99

BUFFY THE VAMPIRE SLAYER SEASON 10 LIBRARY EDITION

VOLUME 1
ISBN 978-1-50670-645-0 | $29.99

VOLUME 2
ISBN 978-1-50670-657-3 | $29.99

BUFFY THE VAMPIRE SLAYER SEASON 11

VOLUME 1: THE SPREAD OF THEIR EVIL
Christos Gage and Rebekah Isaacs
ISBN 978-1-50670-274-2 | $19.99

VOLUME 2: ONE GIRL IN ALL THE WORLD
Christos Gage, Georges Jeanty, Rebekah Isaacs, and Megan Levens
ISBN 978-1-50670-292-6 | $19.99

ANGEL & FAITH SEASON 9

VOLUME 1: LIVE THROUGH THIS
Christos Gage, Rebekah Isaacs, and Phil Noto
ISBN 978-1-59582-887-3 | $17.99

VOLUME 2: DADDY ISSUES
Christos Gage, Rebekah Isaacs, and Chris Samnee
ISBN 978-1-59582-960-3 | $17.99

VOLUME 3: FAMILY REUNION
Christos Gage, Rebekah Isaacs, Lee Garbett, and David Lapham
ISBN 978-1-61655-079-0 | $17.99

VOLUME 4: DEATH AND CONSEQUENCES
Christos Gage and Rebekah Isaacs
ISBN 978-1-61655-165-0 | $17.99

VOLUME 5: WHAT YOU WANT, NOT WHAT YOU NEED
Christos Gage and Rebekah Isaacs
ISBN 978-1-61655-253-4 | $17.99

ANGEL & FAITH SEASON 9 LIBRARY EDITION

VOLUME 1
ISBN 978-1-61655-712-6 | $29.99

VOLUME 2
ISBN 978-1-61655-713-3 | $29.99

VOLUME 3
ISBN 978-1-61655-714-0 | $29.99

ANGEL & FAITH SEASON 10

VOLUME 1: WHERE THE RIVER MEETS THE SEA
Victor Gischler, Will Conrad, Derlis Santacruz, and others
ISBN 978-1-61655-503-0 | $18.99

VOLUME 2: LOST AND FOUND
Victor Gischler and Will Conrad
ISBN 978-1-61655-601-3 | $18.99

VOLUME 3: UNITED
Victor Gischler and Will Conrad
ISBN 978-1-61655-766-9 | $18.99

VOLUME 4: A LITTLE MORE THAN KIN
Victor Gischler, Cliff Richards, and Will Conrad
ISBN 978-1-61655-890-1 | $18.99

ANGEL SEASON 11

VOLUME 1: OUT OF THE PAST
Corinna Bechko and Geraldo Borges
ISBN 978-1-50670-346-6 | $17.99

VOLUME 2: TIME AND TIDE
Corinna Bechko and Zé Carlos
ISBN 978-1-50670-347-3 | $17.99

VOLUME 3: DARK REFLECTIONS
Corinna Bechko and Geraldo Borges
ISBN 978-1-50670-387-9 | $17.99

SPIKE

A DARK PLACE
Victor Gischler and Paul Lee
ISBN 978-1-61655-109-4 | $17.99

INTO THE LIGHT
James Marsters and Derlis Santacruz
ISBN 978-1-61655-421-7 | $14.99

WILLOW

WONDERLAND
Jeff Parker, Christos Gage, and Brian Ching
ISBN 978-1-61655-145-2 | $17.99

GILES

GIRL BLUE
Joss Whedon, Erika Alexander, and Jon Lam
ISBN 978-1-50670-743-3 | $17.99

BUFFY: THE HIGH SCHOOL YEARS

FREAKS AND GEEKS
Faith Erin Hicks and Yishan Li
ISBN 978-1-61655-667-9 | $10.99

GLUTTON FOR PUNISHMENT
Kel McDonald and Yishan Li
ISBN 978-1-50670-115-8 | $10.99

PARENTAL PARASITE
Kel McDonald and Yishan Li
ISBN 978-1-50670-304-6 | $10.99

ADULT COLORING BOOKS

BUFFY THE VAMPIRE SLAYER ADULT COLORING BOOK
Karl Moline, Georges Jeanty, Rebekah Isaacs, Steve Morris, and others
ISBN 978-1-50670-253-7 | $14.99

BUFFY THE VAMPIRE SLAYER BIG BADS & MONSTERS ADULT COLORING BOOK
Karl Moline, Georges Jeanty, Yishan Li, Pablo Churin, and others
ISBN 978-1-50670- 458-6 | $14.99

AVAILABLE AT YOUR LOCAL COMICS SHOP OR BOOKSTORE!

To find a comics shop in your area, visit comicshoplocator.com. For more information or to order direct:
On the web: DarkHorse.com • Email: mailorder@darkhorse.com • Phone: 1-800-862-0052 Mon.–Fri. 9 AM to 5 PM Pacific Time